Becoming and Bonding

Recent Titles in Contributions in Women's Studies

Becoming and Bonding

Contemporary Feminism
and Popular Fiction
by American Women Writers

Katherine B. Payant

Contributions in Women's Studies, Number 134

Greenwood Press
Westport, Connecticut • London

Library of Congress Cataloging-in-Publication Data

Payant, Katherine B.
   Becoming and bonding : contemporary feminism and popular
fiction by American women writers / Katherine B. Payant.
      p. ; cm.—(Contributions in women's studies, ISSN 0147–104X ;
no. 134)
   Includes bibliographical references and index.
   ISBN 0–313–28574–8
   1. American fiction—Women authors—History and criticism.
   2. Feminism and literature—United States—History—20th century.
   3. Women and literature—United States—History—20th century.
   4. Popular literature—United States—History and criticism.
   5. American fiction—20th century—History and criticism.
   I. Title. II. Series.
   PS374.F45P38   1993
   813'.5099287—dc20   92–39268

British Library Cataloguing in Publication Data is available.

Library of Congress Catalog Card Number: 92–39268
ISBN: 0–313–28574–8
ISSN: 0147–104X

First published in 1993

Greenwood Press, 88 Post Road West, Westport, CT 06881
An imprint of Greenwood Publishing Group, Inc.

Printed in the United States of America

The paper used in this book complies with the
Permanent Paper Standard issued by the National
Information Standards Organization (Z39.48–1984).

10 9 8 7 6 5 4 3 2 1

This book is dedicated to my parents,
Mark and Robina Payant.

Contents

Acknowledgments

Papers based on this material have been read at meetings of the College English Association, the Twentieth Century Literature Conference, the Popular Culture/American Culture Associations, and the Midwest Modern Language Association.

I would also like to thank my secretaries, Mary Letts and Rose Rosina, for their patience and assistance, and my sons, Andrew and Philip Pavlik, and husband, Ted Raymond, for their support. Northern Michigan University provided a sabbatical and a faculty grant to help me complete this work.

1

Introduction

Since the early 1970s something very exciting has been happening in the literary world. After several decades of relative silence, Nathaniel Hawthorne's "damned mob of scribbling women" has been operating full steam, producing novels that represent a true renaissance in the world of letters. Most of these novels have focused on a subject seldom documented truthfully in literature—women's experience. Traditional subjects of women's writing, such as courtship and marriage, have been treated differently, and new subjects have opened up—women's development and their relationships with other women, and to their ethnic and cultural backgrounds, for example.

In this new literature, the entire gamut of female experience is being treated with an openness and perception never before encountered. And it is no coincidence that these literary developments have coincided with the women's movement. Although the world of letters has always reflected social changes, seldom has a social movement had such profound impact on literature. Writers do not create within a vacuum: what happens in their society creates a literary environment favorable to certain subjects and stances and may even suggest new subjects.

Like many women readers I came to this new writing around 1970, at the same time that I was plunging into the swirling waters of the budding feminist movement. I read my first feminist novels—*Diary of a Mad Housewife* and *Memoirs of an Ex-Prom Queen*—at the same time I read Simone de Beauvoir, Kate Millett, Germaine Greer, and Shulamith Firestone. Influenced by my years of literary education, I was not sure if what I was reading was literature, but for the first time in my reading experience I fully recognized myself. Members of my consciousness-raising group read many of these works together, passing along titles of novels to each other. That experience was heady for me: books, which I had always loved, were now speaking directly to me in a way they had never done, and were helping me understand and change my life. Like millions of women readers at that time, I used these novels as self-help guides; often they gave me insight and courage to act. "Bibliotherapy," my colleague now calls it.

This renaissance actually sprang from a long women's literary tradition. Women have been active contributors to the history of the novel from the beginning of the genre to the present time. Literary scholars such as Jane Spencer and Elaine Showalter have traced women's involvement in the invention and revision of the novel from the time of Samuel Richardson and Henry Fielding. Early women novelists were constrained by their sex and conventions of the forms in which they operated, but still made important revisions that established a "woman's tradition."[1] Women novelists have continued to the present time to be prolific, and have been especially adept at writing popular generic fiction. Nevertheless, despite their long involvement and prodigious output, few women novelists have entered the literary canon. In fact, the term "women's novel" is pejorative. Until recent times literary scholars gave little effort to studying literature by women; even the women novelists who had become part of the canon, such as Jane Austen, the Brontës, and Virginia Woolf, received scant attention. Especially in the United States, women novelists have found it difficult to achieve critical praise for their work; in a seventy-year period from 1918 to 1988, only nineteen women won a Pulitzer Prize for fiction.[2] Showalter calls the 1950s a particular "low point" for American women writers.[3]

RISE OF FEMINIST CRITICISM

Since the early 1970s the development of feminist criticism—study of literature informed by feminist ideas—has begun to consider writing by and about women in a systematic way. One of the chief occupations of feminist critics has been mining the literary tradition to "rediscover" the so-called lost women writers, women who were perhaps known and widely read in their time but have been lost to succeeding generations. Another equally important activity has been the "reseeing" of the well-known women writers who have found their way into the canon. Feminist scholars have written copiously on Austen, the Brontës, and George Eliot as well as Virginia Woolf. According to the tenets of feminist criticism, these sorts of studies are necessary to understand the importance of gender marking to the literature. The fact that these writers are women becomes an important factor in discussing their work, and previous criticism ignoring the sex of the writer therefore must be suspect. Criticism focusing on women writers has lately become preoccupied with the issue of "difference," revealing the influence of French feminist critics such as Hélène Cixous and Luce Irigaray, who have been influenced by deconstructionism. Is writing by women essentially different from writing by men, and if so, *how* is it different?

Despite all these worthy efforts in examining women's literary contributions, the bulk of the scholarly work has concentrated on women's writing of the past, especially of the nineteenth century. Comparatively few critics have focused on the fiction of today's women writers, especially those who present a feminist sensibility in their work. A few writers have received extensive treatment, the black American Toni Morrison being one, and a few others, such as the Canadian Margaret Atwood and Doris Lessing, a moderate amount of study; but large numbers of popular writers are not significantly represented in the critical literature.

Since the early 1980s, however, scholars have begun to examine developments in contemporary literature by women. Studies include Anne Mickelson's *Reaching Out: Sensitivity and Order in Recent American Fiction by Women* (1979), Joanne Frye's *Living Stories, Telling Lives: Women and the Novel in Contemporary Experience* (1986), Molly Hite's *The Other Side of the Story: Structures and Strategies of Contemporary Feminist Narrative* (1989), Paulina Palmer's *Contemporary Women's Fiction: Narrative Practice and Feminist Theory* (1989), and Gayle Greene's *Changing the Story: Feminist Fiction and the Tradition* (1991). However, little of this scholarship exclusively treats contemporary American women writers. Some older studies, such as that by Patricia Meyer Spacks (1977), concentrate on American writers from earlier decades, such as Mary McCarthy, or British writers; Olga Kenyon and Greene, though including contemporary writers, concentrate on British and Canadian authors.[4] Several excellent collections of essays have been published, for example, Mickey Pearlman's *Mother Puzzles: Daughters and Mothers in Contemporary American Literature* (1989), but these examine specific themes in the works rather than general trends. Few of these studies attempt to examine how the writing reflects popular feminist ideas, being instead applications of feminist literary theory to the literature.

Paulina Palmer's study, for example, analyzes contemporary women's fiction in light of feminist theory. She surveys an impressive number of works, but the majority are by radical feminist British, Canadian, and Australian writers. She tends to dismiss works that do not support her own lesbian feminist politics, and argues that most of today's feminist-influenced works are radical in outlook.[5] It is my contention that in American women's writing, the Women's Movement has had a profound effect on many writers whom one would not call radical feminists—that many American women writers are strongly influenced by feminist ideas but are not "radical." Although sympathetic to feminism in the main, they can be critical of certain ideas or preoccupations of the movement. This widespread and diffuse feminist influence on American women's writing makes it difficult to categorize the literature according to various types of feminist theory.

There are a number of reasons why critics, even feminist scholars, have neglected contemporary women's writing. First, academics want to be respectable in the eyes of their colleagues and because many of these novels have been best-sellers, critics have continued to study older, more respected works. As a feminist friend and colleague told me, "I don't have time for that stuff." A study of Virginia Woolf still carries more clout than one of Erica Jong. Second, most literary scholars are not historians or sociologists, and feel unsure of their ability to assess how contemporary events influence writers.

Present literary fashion also steers scholars away from much contemporary women's fiction. Many of these works are written in what appears to be a realistic mode. I say "appears to be" because some of this fiction does not propose to imitate reality but is a fiction of ideas. This apparent realism, however, is to the critical disadvantage of the works. Today's literary establishment, whether feminist or nonfeminist, privileges postmodern fiction with discontinuous narrative; shifting personas who often comment on the fictional conventions of the work; subtle, impressionistic use of language; and works that reveal a psychoanalytic approach to personality. For example, Nikki Garrard, a feminist critic, while acknowledging the importance of the realistic tradition for women writers, announced the death of the realistic novel as a useful device to present feminist ideas.[6]

Furthermore, fictions of the "fractured self" are more valued than those showing the self as an integrated entity toward which the protagonist struggles in a quest.[7] In short, both traditional and some feminist critics value that which is inaccessible and what nonacademics might call "arty." Though there are a number of women writers producing postmodernist/avant garde feminist novels, including Kathy Acker and Joanna Russ, in this study I am interested in discussing those writers who reflect feminist concerns and are accessible to and read by a larger audience.

Another related, thorny problem arising when discussing contemporary feminism and women's writing is literary scholars' traditional devaluation of political literature. Though great writers from earliest times have considered political questions in their work, traditional wisdom holds that writing which reveals a partisan point of view is suspect as art. Thus, many obviously feminist novels have been dismissed, even by feminist critics, as polemics. Within literary circles there are, of course, honest differences of opinion about this issue, with Marxist and feminist critics arguing that all writing is political because it deals with power relations between people; nevertheless, this traditional view holds sway, especially with critics who operate outside academe. And, alarmists not withstanding, even in academe "politically correct" criticism does not dominate.

For many scholars, writers who adhere too much to doctrines of social determinism, who attribute evil to classes or social systems rather than to our flawed humanity, are not highly valued. And, of course, feminism does attribute evil to social systems—in particular to what feminists see as the oldest and most pervasive social system of all—patriarchy. In a 1985 study of reviews of women's novels, Bronwen Levy found that texts perceived to be making a political statement are often devalued by critics.[8] More recently Alix Kates Shulman, an American feminist fiction writer, and Nikki Garrard have written of this problem. According to both, most women writers who admit to being politically feminist shy away from the term "feminist writer."[9]

A final daunting issue that makes study of feminism and women's writing difficult is the problem of determining how the feminist influence works. Does a writer see her art as a form of praxis, as a Marxist critic would say, a means of promoting feminist ideas to her readers? Does she see herself as an artist/storyteller who describes the world as she sees it, and that way happens to be feminist? Or both of the above? Is she essentially an apolitical person whose work simply reflects current ideas in her society? Many authors do not leave us signposts advertising their intent, and are often reluctant to admit their work is influenced by social and political ideas. They are well aware of the prejudice in the literary world against writing with a political bias. As Shulman says, few fiction writers who confess to being feminist would climb willingly into the vessel "feminist fiction." "Who wants to capsize in shark-infested seas" (72)?

A NEED TO STUDY CONTEMPORARY FEMINIST WRITING

Now, in the early 1990s, it is time to examine more closely the influences of contemporary feminism on today's women writers. How have the content, themes, and style of their work been affected by the Women's Movement and the variety and change within the movement, as well as the thought underpinning it? As Showalter has stated, discussing the history of feminism in literature is a daunting challenge because there is a danger of over- or underfeminization, attributing too much or too little to the sex of the writer.[10] How may these new contents, themes, and styles differ from those of previous women writers? In the case of writers who are overtly feminist, how has this political orientation affected the quality of their work? Finally, what does contemporary fiction say about the universality of women's experience, as well the variety of that experience? Given the racial, ethnic, and class differences among women, can anything meaningful be said in a general sense about being female? In other words, to what degree can we posit a woman's culture that reaches across boundaries of race and class?

Critical Questions

In addressing such issues, I must briefly tackle a number of critical questions raised by feminist critics. The first concerns whether there is such a thing as a women's literary tradition—a body of work written by women,

centered on female experience (but not exclusively concerned with it), directed mainly (but not exclusively) toward women readers.

Since the existence of this long tradition has been demonstrated repeatedly
by various literary historians, I do not propose to summarize their findings
again. However, I do wish largely to exclude, except by occasional reference,
the popular genres of the historical novel, detective story, science fiction,
and so on. Though one can demonstrate that this sort of writing is marked
by gender, it does have formulaic elements which ensure that detective novels
by men or women may resemble each other more closely than novels by
males and females writing mainstream fiction. One popular genre which
has adapted well to feminist issues is science fiction; in fact, since the early
1970s a subgenre of feminist science fiction has developed, perhaps the most
famous practitioner being Joanna Russ. However, scholars have been studying women's contemporary genre fiction for some time, including the influences of feminism on such writing.[11]

A second issue involves the ability of fiction to say anything meaningful
about women's experience, given the fact that language is a construct of
patriarchal culture. This view, embraced especially by those critics influenced
by French feminists such as Cixous, Irigaray, and Monique Wittig, holds
that male-dominated discourse, formulated in logical, rational, linear systems of thinking, is not adequate to express women's experience. The French
feminists have urged women writers to "write the body," to get out of the
narrow paths dictated by male-formulated discourse, through word play to
create "new languages," an *écriture feminine*. French-influenced feminist
critics point out that the traditional plot structure of the novel, evolved over
250 years, dictates that heroines will do traditional things: they will marry
or not marry; they will be victimized by men or they will resist victimization.
Victims or not, they will be constrained by the structures of the realistic
novel, which reflects women's actual situations in patriarchal society, to live
out their fates according to the society's expectations. Some critics have
argued that, given these constraints, the best sorts of forms for the feminist
novel must therefore be science fiction and avant garde fiction.[12]

On the other hand, some feminist critics, most of them American, argue
that while language has been used by patriarchal culture to oppress women,
as a basically neutral construct it can be appropriated by women to accurately document their experience. Therefore, the realistic novel can be a
significant vehicle to convey feminist ideas. They argue that the realistic
novel has far from lost its potential to lead women to new understanding.
For example, in *Living Stories, Telling Lives* Joanne Frye successfully de-
molishes the argument that realistic women writers cannot break out of
traditional plot structures. They can do so by dealing with aspects of wom-
en's lives often left out of earlier women's stories—issues of growing up
female, careers other than marriage, fragmentation of women's lives, and
bonds between women, mothers, daughters, sisters, and friends.

Frye argues that within the confines of the "realistically" constructed plot, women writers can treat such material quite differently than did earlier novelists, the most important difference being the interior life of the protagonist—how she thinks about her experience. In her conclusion, Frye argues the revolutionary potential of women's novels: "[they] do more than 'represent' the available possibilities in women's lives. They do more, even, than create new 'role' models. They take an *active* role in the broader pattern of cultural change."[13] And that is an important reason why we should study these novels—they *have* changed many women's lives.

Other American feminist critics have found problems with the French feminists' call for new languages. In *Sister's Choice* Showalter states that a "muted culture" like that of women can have a "literature of its own" that at the same time is connected to the language and literature of the dominant culture. Women novelists have long been revising the conventions of the novel to produce their own unique works. Showalter declares that the French feminists' dream of a common language "has always been a utopian fantasy."[14] In another recent study, while acknowledging the contributions of the French feminists, Patricia Yaeger criticizes them for ignoring "the radical structures women have invented in the past to protest and to remake a patriarchal discourse their own."[15] My contention is that many of the women novelists of today are continuing these strategies and, in fact, that the political and intellectual movement of contemporary feminism has hastened and abetted that effort.

Mary Jacobus believes that these opposing positions on women's writing are really critical formulations of a basic split between feminists in general: radical feminists who would like to dismantle patriarchy and replace its evil values and thinking with new, more humane institutions; and liberal feminists who would like greater power for women in the present system, in order to reform it from within.[16] I suggest, however, that some feminist thinkers, including several novelists I discuss in this study, appear to combine in their thought the beneficial qualities of both the feminine and the masculine principles, bringing women into the culture from outside it. This approach saves what is good in each tradition, eliminating what Cixous calls the emphasis on difference, on polarity, on sexual battles.[17]

Scope and Method of Study

I have decided to confine my discussion to the novel. Though contemporary women writers certainly have incorporated feminist ideas into short stories and poetry, I believe the novel has had more influence in promoting feminist ideas throughout the culture. In addition, because of its scope, it has a greater capacity for presenting women's quests and the variety and difference of their experiences. One of the dominant forms of the novel during the two decades in question is the quest-romance or *bildungsroman*, a genre aptly suited for presenting feminist ideas.

I restricted myself to American writers. One could certainly write a similar study including Canadian, English, and other women writing in English. Showalter believes that American women's writing is a "hybrid" and exists within a complex cultural network that is becoming international in scope, especially for Afro-American women. Nevertheless, she also believes, and I agree, that the "womanist" novel in the United States is responding to a national literary tradition.[18] Though there is much that is familiar to American feminist readers in writers such as Margaret Atwood and Fay Weldon, there is also a sense of being on slightly foreign soil, a subtle difference in viewpoint. Certainly an interesting subject to pursue would be the similarities and differences in the feminist fiction of various national literatures.

My choice of novels to discuss was also problematic. Because of the extent of my subject—twenty years of American women's novels—I cannot hope to touch on every writer who has reflected feminist ideas in her work, let alone every significant novel; therefore, this study does not purport to be a comprehensive survey. Rather, I will look at major trends and representative writers. No doubt readers will find some of their favorite authors or important novels missing, and to them I can only express my regrets. When choosing authors and works to study, I have included some fairly well known writers, but have excluded others who have been studied critically for some time. I have tried to include a number of writers who strike me as significant but whose work has been neglected. The analyses of the novels attempt to incorporate formal criticism whenever available, but in some cases I have had to rely on reviews for outside opinions on the literature.

In chapters 2 and 3, I examine how women writers have responded to the changing ideas of the Women's Movement in the 1970s and 1980s, as well as the general tenor of these decades. In Chapter 2 I concentrate on the white, middle-class "feminist novel," particularly the *bildungsroman*. More than any other, this type of novel seems to have been the dominant form in the 1970s, clearly illustrating various feminist theories by showing the maturation of a young protagonist seeking to find herself in a hostile, patriarchal world. Some of the theories I relate to the literature include the "social construction of femininity," "the personal is political," and the related issue of sexual politics. Chapter 3 holds that the changing times and nature of feminist theory produced new themes: the restrictions and pleasures of motherhood, and female bonding, including relations between mothers, daughters, sisters, and friends.

I argue that in the 1970s sexual politics and criticisms of patriarchy are featured, whereas in the 1980s cultural feminist ideas gained prominence. As Angela Miles points out in her study *Feminist Radicalism in the 1980's*, the emphasis in feminist thought in the 1970s was on the difference of femininity as weakness, while in the 1980s female difference came to be seen as female value.[19] This change is reflected in novels as well. I also attempt to show, in the wider racial, ethnic, and social range of 1980s novels I discuss, how popular women's fiction expanded its scope and audience. Because feminism is not a monolithic body of thought, in Chapter 2 I provide a brief description of the views of some of the major types of American feminisms.

In chapters 4–6 I examine in detail three different types of women's writing of this period: the radical feminist tradition represented by Marge Piercy; white ethnic writing represented by Irish Catholic Mary Gordon; and black women's writing, illustrated by the work of Toni Morrison. I show how each of these novelists has responded to feminist issues, and how the background of each has influenced that response: in Piercy, a radical feminist/socialist, one could say polemical, approach; in Gordon, a cultural feminist outlook that synthesizes feminist ideas with traditional Christian values; and in Morrison, an Afro-American "womanist" viewpoint that reveals ambivalence about the aims of feminism.

It may be well to explain in more detail why I chose to focus on these three writers. Obviously, I could have chosen others, but Piercy, Gordon, and Morrison illustrate three quite different and thought-provoking fictional approaches to feminist ideas. Piercy unabashedly promotes feminist ideas in her work; her best-selling novels in the 1970s represent a radical feminist viewpoint that can also be seen in the work of Marilyn French. Of the three writers, Piercy is the best representative of that (for some writers) annoying label "feminist novelist." Though her themes and approaches have become more diffuse since the 1970s, Piercy has not lost her allegiance to radical feminist ideas. Mary Gordon, on the other hand, though freely calling herself a feminist, represents a cultural feminist viewpoint more typical of the 1980s than the 1970s. Her attitudes toward the difference of women's experiences seem quite similar to a number of 1980s novelists I discuss in Chapter 3, such as Gail Godwin, as well as some writers of color, such as Alice Walker and Amy Tan. In addition to her interest in women's experience, however, Gordon is concerned with spiritual quests, especially how one may bring together Christian beliefs and feminist thinking, an effort familiar to many Christian women of a feminist bent. Further, the ethnic milieu of most of her work, lower-middle- and working-class urban Irish, is quite different from that of many of the other writers I discuss.

Toni Morrison may seem the oddest choice of the three. Though she is one of the most celebrated American writers, certainly Alice Walker, Gloria Naylor, and Paule Marshall more obviously represent an Afro-American feminist viewpoint. However, I chose Morrison for precisely this reason: though she eschews identification with the Women's Movement, her work shows more feminist influence than she acknowledges. Her emphasis on the strengths and contributions of black women places her squarely in the tradition of cultural feminism. Black women, says Morrison, "are the touchstone by which all that is human can be measured."[20] At the same time, however, that she celebrates the humanity of black women, she indirectly and sometimes directly expresses ambivalence about the effects of some white feminist ideas on black women; she is also less willing to sweepingly condemn black males than some black feminist writers. Though she is often critical of black men's treatment of black women, her primary project is to expose the evils of slavery and racism, which she sees as an underlying cause of such treatment. The complexity of Morrison's treatment of gender issues makes her a fascinating subject for feminist analysis.

Throughout this study I tie developments in the literature to the changes in the Women's Movement during this twenty-year period and, when necessary, discuss the ideas of feminist theorists that seem to find their counterparts in the literature. Some of this information will be found in the text and some in the notes. However, for the most part, I do not attempt to identify individual theoretical sources for the fictional works I analyze. Though many of the fictional ideas find their counterpart in the theoretical literature, my argument is not that women writers read feminist theory and then wrote novels to illustrate that theory. The connection between political and social change and fiction is seldom that obvious, although no doubt this sort of direct influence sometimes happened, especially in the case of radical feminist writers. Rather, I am arguing that the feminist theories I discuss here were (and are) widespread, popular ideas about women's experience that writers encountered in their contacts with other women and in the popular media, as well by reading feminist thinkers. They saw the relevance of feminist ideas to women's experience and gave them fictional shape.

A final caveat: as I have explained, I do not intend to imply that all the writers and works I discuss are "feminist" in the sense that they consciously promote feminist values or write with a polemical purpose. Even Piercy identifies herself foremost as an artist, a teller of stories. What I *am* arguing is that all these writers have been influenced by feminist ideas about women's experiences, that they are women of their times, and that their writing reflects, either consciously or unconsciously, the new ideas about women. In her article in *Ms.*, Alix Kates Shulman states that if one defines "feminist fiction" as "fiction by political women for whom the contemporary women's movement was one of the major experiences of their lives," then the list of writers and works will be slim. If one takes a more expansive viewpoint, then feminist fiction becomes

fiction that does not admire patriarchy or accept its ideology. Nor does it portray its male characters as naturally more exciting, more important, or more valuable than its female characters. In addition, the female characters are valued enough to be presented in their full humanity, whether they be villains or heroes, and the sympathetic female characters are neither nice nor necessarily beautiful. (72)

With this definition in mind, all the novels I discuss in this study can be called "feminist."

I hope this study will be of interest to a number of readers: feminist critics who may not yet have read much contemporary women's fiction; other academics, such as historians and sociologists, who want a general introduction to how a social/political movement affects an art form; and any educated reader who has read some of these novels and would like to read critical discussion of them. Because I speak to several audiences, I do not assume a great deal of knowledge about literary theory, and those who seek applications of poststructuralist theory to the literature will not find them here. What I am interested in is how the literature reflects the new, widespread notions about the nature of women and their experiences.

To my mind, this stress on highly technical theory is a major problem with literary criticism today, both feminist and nonfeminist. Much of it is complex and theoretical, requiring extensive acquaintance with ideas of deconstructionism and other postmodern theories, and thus is inaccessible even to well-educated readers. As many feminists have warned, we academics tend to speak only to each other in our own privatized language. One result is that our messages reach very few people—for a political movement like feminism, a turning inward that can only spell disaster.

NOTES

1. Jane Spencer, *The Rise of the Woman Novelist* (Oxford: Basil Blackwell, 1986); Elaine Showalter, *A Literature of Their Own: British Women Novelists from Brontë to Lessing* (Princeton, NJ: Princeton University Press, 1977); and *Sister's Choice: Tradition and Change in American Women's Writing* (Oxford: Clarendon Press, 1991).

2. *The World Almanac and Book of Facts* (New York: Pharos Books, 1992), 326-327.

3. Elaine Showalter, *Modern American Women Writers* (New York: Charles Scribner's, 1991), xii.

4. Patricia Meyer Spacks, *Contemporary Women Novelists: A Collection of Critical Essays* (Englewood Cliffs, NJ: Prentice-Hall, 1977). Olga Kenyon, *Women Novelists Today: A Survey of English Writing in the Seventies and Eighties* (New York: St. Martin's Press, 1988); *Writing Women: Contemporary Women Novelists* (Concord, MA.: Pluto Press, 1991).

5. Paulina Palmer, *Contemporary Women's Fiction: Narrative Practice and Feminist Theory* (Jackson: University Press of Mississippi, 1989), 3. Palmer states in her introduction that she is a radical feminist, and no doubt this has affected her choice of works.

6. Nikki Garrard, *Into the Mainstream: How Feminism Has Changed Women's Writing* (London: Pandora, 1989), 108. Garrard says that the realistic domestic novel is "insular" and "sealed off," an inadequate vehicle to express "larger preoccupations."

7. Palmer, 7.

8. Bronwen Levy, "Women and the Literary Pages: Some Recent Examples," *Hecate* 11 (1985), 6-7, 11.

9. Garrard, 106-107; Alix Kates Shulman, "Books: The 'Taint' of Feminist Fiction," *Ms.* (November/December 1991), 72.

10. Showalter, *Sister's Choice*, 18.

11. Anne Cranny-Francis, *Feminist Fiction: Feminist Uses of Generic Fiction* (New York: St. Martin's Press, 1990), believes that some of the popular genres are easier to adapt to feminist themes than others. For instance, science fiction/fantasy adapts well to feminist concerns; detective novels are more problematic; and romance is the most difficult, due to the inherently conservative nature of the male/female relationship in romance novels.

12. This is the position of Thelma Shinn in *Radiant Daughters: Fictional American Women* (Westport, CT: Greenwood, 1986), 185. Ellen Morgan and Joanna Russ in earlier essays—"Humanbecoming: Form and Focus in the Neo-Feminist Novel" and "What Can a Heroine Do? Or Why Women Can't Write," in *Images of Women in Fiction: Feminist Perspectives*, ed. Susan Koppelman Cornillon (Bowling Green, OH: Bowling Green State University Popular Press, 1972)—stated the same belief.

13. Joanne Frye, *Living Stories* (Ann Arbor: University of Michigan Press, 1986), 199.

14. Showalter, *Sister's Choice*, 7.

15. Patricia Yaeger, *Honey-Mad Women: Emancipatory Strategies in Women's Writing* (New York: Columbia University Press, 1988), 16.

16. Mary Jacobus, "The Difference in View," in *Women Writers and Writing About Women*, ed. Mary Jacobus (Totowa, NJ: Barnes & Noble, 1979), 10-21.

17. *Hélène Cixous*, "The Laugh of the Medusa," trans. Keith Cohen and Paula Cohen, *Signs* 1 (Summer 1976), 875-893.

18. Showalter, *Sister's Choice*, 20.

19. Angela Miles, *Feminist Radicalism in the 1980's* (Montreal: Culture Texts, 1985).

20. Quoted in "Toni Morrison," in *Modern American Women Writers*, 17.

2

The Bildungsroman *of the 1970s: Growing up Female in Patriarchy*

Many histories of the contemporary feminist movement have now been written, but few communicate the excitement of the times, the heady sense of a new world in the making. In retrospect, one can see that the wave of feminism which swept the nation in the late 1960s was inevitable. This new movement was rooted in changes and contradictions present in the lives of modern women. Though by the early 1960s more women than ever before were working outside the home, and the birth control pill had given them a new freedom, women were still viewed by the larger society mainly in their roles as wives and mothers. It was those obvious contradictions that drove women to begin questioning their roles in society and society's attitude toward them.

This was not the first wave of feminism in the United States, of course. The First Wave, as feminist historians term it, began before the Civil War, narrowed to a focus on suffrage, and subsided after the vote for women became law. As many visionary feminists had warned, suffrage did not change the situation of the American woman. Women were still envisioned mainly in their traditional roles; as political analysts noted, they tended to vote as their husbands did. Younger women in the 1920s rejected the "suffragette" image of their mothers, believing that women's emancipation had been achieved. Feminism was associated with unattractive, unmarried women; some young women writers declared feminism "old hat."[1] During the 1930s the Great Depression certainly did not aid the cause of women's rights; jobs were scarce, and women were expected to be the buttress of their families and support their men. Among leftist groups, women's rights were downplayed, seen as secondary to the "more important" issue of economic justice.

World War II was an important event in the 1960s rise of feminism in that although the women who took jobs during the war years were urged to return home, quite a few did not, and remained in the work force. This group of women, low paid and always first fired during economic downturns, belied the 1950s general social dictum that a woman's place was in the home. The "cult of domesticity" that swept the nation in the 1950s had a number of manifestations: earlier marriages, larger families, and fewer women going to college, all supported by an ideology reflected in the popular culture of television, magazines, and films. Pop Freudian interpretations of woman's role abounded: women were supposed to find their primary meaning through domesticity, and those who were dissatisfied were told by their psychiatrists and the culture that they should adapt. This vision of the family, supported by a loving, sacrificing mother, provided a nostalgic refuge from the anxiety of the Cold War.

Not all was quiescent, though, as shown by subsequent events. There was a base of working women; some who were involved in politics; and there were still large numbers of educated women, who became the leaders of the Second Wave of feminism.[2] These women knew about earlier feminist movements and were able to look critically at the cultural admonitions and ideology surrounding them. When their personal discontent combined with the new atmosphere more conducive to social change sweeping the nation in the 1960s, this new social movement was truly inevitable.

The public phase of the movement can be traced back to the Presidential Commission on the Status of Women established by President Kennedy in 1960. Headed by Eleanor Roosevelt and composed of leaders from the political parties, labor, business, and academe, the commission worked for several years and in 1963 made a number of quite conservative recommendations.[3] In the years after the commission's report, little change took place in the federal government's approach to women's issues, and so in 1966 a group of disgruntled women in Washington, D.C., at a convention of state commissions on women gathered in Betty Friedan's hotel room and formed the National Organization for Women (NOW).[4] NOW's goal was "participation in the mainstream ... in equal partnership with men."[5] Although NOW came to be described as radical by the media, within the movement these women were considered "conservative" feminists, seen as more concerned with the problems of women in public life than they were with controversial areas such as the family.[6] Sometimes referred to as "egalitarian" or "liberal" feminists, this group, at least initially, believed that women's status would be improved by granting equal rights under the law and opening up opportunities for women in politics and business.

The other, more radical group of feminists came from the antiwar and civil rights movements. They were younger, more unconventional (some were the "bra burners" hyped by the media), and more likely to challenge traditional notions of women's roles in the family.[7] At the same time that NOW was being formed, these women were beginning to discuss their restricted position in the New Left movement and the oppressive attitudes of so-called radical men toward them. As many of them later said, they "manned the barricades" with the men, but were expected to run the mimeograph machines and make coffee. As the 1960s progressed, more and more of these young women either deserted the New Left movement entirely or began to divide their time between women's causes and other radical causes. The earliest consciousness-raising groups were formed by these women, and the idea spread to more moderate women. It is rare today to find a feminist over forty who was not a member of a consciousness-raising group in the 1960s and early 1970s.

Although I speak here of "conservative" feminists and "radical" feminists, it is important to recognize that as early as the late 1960s there were many different points of view developing within the movement. In fact, Josephine Donovan, in *Feminist Theory: The Intellectual Traditions of American Feminism*, discusses six different types of American feminism: Enlightenment liberal feminism, radical feminism, cultural feminism, Marxist or socialist feminism, existential feminism, and psychoanalytical feminism.[8] As Donovan points out, ideas in these several viewpoints overlap; there is a good deal on which all feminists agree. And in many cases a feminist thinker could subscribe to parts of several theories while rejecting other ideas within the same theories. In the case of the literature, the same situation obtains but even more so than with the scholarly writing. Unlike academics, few fiction writers, even those who publicly identify themselves as feminist, align themselves with a particular school of feminism.

Keeping all this in mind, it will not always be possible to place a writer or novel into a particular feminist framework; some of the writers I discuss seem "radical feminist" in their approach but appear to reflect other points of view as well. Some writers reveal feminist ideas in a more general, diffuse sense. The point here is that theories about the nature of woman and her place in patriarchal society originated mainly among scholars and academics, then found their way through scholarly writing into the society at large. These ideas have become commonly accepted among large segments of society, including fiction writers, who reflect them in their work.

From its earliest days, this new women's movement was in large part an intellectual revolution, a personal revolution in thinking, reading, and writing. True, it had its public side, with marches and manifestos, with more women gaining courage to enter public life, whether by getting a job outside the home, going back to college, or running for public office. However, in order to gain the confidence to do these things, women needed new ideas and ways of thinking about themselves, ideas provided by the growing body of feminist writing. Women read these works, passed along their titles to friends, and discussed them in their consciousness-raising groups. As they discussed their own experiences in the light of the feminist theory, each began to form her feminist consciousness.

Several of these works had been available for some time. Simone de

Beauvoir's seminal work, *The Second Sex*, appeared in 1952, and in 1963 Betty Friedan published *The Feminine Mystique*, a study of the predicament of the middle-class housewife. Neither book made an immediate impact, however; they were "discovered" by feminist readers only in the late 1960s. Some feminist writers, on the other hand, say they read these works earlier and were influenced by them in their own writing.[9] Despite the initial slowness of these crucial works to catch on with a larger audience, by the early 1970s the feminist movement was producing its own body of scholarship to add to the feminist writing of previous decades.

In academe, scholars in the humanities and social sciences began addressing women's topics, producing works such as Kate Millett's *Sexual Politics* (1970), an influential study of antifemale attitudes in the culture and in the work of the male writers in the literary canon. *Sexual Politics* is, no doubt, one of the few works of criticism read by large numbers of nonacademics. In my own small northern Michigan town, in my consciousness-raising group composed of teachers, artists, other professionals, and housewives, we avidly discussed it and other works at the same time that we explored our experiences as women. The tie-ins were excitingly obvious to us. Equally exciting were the new novels by women writers that spoke to the experiences of being a contemporary woman, and we began to read and discuss these, too.

EARLY FEMINIST NONFICTION WRITING

Although it is beyond the scope of this study to give a detailed account of the evolution of feminist thought, it is necessary to make some reference to this developing body of theory in order to see how it connects to the literature. Besides *Sexual Politics*, there were dozens of books and articles published in the early 1970s that influenced the fiction of the period. Scholars and popular writers traced misogyny throughout history, documented the lack of women in public life, the poor wages of working women, educational discrimination and poor health care for women, violence against women, the sexual double standard, and the objectification of women in the popular media and pornography. Special attention was paid to impossible standards of beauty, which caused women to hate their own bodies.

Though all these concerns were important in nonfiction feminist writing in the early 1970s, even more important was the nature of woman herself. Why do women not achieve in the public sphere at the level of men? Why do women seem different from men—weaker, softer, less active and confident? Few feminist thinkers at this point were considering these perceived differences as possible strengths rather than debilitating weaknesses. To answer such questions, feminists debunked Freudian explanations for woman's nature: that anatomy was destiny, that a woman's biology was bound to keep her from achieving in the public sphere. Millett attacked Freud, as did Germaine Greer in *The Female Eunuch* (1971) and Shulamith Firestone in *The Dialectic of Sex: The Case for Feminist Revolution* (1970). Each gave a similar explanation for "woman." Woman is what she is, for good or ill, because society has made her that way.[10] This was not a new idea, of course, having been suggested by Mary Wollstonecraft in the eighteenth century, but these writers popularized it, challenging old assumptions of millions of people about the nature of the sexes. Feminists today call this concept the "social construction of femininity" or "gender," gender being the socially conditioned aspects of one's behavior distinct from biology.

If "woman" was not something biologically determined, then how society "produces" her became very important.[11] Thus feminist thinkers wrote a great deal about the socialization of girls in the family: the differences between the way girl and boy babies are treated from birth on. Other feminist scholars studied the effect of the literary and popular cultures on women's acculturation—the effect of mythology and folklore, popular fiction, movies, and music. As we shall see, all these concerns found their way into the novels of the period.

Since the usual explanations for women's nature said that women are naturally suited for their nurturing role as wives and mothers, feminist theorists paid a great deal of attention to traditional marriage, even more than the lack of women in the public world, discrimination in the workplace, and related political issues.[12] Feminist thinkers soon focused on woman's role in the family, a role they saw as created and buttressed by patriarchal society, as central to her oppression. For example, Juliet Mitchell in *Women's Estate* (1971) argued from a Marxist position that woman's position in the family is similar to that of the wage earner in capitalism; and if she works outside the family, she finds herself doing double duty, working for a pittance in one job and for nothing in the other. It was early agreed by all varieties of feminists that woman's role in the family would have to change if women were to become "liberated" to play a larger role within society. Thus we find popular essays like Vivian Gornick's "The Conflict Between Love and Work" and the debunking of romantic love by many radical feminist writers.

As Greer, Firestone, and others saw it, romantic love was a myth used by society to provide free labor to nurture the nuclear family; women themselves used the myth to rationalize the loss of power and freedom demanded by traditional marriage. For this loss they gained (supposedly) the love of their families, economic security, and the prestige of having a husband, society treating the unmarried woman as a pitiful object. Therefore, a pressing necessity of the new feminist movement was to help women recognize a central idea: the personal is political. If society is a patriarchy, dominated by males in both public and private spheres, what happens in a woman's marriage or relationship with her lover is a paradigm for the society's oppression of women as a class.[13] Therefore we see many articles on the oppressive nature of marriage for women, two humorous examples being Judy Syfers's "Why I Want a Wife" and Pat Mainardi's "The Politics of Housework." In much of this writing, men and misogyny were seen as the enemies, the traditional sex role division being obviously of great advantage to men, who profit from having unpaid labor in their homes and always having someone to feel superior to. The feminist movement's questioning of woman's position in the family was quite remarkable because previous feminist thinkers had seldom challenged this role.

Another important idea in this early feminist writing was the "objectification" of woman as body/sexual being. De Beauvoir and others pointed out how throughout history woman has been seen by the culture as primarily a passive object of man's desire, created for and suited for the begetting and raising of children. Such a view promotes passivity in women because it is not necessary for them to "do," but only to "be."[14] Literature, religion, and philosophy have all promoted this view of women, causing women to consider themselves as objects, to concern themselves with adorning their persons in order to obtain mates, and thus to fulfill their cultural roles. According to this view, early in their lives women abandon ambitions in the larger world when they perceive they are valued mainly for their bodies' beauty and their ability to create children. A consequence of this abandonment is a loss of self-esteem because young women know well that the larger society values achievement in men, not personal beauty.

TYPES OF FEMINISMS AND THE LITERATURE

Despite my earlier reservation concerning the difficulty of applying specific feminist labels to the literature, it may be useful to describe briefly some of the main ideas of several of these "feminisms," since I will occasionally suggest connections between the literature and a particular type of feminism. In the early writing considered above, and in the writing that followed, certain positions and ideas emerged that were associated with different schools of feminism. The mostly mainstream literature I examine reveals two general types of feminist ideas: radical, which I associate mainly with the 1970s; and cultural feminism, which seems more prevalent in the writing of the 1980s. With the exception of Marge Piercy, one does not see too much interest in socialist feminist ideas in this literature, and although certainly one can see reflections of psychoanalytic thought, this is not a dominant preoccupation of these writers.

First, as I have said, types of feminisms are not monolithic; individual thinkers differ on various issues. For example, radical feminists differ on whether woman's oppression is partly biological, as Firestone suggests, or dependent entirely on society's system of gender roles. This issue is divisive because it leads some radical feminists to argue that women indeed are superior to men, whereas others believe the idea of sexual superiority is to be avoided. Some radical feminists include a socialist critique of society and urge solidarity with other oppressed people, including men, whereas others discourage women from working with men altogether. Many radical lesbian feminists believe that sex with men is bound to be oppressive for women, and urge a lesbian lifestyle as an alternative to the brutalization they see in heterosexual relationships; for them sexual relations with women are the only true form of feminism. Other radical feminists believe that women can have relationships with men that are not exploitative.[15]

Nonetheless, despite these considerable differences, radical feminists agree on many ideas. First, they believe that male domination of females, or patriarchy, was the first "class system" in human history, and that this oppression of females by males became a model for later oppressions of one group by another. Institutions such as slavery and colonialism of non-Western people look back to sex oppression. Most radical feminists believe that male domination originates not in biology but in gender roles learned in the family and reinforced by society.[16] Unlike Marxist feminists, radical feminists argue that woman's exploitation by males, by her family, and by society is not primarily economic but psychological. Women are conditioned to seek self-fulfillment through love and approval within private relationships; men are conditioned to quest for their selves through action and creation in the public world. As we saw in the early writing, it is believed that this process produces women who lack self-esteem and continually try to find it through romantic love with men. It produces men who derive immense ego satisfaction from feeling superior to women, a satisfaction making it very difficult for them to give up power. For most radical feminists, a socialist revolution will not touch sexual oppression, as witnessed by socialist societies, such as China, where women remain subordinate to men. This is not to say that society does not need radical economic reforms, only that the problem is not primarily economic.

Radical feminists have a great deal in common with cultural feminists. They believe that traditional family life must be changed, including the raising of children, and that so-called female qualities of nurturance, intuition, and sensitivity to suffering, if allowed to thrive in the public sphere, will save the human race. In other words, if the basic model of sexual oppression were eliminated, then humankind could begin to eliminate other types of domination—war, imperialism, racism, and environmental damage. Thus, the basis for all revolution is liberation from sexual oppression, which will involve radical changes in people's thinking.

Although cultural feminist attitudes were certainly present early on (in fact, they can be traced back to the thinking of such great nineteenth-century feminists as Margaret Fuller and Elizabeth Cady Stanton), they are more noticeable starting in the late 1970s, and become prominent in the 1980s. Unlike liberal feminism, which tends to denigrate traditional female qualities, such as the desire to nurture, cultural feminism celebrates traditional female qualities. Liberal feminism attributes the differences between the sexes to lack of opportunity for women in the public sphere, stresses work within the political system to create opportunities for women in employment and politics, and shies away from suggesting radical changes in family structure.

Like radical feminists, cultural feminists believe that for woman's lot to change, sweeping changes need to be made throughout the society, including bringing men fully into the nurturing of children. They believe that women's life experiences make them more humane and urge an infusion of superior female values into the world beyond the home, creating a society in which poverty, war, and racism would become outmoded relics of the dead patriarchy. This sort of feminism sees a total cultural revolution and a utopian new age emerging in which both sexes would benefit from the female values of nurturance, reverence for the land, and rejection of hierarchical and power-based modes of rule. One significant difference between radical and cultural feminists is that at least in the early days radical feminists tended not to celebrate traditional female roles such as motherhood, seeing such attempts as sentimentalizing a mostly tedious task. They did not sanctify domesticity—early in the movement they called housework "shitwork," perhaps rightly feeling that if housekeeping is admitted to be sometimes pleasant, women will end up always doing it.

Virtually all types of feminism agree on women's oppression by men, and the institutions of society as contributing to this oppression; their difference lies in the degree to which change can be effected through the present political/economic system and the nuclear family. All feminists believe that the law, education, the media, religion, and health policies such as restrictions on abortions encourage the domination of women by men. For example, prostitution and pornography, which are tolerated by society, degrade women's bodies, encouraging men to think of women as objects. Radical feminists warn that the so-called sexual revolution of the late 1960s mainly made more women sexually available. It did nothing to change the basic status of women. Susan Brownmiller's and others' studies argue that rape or the fear of rape is a social institution which makes every woman vulnerable, restricting her freedom.[17]

HISTORICAL PRECEDENTS

In the literature of the 1970s many of these issues came into play, but probably the most important were (1) how a woman was created and (2) the oppressive nature of her existence in patriarchy, especially in traditional marriage. These ideas took little time to appear in the fiction; by the late 1960s we can see their unmistakable influence in women's novels, which usually took the form of the *bildungsroman*, or novel of development.

Actually, literature examining women's development and roles, particularly in marriage, was not new. Feminist literary historians have uncovered an "anti-tradition" going back to the eighteenth century and the earliest days of the novel. Elizabeth Boyd Jordan has documented the evolution of the novel of female development, particularly the role of marriage. Early examples of this genre were based on medieval traditions of sentimental romance and had "fairy-tale endings," as in Richardson's *Pamela* (1740), where virtue is rewarded—virtue being equated with passivity and sexual ignorance—and marriage provides closure to a woman's development. This tradition was continued by women writers such as Fanny Burney in *Evelina* (1778). Later writers, however, such as Maria Edgeworth and Jane Austen, gave us a new sort of protagonist who was expected to be more than passively ignorant of the world, although marriage as the goal of her moral development was never questioned. The heroines of Charlotte Brontë also broke with convention, Jane Eyre being one of the first fictional woman to "strain at the everyday social limitations of average women," though Brontë ultimately turned to the standards of romantic fiction and united Jane in marriage with her beloved Rochester.[18]

Other nineteenth-century writers also struggled against traditional conventions. For example, Elizabeth Gaskell in *Mary Barton* (1848) deals with the importance of a woman's job in forming her character. George Eliot and two male writers, George Meredith and Thomas Hardy, question the institution of marriage. In Eliot's *The Mill on the Floss* (1860), achieving the female "virtues" of ignorance and passivity is a self-denial that leads not to rewards but death; however, in *Middlemarch* (1871-1872) Eliot's view is more positive, showing marriage as both a disappointment and an opportunity for moral growth. Meredith's *The Egoist* (1879) and *Diana of the Crossways* (1885) feature heroines who question their marriages to men whom today we would call "male chauvinists." According to Jordan, the strongest questioning of traditional ideas about marriage's effects on women came from Hardy, who shows marriage to be a crippling social institution.[19]

Though historical studies demonstrate evidence of older fiction that questioned traditional views of women's moral development and the effects of marriage, in much mainstream literature conventional views of the development of women prevailed. The view that marriage is the goal and end of a girl's development held sway well into the twentieth century, and much of the literature considered important and "serious" did not treat woman's development at all. We see few examples of *Portrait of the Artist as a Young Woman*. Thus, despite the anti-tradition outlined above, the recent outpouring of female *bildungsromans* critical of traditional female development is quite extraordinary.

In fact, in *The Female Imagination* Patricia Meyer Spacks states that prior to the Women's Movement there had been no novels celebrating female adolescence, seeing it at best as a time to adjust to one's inevitable role and at worst as ending in madness. This is largely because of the limited range of acceptable behavior open to young women.[20] As Elizabeth Abel says in her anthology of essays on the female novel of development, "Even the broadest definitions of the *bildungsroman* presuppose a range of social options available only to men."[21] This is true not only in the older versions of the form, when the best a young woman could do was to make a good marriage, but to some degree in the more recent versions as well. In fact, one of the central issues of the 1970s *bildungsroman* is the strong internal and external pressure young women feel to consider marriage their most important option. A significant difference, however, between these novels and earlier ones is that the more recent works implicitly assume that if the protagonist can understand her past and the workings of her culture, she can break away from socially imposed restrictions. Opportunities do exist to "rewrite the story," if only she has courage to take them.

Two important 1960s predecessors to the 1970s *bildungsroman* are Doris Lessing's *The Golden Notebook* (1962) and Sylvia Plath's posthumously published *The Bell Jar* (1963). Though Lessing is British (formerly from Rhodesia), she deserves mention here because *The Golden Notebook*'s Anna Wulf and Martha Quest of the *Children of Violence* series seem prototypical heroines of later feminist novels. In these works, Lessing touched on many themes found in contemporary American women's novels: conflict between career and one's womanly role, desire for independence and emotional need for men, and the most important theme, exemplified in the central metaphor of the colored notebooks in *The Golden Notebook*: fragmentation of the modern woman's life due to the myriad expectations of society. Though Lessing has repeatedly disavowed the feminist label, saying that gender issues are less important than global issues of world peace, feminists have embraced her as one of their own; according to Gayle Greene, Lessing has had a profound influence on later feminist writers of both nonfiction and fiction. Isadora Wing of Erica Jong's *Fear of Flying* names Anna Wulf as a writer who failed her as a role model, and Lisa Alther, another writer I discuss in this study, cites her debt to Lessing.[22]

Like Anna Wulf, Plath's Esther Greenwood of *The Bell Jar* is torn, finding that although the world supposedly is open to her as a modern young woman in the 1950s, there is actually little place for a woman who wants to "live in both the country and the city"—or, as contemporary jargon puts it, "to have it all."[23] Esther thinks she wants a career as a writer or scholar, but she hates the implication that, unlike a man, she will have to give up her sexual identity for it. The profound conflict she feels leads to a suicide attempt and a stay in a mental hospital. Though the ending finds her leaving the asylum, we know that in the outside world the bell jar, a symbol of madness and her isolation as a woman artist from her society, is waiting to descend again with "all its stifling distortions" (197). Greene believes this ending shows Esther's lack of understanding of the larger political/ cultural causes of the bell jar, and is also an ominous indication of Plath's own unresolved pain that led to her suicide (67-69). Plath needed the knowledge a feminist critique of her predicament would have given her.

As I have stated, more recent *bildungsromans* take a much more positive view of the possibilities for self-realization for today's young woman. The "mad housewife" protagonist faces many of the same conflicts as Esther, but real madness is never a possibility. There is a close similarity, however, between the satiric/ironic style of *The Bell Jar* and that of later novels. Esther often sees her situation and the world around her as slightly absurd, and so do feminist writers of the 1970s. There is much that is funny about growing up female; in fact, some of these novels move beyond irony to outright slapstick humor. Spacks believes, however, that irony often conceals suppressed anger; and if that is so, these novels contain a good deal of it. Women writers, says Spacks, have always been masters of "evasion" and the "devious" (28).

In the United States the feminist critique lacking in *The Bell Jar* began to appear in the late 1960s and early 1970s in series of novels that have been called "Jewish-American Women's Novels" and "mad housewife" novels (though not all protagonists were Jewish or housewives).[24] These books examined upper-middle-class women's lives—why women were dissatisfied with the roles assigned them by society. Examples include *Diary of a Mad Housewife* (1967) by Sue Kaufman, *Such Good Friends* (1970) by Lois Gould, and *Up the Sandbox!* (1970) by Anne Richardson Roiphe. Tina Balser, the heroine of *Diary*, is in some ways typical of these protagonists and the ones to follow in the 1970s: Isadora Wing of Erica Jong's *Fear of Flying* (1973), Sasha Davis of Alix Kates Shulman's *Memoirs of an Ex-Prom Queen* (1972), and Stephanie of Francine du Plessix Gray's *Lovers and Tyrants* (1976). Tina is affluent, upper middle-class, and college educated, has two children, and is married to a professional.[25] In these novels the protagonist is torn between her role as housewife and mother and her vaguely realized aspirations, career and otherwise. Her situation is a literary illustration of Friedan's "feminine mystique." Suffering from the existential "angst" of contemporary male characters, like John Updike's Rabbit Angstrom, she finds it difficult to break away from the restrictions of her feminine role. Sometimes she takes a lover, as Tina does, but predictably finds this brings no fulfillment. Sometimes, like Isadora and Stephanie, she runs away from the stultifying boredom of her married life.

THE 1970s *BILDUNGSROMAN*

As one examines the outpouring of women's novels in the 1970s, it is clear that one form predominates: the *bildungsroman* or novel of the development of a young protagonist coming into conflict with society and finally taking her place in that society. Even those "mad housewife" novels which concentrate on the adult life of the protagonist usually have a section where she reflects on her childhood and adolescence. As Barbara White has demonstrated in *Growing up Female: Adolescent Girlhood in American Fiction*, recent women writers have adapted the *bildungsroman*, which usually focuses on a child or adolescent, to an adult woman.[26] In a sense, these protagonists are children who must undergo a metamorphosis in order to become free adults in a society that has denied them full personhood because they are women.

Two other important examples of these 1970s novels are *Small Changes* (1972) by Marge Piercy and *The Women's Room* (1978) by Marilyn French. Both these novels are *bildungsromans*, containing some material on the protagonists' earlier lives but concentrating on their development after the teen years. Many critics have pointed out the suitability of the *bildungsroman* plot for this type of novel. If one is to criticize the social construction of femininity, then one must discuss how women are socialized from girlhood on. One important difference between these two novels and the others is that French and Piercy write from a definite radical feminist viewpoint, using their heroines' lives to illustrate specific aspects of feminist theory. I will discuss *The Women's Room* later in this chapter and Piercy's work in Chapter 4.

FEMALE DIFFERENCE AS WEAKNESS

One theme recurs so often throughout these 1970s novels that it deserves early mention—the idea of femininity as weakness. Much feminist theory of the early 1970s tended to see femaleness as not only a disadvantage to a quest for self but also as a negative condition to be eradicated or overcome. Traditional feminine qualities such as dependence on others, passivity, and the desire to nurture were seen as debilitating.[27] A woman searching for self should reject that which is exclusively female and try to develop a more androgynous personality. One sees in the mainstream literature of this period a similar emphasis on the negative qualities of feminine characteristics and experiences. They limit the protagonist in all kinds of ways, making her a kind of emotional and mental cripple. Occasionally, there is a hint of cultural feminism, a view that some traditional qualities women possess might enhance their lives as well as the culture as a whole, if they were given more value; however, for the most part 1970s feminist fiction seemed to view being female as a negative condition.

Childhood—The World Unlimited

Without exception, the 1970s *bildungsroman* spends little time on the protagonist's childhood. This is generally a happy time of freedom, of continuing expansion of the girl's sense of self, ability, and her world. She is bright, does well in school, is a tomboy, has confidence in her body, and plays with neighborhood children, boys and girls, on terms of complete equality. Sometimes, though, she is aware that she is considered inferior to boys, both by boys and sometimes by her family, who seem to value their sons more. Sasha of *Memoirs of an Ex-Prom Queen* tells us that about age ten

If a girl was spotted on their territory the boys felt perfectly free to: give her a pink belly, or lock her in the shed, or not let her down from a tree, or tie her to the flagpole, or lash at her legs with reeds.... They did it for fun. They did it to prove themselves. They did it because they hated us.[28]

Adolescence—The World Limited

In earlier decades psychologists did studies that showed a diminishment of a girl's scholastic achievement as she got older and realized her destiny as a woman.[29] Similarly, the protagonists in these novels come up against social restrictions with the onset of puberty and begin to realize their differences from boys: that they are destined for lesser things, that they are sexual prey, and that they are sexually weak in comparison with males. The onset of menstruation, for example, is seen as exciting but also limiting. Now, for a few days each month, they can get out of gym class (which they often hate) but also are more limited in their bodily freedom, must wear an encumbering harness around their waists. Most of them seek compensation for this diminishment by capitalizing on their femininity. Ginny Babcock in Lisa Alther's *Kinflicks* (1975) trades in her football pads for a flag swinger outfit, realizing the power of her new body to ensure her popularity.

Reflecting the feminist interest in the process of female acculturation, novels of the 1970s spend a good deal of time on adolescence. The most difficult aspect of this process is learning to deal with the dominant sex in the world of dating. An important target is the sexual double standard, which can cause much unhappiness and anxiety in teenage girls. Ginny, at the time of telling her tale a twenty-seven-year-old housewife, has come back home to Hullsport, Tennessee, to be with her dying mother. This experience occasions serious thought on her own mortality but also brings back her past. This plumbing of the past is an important aspect of every feminist novel, a type of consciousness-raising leading to new insights into self.

Ginny recalls her romance with handsome but dull Joe Bob Sparks. As flag swinger for the Hullsport High marching band, Ginny's perfect match is halfback Joe Bob. However, to be his steady will involve more than French kissing, and of course it is up to the girl to "call the shots" in such a relationship:

I put the ring on my thumb, but there was still room for another finger or two.... Hullsport High tradition required that each new material commitment between a couple signal a new array of carnal privileges. We both knew . . . that the unexplored territories below the waist were now up for grabs.[30]

Joe Bob, with his magnificent physique, is the sex object par excellence; however, Ginny's good reputation is equally desirable: "Would Joe Bob still respect me if I went all the way with him? Would I become like my old grade-school chum, Maxine Pruitt . . . whom Joe Bob and his friends referred to with snickers as 'Do-It' Pruitt?" (54). Other feminist novels also contain characters like Maxine Pruitt—the girl of easy virtue who is the victim of society's double standard, but so far no writer has made such a character her protagonist. Though Alther views her subject with irony and sometimes even with ribald humor, she also communicates the tension experienced by the adolescent girl in her desire to be popular yet respectable. She knows she must catch a boyfriend, and ultimately a husband, to be valued, but to do this she must not give away too much of her precious body—which is, after all, all she really is.

Alix Kates Shulman in *Memoirs of an Ex-Prom Queen* adopts a similarly ironic tone in dealing with teenage dating and mating. Her heroine, Sasha Davis, who grows up in Cleveland in the 1950s, also must confront the double standard. She manages to hold off her boyfriend, Joey, for some time, but succumbs the night she is voted Prom Queen. Her exalted position convinces her she can get away with anything: How could a Prom Queen get a bad reputation? That night in Joey's car Sasha thinks, " . . . being Queen, I dared to believe I could get away with it. There was something regal about going all the way" (68-69). Later, though, she is forced to acknowledge Joey's new power to injure her. As Barbara White points out, letting Joey have power over her and use her when she feels no answering pleasure shows how Sasha is on her way to being objectified (158).

More than one critic has pointed out that until recently, one of the few ways a young woman could rebel was to have sex with someone her parents, especially her mother, would disapprove of or to act out sexually in some other way, such as dressing provocatively.[31] For the most part, women's adventures in these novels are sexual, though one could argue that this does represent an important change from a time when a heroine did not have sexual adventures. These protagonists resist to some degree their society's admonitions that they should not experience sexual pleasure.

At this point it is important to stress how strongly these novels call for reader identification. The writers are directing their stories toward the woman reader who has also been through such experiences. Such novels induce the reader's anger at how she was "programmed" into the female role, and at the same time make her laugh at her attempts to get a date for the prom while preserving her virginity. Speaking from my own experience and that of many women friends, I know that books like these played a key role in our consciousness raising, and thus have aided in bringing about changes in our lives, perhaps more so than feminist nonfiction. For some novelists, such as Marge Piercy (see Chapter 4), achieving this reader "re-seeing" has been an important part of their purpose.

College Days

Since these *bildungsroman* protagonists are from affluent middle-class families, they usually attend college after high school. Here, too, they find that patriarchal values dominate. Though most of them respond strongly to the new world of ideas, it becomes clear that this experience does not mean the same thing to them that it does to male students. They are not preparing for their lives' work in same way as young men, or they are doing so only in the sense that they are in college to find a mate who will then be their lives' work. In their peer groups they feel pressured to be more concerned with boys and dating than with studies; thus they respond as Esther does in *The Bell Jar*, pretending to be more interested in men and dating than they actually are. Ginny abandons herself to the mentorship of her professor, Edith Head, a brilliant yet cold and austere philosophy professor, whose chief delight, besides the world of ideas, seems to be "taking her cello between her legs" at campus musicales (240). Miss Head, like Esther's asexual mentor JayCee, serves to remind Ginny of the fate of women who pursue a career.

Several other protagonists find themselves embroiled in affairs with male professors who prey upon their naïveté. Sasha, for example, becomes involved with her exploitative philosophy professor, Dr. Alport. After the relationship ends, Sasha's "on-the-rebound" marriage is a kind of retreat into security. And protagonist Theresa, in Judith Rossner's *Looking for Mr. Goodbar* (1975), is cruelly rejected by her English professor, Martin. Rossner implies that some of Theresa's later promiscuity is the result of the poor self-esteem this experience engendered in her. These and other seductions of young women by professors and employers in feminist novels imply that patriarchy makes it natural for men in authority sometimes to seduce women: the situation is simply an exaggeration of all male/female relations within the culture. In such situations women find it difficult to resist because they have been culturally conditioned to be attracted by the man's air of authority.

Marriage and Motherhood

The 1970s *bildungsroman*, after recounting the protagonist's childhood and adolescence and her struggles with social restrictions against females, moves on to the marriage and motherhood of the young woman, where patriarchal values are most vividly seen. This is the "mad housewife" part of the story found even in those novels where marriage occupies only a small part of the protagonist's quest. Here the narrative centers on the clash between the protagonist's desires for herself and society's expectations of her. Sometimes the heroine marries because she is in love, and sometimes simply because she sees little else to do with her life. However, in every case a central reason she marries is that marriage is expected and as a single women she will be considered a failure.

These novels show marriage to be oppressive, as feminist theory says. Whereas the protagonist might have functioned with her husband-to-be on terms of equality during courtship, since marriage makes her economically dependent, she finds she has lost all power in the relationship. As Marxist-feminist theory holds, she is truly the wage earner, with her husband as the capitalist employer. Sasha realizes she cannot cross her husband, Frank, for this reason. Similarly, Ginny discovers she is now her husband's toilet washer and sexual servant—she earns her "bed and bored," says Ginny. Not only are they dominated by their husbands but their day-to-day life is incredibly tedious. The writers' messages are the same as in *The Second Sex* and *The Feminine Mystique*: housewifery is repetitious, isolating, and mind deadening. As de Beauvior says, unlike the tasks of men, it produces nothing, being an endless series of activities leading nowhere. The only really creative and enjoyable part of housekeeping is cooking, and the product of that activity is consumed rapidly and forgotten.[32] Besides the repetitious nature of housework, the day-to-day care of small children is not the supreme joy the women's magazines would have it seem, and our society gives women neither preparation nor help in assuming their tasks.

Such novels confirm what feminist social historians have pointed out about the change in society since the industrial revolution and the relatively recent development of the nuclear family. Since the change from farming and home manufacturing, when all the family worked together, to an economic system where men work outside the home in factories and offices, woman's role in the larger life of society has been increasingly restricted. This has proved to be limiting and frustrating for the educated, middle-class housewife. Her life may be immeasurably more physically comfortable than her foremothers', but it lacks challenge for her faculties.[33]

Though the 1970s' *bildungsroman* says all this in ironic fashion, the underlying emotion is anger—society has played an elaborate hoax on women, educating them, telling them they are free, and then leaving them with little to do but care for their families. Usually the protagonist tries hard to become what her society says she should. Sasha wants to be perfect, a "Supermom"; she pores over women's magazines and Dr. Spock, discovering cures for diaper rash and colic but finding little help for the dissatisfaction and inadequacy she feels: "The books I had taken from the library in preparation proved, like *The Questions Girls Ask* and *Girl Alive!* to be mere parodies of life" (250). Ginny tries traditional women's activities but feels like an outsider:

Now girls," [the Tupperware lady] began urgently, "I know you've all been waiting to hear about the grr-eat new Tupperware products that have just come out, designed as always to help today's busy homemaker. . . . A dizzying succession of plastic bacon keepers, cauliflower crispers . . . swirled from hand to hand. By the end of the "party," everyone in the room had committed herself to dozens of plastic objects. Except me. I had bought nothing. I was overwhelmed with all the things my kitchen lacked. (385)

We see here another part of Friedan's critique of woman's role; she becomes part of the voracious consumerism that is so important to American capitalist society. A housewife's life is given meaning through her ability and duty to acquire as many objects as possible to secure the comfort of her family.

The women in these novels feel restricted not only by society's expectations but also by their own internalization of those values. They really want to succeed at being the women the society says they should; such success will offer them approval and security. Isadora says:

I suddenly had a passion to be that ordinary girl. To be that good little housewife, that glorified American mother, that mascot from *Mademoiselle*, that matron from *McCall's*, that cutie from *Cosmo*, that girl with the *Good Housekeeping* Seal tattooed on her ass and advertising jingles programmed in her brain.[34]

As feminist social critics have told us, the messages of the media do not go unheeded in the psyches of these well-educated women, who intellectually may reject them as absurd but have internalized them at a deeper level.

In keeping with earlier feminist theories that view motherhood in negative terms, as preventing women's attempts to realize themselves, these novels portray motherhood as a powerfully restrictive force.[35] Thinks Margaret in *Up the Sandbox!*, "If I were younger, I would join the student revolutionaries. . . . As it is, Elizabeth needs a daily bath."[36] Yet the writers do acknowledge the power of mother love, its physical pleasure and pain: Sasha says: "She purred and giggled as I suckled her. She had her preferences, did my daughter, and when something made her cry she broke my heart with her great stores of tears that flooded her enormous green eyes and overflowed their thick banks of black lashes like swollen rivers" (254). This painfully true paradox about motherhood—that it can be a tender trap—is one reason why these novels were so effective with a 1970s audience of women. Children are so immensely restricting and can be boring to be with every day, and yet the emotional and physical pleasures they provide are profound. This paradoxical nature of motherhood would be explored in greater depth by women novelists during the 1980s.

WOMEN'S BODIES/SEXUALITY

Early feminist theory critiqued Western culture's identification of women with the natural and physical, pointing out that Platonic thought and later Christian ideas perpetuate the contrast between man as mind/culture and woman as body/nature.[37] As I have stated, feminists have pointed out how such ideas limit the woman in her development of a good self-concept and also affect how men in the culture see her. There is also a paradox here, however, because while cultural ideas tell a woman her body is all-important, she is also told that "decent" women deny sexual feelings. Therefore a feminist heroine must free herself from societal views of herself as primarily a sexual creature, fit only for marriage and babies, and at the same time find pleasure and ease with her sexuality. As Isadora realizes, she must integrate the physical and intellectual parts of her being in order to, as Anne Mickelson says, "resolve the conflict between the creative woman and the wife."[38]

Another complication that prevents a protagonist from achieving a free, joyful sexuality is the sexual politics of the typical male-female relationship. The adolescent female must preserve her virginity until marriage or at least love is achieved, while her male counterpart is encouraged to regard her as prey. When she succumbs to his desires, he has "scored" in the game. After marriage, she is economically dependent and so must submit to maintain her status. Thus, as early feminist theorists pointed out, each marital sex act becomes at worst a rape and at best a kind of prostitute-client situation. The sex act itself is the arena where the drama of sexual politics is most clearly played out. To those critics who argue that politics is not involved in the loving relations between husbands and wives, feminist critics would reply that the lack of equality in a traditional marriage makes this "love" problematic.[39]

More than any previous literature by women, these novels of the late 1960s and 1970s dealt forthrightly with women's sexuality—their desire for sex and the physical result, children. They say that women desire and enjoy sex as much as men do. Nevertheless, these protagonists are not always comfortable with their bodies, society having inculcated them with impossible images of beauty and a good amount of self-hatred. Often they are ashamed of or disgusted by their physical selves because, unlike males, whose phalluses are celebrated in art, women are taught to despise their genitals. Margaret in *Up the Sandbox!* compares her tiny daughter's genitals with her own "pulsating, discharging, odorous, membranous opening...." She wonders why "we couldn't preserve the sculptured perfection of our own immature genitals" (17).

Still, these women are aware of their self-hatred and are trying to learn to love themselves and their bodies. They take guilty and/or joyful pleasure in their sexuality; they masturbate, sometimes because their sexual partners do not satisfy them, and sometimes just because it feels good. For instance, in one of the most erotic passages in *Fear of Flying*, Isadora satisfies herself: "Lonely, lonely, lonely, She moves her fingers to that rhythm, feeling the two inside get creamy and the clitoris get hard and red. Can you feel colors in your finger tips? This is what red feels like. The inner cave feels purple." (121). Nancy Regan says passages like this reveal "women's reinhabitation" of the body. Though this self-absorption could be called narcissistic (some radical feminists would say only by those who wish to perpetuate the "myth of the vaginal orgasm"), Regan believes that self-love, including love of one's body, is the first step toward self-actualization, toward living *through* the world in one's body.[40] Women's concern with self-love in these early days of the contemporary feminist movement is similar to the "black is beautiful" thrust of the black liberation movement in the 1960s.

In *Feminist Studies*, Molly Hite discussed the new frankness about female sexuality in fiction by women. Prior to the rise in feminist consciousness, says Hite, female sexuality was avoided by women novelists or was interpreted by male writers through their own eyes. Women were seen as sexed objects of male desire, which had the effect for the woman reader of distancing herself from her self. According to Hite, there is something culturally subversive about women "writing the body," as the French feminists say. On the one hand, it co-opts the identification of woman as primarily body, and at the same time it avoids the dualism that tends to separate mind and body, suggesting that somehow the body is inferior to the mind. When a woman speaks self-consciously as a woman about "female desire, female sensuous experience generally, her performance has the effect of giving voice to pure corporeality, of turning a product of the dominant meaning-system into a producer of meanings."[41] Because a woman's experience of sex is so associated with passivity, a woman speaking about her own body is naming her own experience and making it hers—an act of personal and cultural liberation.

The road to a free, joyful sexuality is rocky, however, for these protagonists. Often their early attempts at sex with men are unsatisfying, but they usually come to enjoy and desire sex with men. Some experiment with sex with women and find there tenderness not experienced with men (I intend to discuss lesbianism in the literature in Chapter 4). In general, though pleasurable and alluring, heterosexual female sexuality can be a snare because of society's attitudes. Because sexual pleasure can lead to social disapproval or even pregnancy, it is dangerous. In marriage it leads to babies, which, because one loves them with a physical passion, in turn leads to restrictions on careers and personal movement. Sheila Ballantyne in *Norma Jean, the Termite Queen* (1975) illustrates these ideas of woman as body and sexuality as a snare. Norma Jean feels like an immense breeder who is losing her mind in the relentless physicality of her life. Just as a termite queen pours forth "rippling eggs" from her body, Norma Jean feels that her whole purpose seems to be the care and feeding of the species.[42] Her problem is that, unlike the termite queen, she is able to question her role.

Like feminist theorists, feminist novels of the 1970s say that sexual liberation for women in the contemporary era is a sham. Because women have been taught to desire sex only in the context of a loving relationship, they cannot enjoy the kind of ribald, unfettered sex associated with males. In *Fear of Flying* Isadora fantasizes about a "Zipless Fuck," an encounter with an anonymous male, unencumbered by zippers or by any emotion other than physical passion. However, when faced with the opportunity, she cannot go through with it: without feeling, she experiences loathing and in fact is outraged at the presumption of the male—a young train attendant who thinks that since she is traveling alone, she is fair game.

In the final analysis, though sexuality and love are snares, they are life-enhancing. No protagonist of these mainstream novels *finally* desires sex unencumbered by feeling: to do so would be to adopt male values. She may fantasize about it, but she sees such an attitude as a kind of enslavement to the deadening values of a system that uses people. It might also be noted in passing that despite the debunking of romantic love found in feminist nonfiction, most of the heterosexual protagonists of the 1970s never give up on the possibility of love between the sexes. In fact, at least one, Isadora in *Fear of Flying*, returns to her husband. Some critics felt that this sort of conclusion pandered to romantic convention and weakened the novels' potential for social change. There *is*, however, an acknowledgment in all these novels that love can enslave women and that its nature is ephemeral.

CAREERS

Though a central concern of early contemporary feminism was the difficulties of women in the working world, few of the novels of the 1970s focus on careers as a central theme. Many of the protagonists are housewives, and others, though working outside the home, seem far more preoccupied with their families and lovers than with their jobs. For example, Isadora and Stephanie are a writer and teacher, respectively, yet their personal lives, especially their sexual fantasies, occupy much of their thoughts. When a career is included, such as Miriam's profession as a systems analyst in *Small Changes* (see Chapter 4), it seems an issue mostly because of how it impinges on her family life. Gail Godwin's heroines in *The Odd Woman* (1974) and *Violet Clay* (1978) are professionals (professor and artist) and, as expected, their jobs are central to their identities. However, in both cases, Godwin uses the career to illustrate how the women make connections between the ideas present in their work and their personal lives. For example, Jane Clifford of *The Odd Woman* (odd meaning unattached) would like to see her life correspond to the patterns she studies in English novels of the eighteenth and nineteenth centuries. It does not, of course. Life is too messy and open ended to have the kind of closure of a novel.

This preoccupation with personal relationships, sexual politics, is central to the early Women's Movement's rallying cry, "The personal is political."[43] As I have explained, this slogan means simply that all relations between the sexes, including sexual relations, are political, based on the collective oppression of males over females dictated by patriarchy. Therefore the struggles between women and their lovers and husbands, and the analysis of these struggles in consciousness-raising groups are central to the liberation of women in the larger society. Many of the novels I discuss are in fact the fictional equivalent of consciousness raising. Many consciousness-raising groups were structured in the same way as these novels, beginning with analysis of women's experiences in childhood and moving on to adolescence, marriage, and so on.

Despite feminism's assertion that "the personal is political," some women critics have harshly condemned the lack of a career as a deep involvement in the lives of these late-twentieth-century characters. Such critics complain that, like the cultural stereotypes, these protagonists seem to care about nothing but men and children. Arlyn Diamond took both Anne Richardson Roiphe and Erica Jong to task for not creating heroines with more genuine interest in the world beyond their private lives and more liberating fantasies than sexual ones. Further, since housework is not acknowledged by the larger society as a worthy social task, "discussions of freedom for women must for now be tied to the idea of a job in the public world."[44]

Today, with the evolution of cultural feminist ideas and the movement's recognition that female concerns are significant, such comments seem dated. Also, while much of what Diamond says is true about both novels—they do not focus on work, and their heroines do use sexual fantasy as an escape— she does not seem to recognize that for women of the 1970s, the problem of reconciling love and work and the kind of conflicts treated by these books *did* reflect the reality of the period. It is, in fact, the most important issue still facing many women—how to reconcile the demands of their public and private worlds, for most women seem unwilling completely to give up the idea of romantic love or family life for involvement in the public sphere. And the ideas of radical feminists who urge alternatives to the nuclear family have simply not caught on with significant numbers of women, novelists as well as other women. Though the "nuclear family" may be only an ideal for large numbers of people, it is still a powerful social fantasy.

CONTACT WITH THE FEMINIST MOVEMENT

In these popular feminist-influenced novels does the protagonist become involved in feminism herself? Since she grows up in the 1950s and early 1960s, the narrator must superimpose her new feminist sensibility on her early experience. Later, some protagonists, such as Isadora, Stephanie, and Norma Jean, discuss feminist ideas with their friends, or read feminist writers, but they do not join discussion groups or participate in public demonstrations. Since these novels are often autobiographical, I suspect that the degree of public involvement of the protagonist depends partly on that of the writer. Marge Piercy, early on a feminist activist, does feature protagonists who participate in feminist political action.

An exception to lack of political involvement is Alther's *Kinflicks*, wherein Ginny and her lesbian lover, Eddie, become involved with 1960s radicalism and feminism. After Ginny leaves Worthley College and Miss Head, Ginny and Eddie follow one typical path to feminism, from antiwar demonstrations to an awareness of male domination in the movement. They move to a commune in Vermont, where the women soon set up their own farm because all the men want to do is "fart around in the gardens all day" and then come in to hot cooked meals (297). In this part of the novel, Alther gently satirizes some of the more radical aspects of the feminist movement. Despite their separation from the men, the women's farm quickly adopts the traditional divisions of labor, with some women doing all the outdoor work and Ginny staying in the cabin and playing the wife role to Eddie as husband.

When the woman try to gain more communards by holding a "Free Women's Weekend," Ginny feels like an outsider as she strolls from workshop to workshop, experiencing estrangement from her sisters. She cannot imagine why women would *want* to see their own cervixes in a mirror, and at the "Women and Rage" workshop, when she watches a woman cry and pound the floor in agony over a rejecting lover, feels embarrassed by such "unearned" intimacy (322). When conflicts develop with the local men over their right to hunt on the women's property, Ginny notices that the pacifist feminists are not above using violent tactics to keep the men away.

However, Alther tempers her criticism of some aspects of the feminist movement in the "mad housewife" section of the novel, "Wedded Bliss." As we have seen, Ginny finds married life with her straight, dull snowmobile salesman husband, Ira, as restricting as her affair with Eddie. The point of *Kinflicks* is that women must be free to conduct their personal quests and not settle for a path dictated by others. *Kinflicks* and other 1970s novels made clear the variety of points of view within the feminist movement. Alther's ambivalence toward radical feminism has caused radical feminist critic Paulina Palmer to call *Kinflicks* ideologically inconsistent.[45] However, it can be judged this way only if one assumes Alther's purpose was to promote radical feminist ideology.

Though they may not be feminist activists, protagonists are aware of feminist issues and how they are trying to pattern their lives according to society's expectations. Isadora thinks, "Somewhere deep inside my head . . . is some glorious image of the ideal women, a kind of Jewish Griselda. She is Ruth and Esther and Jesus and Mary rolled into one" (230). When a woman moves toward her own freedom, she also may see herself as a representative of other women. As Stephanie begins her odyssey, she tells herself that she "rebels for all women, because we are killing ourselves in our doll's houses" (223). All these heroines are conscious of themselves struggling for identity and self-knowledge *as women*, the implication being that as long as society remains patriarchal, one's sexual identity determines and colors all her experience.

THEMATIC CONCERNS: INTIMACY VS. INDEPENDENCE

Feminist theory holds that women's socialization produces people who seek identity and fulfillment in their relationships with others. In these early feminist novels, one of the main conflicts is between the heroine's need for independence and her dependence on others, especially men, for love, security, and identity. In fact, the other conflicts in the heroine's life—romance, marriage, motherhood, career—are part of this central theme. The protagonist is acutely aware of her need for love and how it conflicts with her other aspirations. Intellectually, she realizes she has intrinsic worth without a man, but emotionally she cannot seem to shake her desires, and continues to attempt to define herself relationally.

This same point is made by the feminist psychologist Nancy Chodorow in her studies of female development. Chodorow says that female children identify more strongly with their mothers than do male children, who, in the preoedipal stage are forced to differentiate themselves from the female. The boy must abandon his infantile dependence on his mother and identify with other males; the girl child, realizing she is female, does not need to do this. She will continue her close relationship to her mother. On the other hand, she will be attracted in the oedipal state to her father, representing the male principle. As she develops, it is more difficult for her to establish definite ego boundaries; she continues to see her self "in relationship," and constantly vacillates between the need to break away and establish self and her desire for human connection. Chodorow asserts that few women find this connection with men, who for a host of reasons cannot supply the emotional support and closeness women need. Thus, women form close bonding relationships with other women when they discover that men cannot fulfill their needs.[46] (I will take up the question of mother/daughter relationships and female friendships in Chapter 3.) It is true, however, that the protagonists, though constantly seeking self, at the same time seek bonding in their relationships with men, efforts that work at cross-purposes.

Despite their attempts to achieve closeness to others, they often feel unbearably lonely. From de Beauvoir on, feminists have explored the theme of woman's "Otherness," a feeling women have of being different, isolated, marginalized to the edges of their culture.[47] The protagonists of these novels feel an acute sense of estrangement, from men because the men in their lives see them as essentially different, and from many women who are following traditional women's roles. This sense of estrangement from both sexes makes for difficulty in establishing a firm sense of identity. Protagonists sense their difference early in their lives.

FEMININITY AS DISGUISE

Because of their weak sense of self, protagonists operate in a series of disguises. By the end of her story Ginny realizes that her life's pattern has been the adoption of one disguise after another, none of which seem to fit. According to the authors of the 1970s *bildungsromans*, women try to adapt to their society's wishes for them by wearing masks, a common idea in feminist theory as well.[48] In fact, one could say that each story describes a process by which the heroine gains awareness of the roles she has been playing. Since others seem to see her only as a representative of these roles, she can have a terrifying lack of identity: Isadora's lover tells her, "In the mornings, I can never remember your name." And so she spends her nights "lying awake...next to him trembling and saying my own name over and over to myself to try to remember who I was" (275). All these novels assume the possibility of a unified self that an individual discovers through a personal search, a possibility that more psychoanalytical approaches would reject.

Stephanie in *Lovers and Tyrants* also oscillates between "the irreconcilable poles of lover and liberation, security and freedom." She longs for liberation and at the same time she craves union with those she loves and needs. This need for love can be tyrannical. Like Isadora, she finds herself incomplete without union with another, and when she makes love with Elijah, she momentarily loses her estrangement and becomes one with him:

She stares at him beneath her, her reflection, her mirror image, Stephanie is plunging in and out of the pool, lapping her own image, she is two people, she is man and woman, she is the great round ball of light before it is divided into man and woman, she is Eve fucking Adam before she is detached from him.... (274-275)

As she continues, she thinks of the tyranny of the body, how this need for union, which banishes loneliness, also destroys freedom. Once again, as in the other novels, sexuality becomes a sort of bondage. In the morning, of course, she is once more free but alone. Sexual union provides only a brief respite from the sense of "otherness."

THE WOMEN'S ROOM

Any discussion of the 1970s feminist novel should include Marilyn French's *The Women's Room* (1978), a best-seller despite the fact that it is more radical than any of the novels I have discussed. In the late 1970s it occasioned a good deal of talk between women and men. Men hated it, but women, for the most part, though sometimes finding fault, admitted they could not put it down. One prominent difference between this novel and the others discussed so far is its total lack of irony. In *The Women's Room* there is nothing to laugh at in growing up female in our society; in fact, the atmosphere of the novel is unrelievedly gloomy, a catalog of oppression of women by men.

The Women's Room is the *bildungsroman* of Mira, whom it follows from childhood to middle age, as she progresses from a vague sense of dissatisfaction with her role as a woman to full-blown feminist consciousness. Contrary to the idea of a novel of development being a story of "growing up," in *The Women's Room* characters "descend" into femininity.[49] Because of a devastating near-rape as a girl, Mira marries young, feeling that a woman needs a man for protection. This idea, that women marry for protection against other men, is found in Susan Brownmiller's *Against Our Will*.

French presents a radical feminist view of traditional marriage. Because a woman is economically dependent on a man, she has little say in major decisions; she functions as a domestic and sexual servant. Mira's husband, Norm (his name suggests he represents the all-too-typical characteristics of his sex), is cold, distant, and consumed by his career. Although he is not evil in himself, he has appropriated the evil, masculine qualities of his society. Judi Roller states that some radical feminist writers like French use males to represent ideas—for example, that male dominance in the family can be compared to the dominance of the United States in world politics.[50]

French depicts the housewife role as confining and self limiting; Mira yearns to affect the world in some way, but she knows women do not make change: "Men . . . did these things. Pompous and self-aggrandizing, they tried to erect permanently in the outside world symbols of the penile erection they could not maintain in the flesh."[51] There are, however, compensations for being a woman. Mira enjoys the pleasures of creating a beautiful home for Norm and her two sons, and as a way of making sense of her limited existence, she develops a kind of passive serenity, based on her belief that women *are* necessary. Because they are not able to make money or change the world, they can be in touch with life in a way that striving, driven men cannot. In these ideas French seems to be anticipating 1980s cultural feminist notions of female power. Women maintain the day-to-dayness of the world: "It was women who kept the world going, who observed the changing seasons and kept the beauty high, women who cleaned the world's house . . . " (269). The pity is that in this world no one, not even women themselves, recognize their power.

Since in patriarchy women are mainly sexual objects for men, once Norm loses interest in Mira's body, he discards her for a younger woman and she becomes a displaced homemaker. Like many women during this time, her frightening freedom leads Mira to the world outside her home and finally to feminist ideas. At this point the novel becomes a wide-ranging critique of patriarchy, more so than many of the other "mad housewife" novels. Through Mira's and her friends' experiences at Harvard in the late 1960s, we see male dominance in the classroom, in the medical profession through seducing psychiatrists, and in the legal system through insensitive police who treat Mira's raped friend as cruelly as the rapist had. The military is represented by Duke, a West Pointer, who says, "You have to keep things in separate categories. I believe in this country, I believe in a well-trained army. Sometimes the politicians make a mistake [in Vietnam]. You just have to do your job and hope the politicians will find a way to correct it" (443).

Through Mira's growing feminist consciousness, French says that what is wrong with America is related to what is wrong with the relations between women and men. In the American capitalistic system a few white, upper-middle-class males hold all power and tyrannize over nonwhites, workers, and, above all, women. It is a society that deems logical, rational, masculine thought superior to intuitive, emotional, feminine thought; Mira believes the former modes of thinking are intrinsically evil because, eschewing intuition and emotion, they can be used to justify all manner of evil, including the Vietnam War. French takes pains to point out that the male radicals Mira knows are part of this evil. When Mira finally takes a chance and lets herself love Ben, a social scientist with seemingly nonsexist attitudes toward women, she is bitterly disappointed. Ben gets a chance to go to Africa, and he assumes that Mira will give up her dissertation, follow him there, and have a child with him.

The end of *The Women's Room* finds Mira alone, over forty, with a second-rate teaching job (no first-rate university will hire a woman her age), walking the beach near her home, fighting madness. Although she has achieved economic independence, she is still worse off than when she was with Norm. At night she is plagued with dreams in which male intruders menace her. Here French seems to imply that women must follow the conventions or end up poor and lonely. This depressing result of sex role liberation—unhappiness and loneliness—is also true of Mira's friends who have provided her support and love throughout her years of growth. No heterosexual woman in the novel achieves a happy life; only the lesbians form lasting bonds with other human beings.

This conclusion seems to adhere to the earlier pattern mentioned by Elizabeth Abel in her introduction to her study of the female *bildungsroman*. If a woman's story does not end in marriage, then it may, because of social restrictions, conclude in "an isolation which may end in death," in this case a kind of emotional death (8). Mira says, "Some days I feel dead, I feel like a robot treading out time" (686). In this sense, then, *The Women's Room* does not depart from patterns of women's lives in earlier novels. However, there is a difference. Though the same things have happened to her as to many women, Mira has a different, more aware interior life. Though the novel ends on a despairing note, Mira does achieve self-knowledge.

OTHER POSSIBILITIES—HOPEFUL CONCLUSIONS

Later feminist novels and even some earlier ones do not always take such a gloomy view of the protagonist's and woman's possibilities. *Up the Sandbox!* was probably the least satisfying in terms of providing a way out of the confining female role. The ending finds Margaret pregnant again and happily resigned that she will not live any of the fantasies she indulges in while pushing her baby carriage. *Fear of Flying* concludes with Isadora going back to Bennett, her husband, but with increased understanding of herself and the meaning of her past. *Memoirs of an Ex-Prom Queen* ends with Sasha cutting her hair, a symbolic act, and lifting the telephone to call her writer friend Roxanne, who has never become tied down with a husband and children. Similarly, Norma Jean in *Norma Jean, the Termite Queen*, though still with her husband and children, at the end of her story is beginning to create a life for herself by taking up her premarital vocation, potting.

The conclusion of *Lovers and Tyrants* finds Stephanie in Las Vegas at a glitzy casino floorshow. She wonders if her odyssey has given her self-knowledge and a sense of direction:

... the writer is like a courtesan, dropping perfumed handkerchiefs about the floors of a great house so that the cavaliers can find her room. I have dropped all these clues to myself and where am I now? (315)

She has made progress, however. By plumbing her past she has identified those forces which have held her spirit in bondage: "The magic word is the jailor's name. Identify the enemy, and then you may begin to love him. Make an effort to remember to remember to remember the kingdom of your history. And if you can't recall it, invent it" (315). This eloquent plea for women to remember their pasts in order to free themselves in the present (and to know the enemy) is an important idea behind 1970s consciousness raising.

As Stephanie looks at the sequined acrobat performing over her head, a strangely yet significantly androgynous being, he/she takes on the image of a metamorphosing angel:

We can all be reborn. I am better off now, much better off, I am total, complete, like the great round ball of light before it was divided. I can be more, I can be two, I can be the Other. Children can also be cannibals, sons and lovers can be killers. ... I shall live alone, or with others, for myself... this time I've exorcised myself of one hell of a bunch of oppressors. The stars are thickening. The night is ashine with splendor and with hope. Here, at last, is a beginning. (316)

Though some critics called this ending too florid and too obvious—the idea that we can be oppressed by our society and those we love is hardly new[52]—for many women readers of the 1970s, these ideas *were* new and did express their own desires for self-knowledge and rebirth.

Perhaps, though, of all these novels it is *Kinflicks* that provides the most satisfying resolution. Throughout the novel, Alther has alternated between Ginny's present, while she waits for her sick mother to die, and her reminiscences of her past. Ginny has always felt guilty around her mother, who had chosen a traditional lifestyle. However, the intimacy they share during the mother's last days shows Ginny that her mother regrets her missed opportunities. At the same time that Ginny comes to terms with her feelings of guilt, she realizes that the experimentation of the past ten years has been essential to her growth.

Poised on the brink of her future, Ginny grapples with the frightening knowledge of her freedom. She has been caring for some baby birds who obviously represent herself and her mother; immediately before her mother's death, the last bird dies, killing itself by flying into a closed window, even though the window next to it was open. Unlike the bird, Ginny now sees the open window. After her mother's death, Ginny briefly contemplates suicide, a kind of existential crisis; but finally she embraces life, packs her things, and leaves Hullsport, "to go where I had no idea" (518). This sort of conclusion, typical of almost all these novels, is satisfying to the woman reader of the 1970s who, after her feminist consciousness was raised, had come to terms with her past and was hopeful, yet anxious about the future. As Bonnie Hoover Braendlin points out, Gray's concluding symbol for Stephanie's journey, the androgynous acrobat on a tightrope, suggests that the future will be exciting but fraught with danger.[53]

A CRITICAL ASSESSMENT

It has now been more than twenty years since the first of the 1970s *bildungsromans* appeared. How can we assess the artistic significance of these novels? Will any of them be accorded a place with the important novels of our time, or will they be viewed as dated responses to a situation peculiar to a particular place and time—the predicament of the educated, middle-class housewife in the nuclear family of the 1960s and 1970s—interesting only as a literary response to a sociological problem? In examining these questions it is useful to consider what contemporary reviewers have said of these novels at the time of publication, as well as what later critics have said.

One charge that was frequently made is that these novelists relied too much on their own experience, that in fact, feminist novels are only thinly disguised autobiography, not fiction at all. Because they are so close to their material, these writers have lost their artistic distance, and this is why males are portrayed so unsympathetically, for instance. These women have had bad experiences, and their views are therefore distorted. Such criticism is puzzling, since one would think that the autobiographical nature of most first novels had long been established. One needs only to cite examples of classic male bildungsromans such as Goethe's *Wilhelm Meisters Lehrjahre* and D. H. Lawrence's *Sons and Lovers*. I suspect that in the case of these female-authored novels, critics seized on this old saw in large part because of antipathy to the material (women's experience) and message (feminist themes).

It seems to me that in this case each novel should be judged separately, rather than making a blanket charge condemning them all. Does the writer successfully distance herself, so that the reader is not uncomfortably aware of her life? I would agree, for example, that sometimes I am bothered by the confessional tone of Jong in *Fear of Flying*, which has been likened to being in an elevator with a woman who will not let you out until she tells you her life story.[54] In other cases, notably *Kinflicks* and *Lovers and Tyrants*, the autobiographical material seems to be transformed into something beyond itself.

A more serious charge that has been made of these novels is their weak characterization of males. In her study *Women Writing About Men*, Jane Miller says that women in the past have portrayed men equivocally, as "protectors, our representatives and our opponents."[55] This may have been the case in the past, but most feminist writers of the 1970s portrayed men unequivocally as the oppressor. Fathers, when they appear at all, are usually indifferent to their daughters and teach them traditional values that hamper them in their search for self. Other males, usually lovers and husbands, are even worse. Protagonists may desire them, but they fail again and again to provide love, support, understanding, or even good sex. They are obtuse and self-centered, not understanding their wives' needs for self-realization. They are critical: Jonathan of *Diary of a Mad Housewife* tells Tina, "You look just terrible. Your color's rotten" (3). They are bumbling: in *Kinflicks* Ira dons a leather jockstrap and attempts to hang with Ginny from a rafter to help her reach orgasm. They are cruel, like Tina's lover, George. Above all, they are cold, unable to express love. They have so absorbed traditional values about what is proper male behavior that they have lost the ability to feel. Bennett Wing, Isadora's psychiatrist husband, can "screw" for hours, but he cannot make love: he never kisses her. Even so loving a husband as Paul in *Lovers and Tyrants* cannot really understand Stephanie's needs.

Insofar as they represent patriarchal values or the corrupt capitalist system itself, these male characters can fairly be accused of being stereotypes, as some critics have done. Nevertheless, the fact is that many of these males are recognizable human types. In any case, from the beginning of the form novelists have used characters to represent ideas and to make statements about groups of people. If feminist writers of the 1970s used their characters to express what they believed about men, then one must assume that some writers viewed men as cold, self-centered, oppressive, yet weak. A later, more psychoanalytic view that individual men are not to blame for the state of affairs between the sexes, since masculinity is also a construct of society, was not much in evidence in the 1970s. This is a view that feminist writers were to express more clearly in the 1980s.

Despite these defensive comments, male characterization *is* a primary weakness of these novels. If one knows males who are capable of sensitivity and compassion, then Marilyn French's *The Women's Room* is weakened both as fiction and as polemic. Mickelson says one must take issue with the view that men do not suffer under patriarchy and that they cannot change (221). French impatiently defends her writing against such charges: "The men are there as the women see them and feel them—impediments in women's lives." She argues that we never question when a male writer creates weak female characters.[56] The point is, of course, that feminist critics are questioning female characters created by males, and it therefore behooves them to point out similar weaknesses in women's writing.

This leads us to a related criticism of feminist writing—that it is propaganda disguised as art. This charge has been made particularly of radical writers like French and Marge Piercy (Chapter 4); it is said their zeal to illustrate the injustices suffered by women weakens their art—for example, that too much attention to feminist theory causes them to lose sight of their characters and plot.[57] In *The Women's Room* French catalogs the entire feminist list of crimes against women: emotional crimes such as the stifling of a young girl's newly found sense of self, belittling of female values by insensitive males, ignoring of wives' need for intimacy by husbands, social crimes such the poverty of divorced women, the difficulty of older women in finding jobs, the degradation of black women, and the physical crimes: beatings, rapes, and even the crime of making a woman hate her own body— to feel it is too fat, too old, in some way inadequate. Because she wants to include every possible injustice, as has been said of the novels of Marge Piercy, *The Women's Room* becomes predictable.

Patrocinio Schweikart states that reader-response theory can be useful in assessing our reaction to feminist writing. Readers must grant the woman writer the "light of her own premises," the fact that the "exclusions" and "necessities" she endured "were conditioned by her own world."[58] Marilyn French's view of the world is *her* unique view, conditioned by her experiences and milieu. Schweickart suggests that our response to women's writing should be "dialogic," an effort to communicate at a "minimal distance" in a head-to-head conversation. When I grant her the right to have her perceptions as a woman and a writer, then I find I can argue with her as a reader and yet respect her achievement.

Even though it is "predictable," I cannot deny the power of *The Women's Room*. The book sold millions, and "countless" women wrote to French to tell her of how she had described their own lives. Even faultfinding critics grudgingly acknowledged the novel's power:

It is a novel that lacks grace, restraint, good manners, and acceptance of the realities and pleasantries of life. It forces confrontations on the reader mercilessly. ... As a polemic the book is brilliant. It forces the reader to accept the reactions of the women as the only possible ones.[59]

And Christopher Lehmann-Haupt feels the book does characterize well and rings with truth: "Her story is true. At least it seems true. If it doesn't imitate a truth in the real world, it creates a real world of its own."[60] Such varied reactions indicate the disparity in people's perceptions of male-female relations.

DOUBLE STANDARDS IN CRITICISM

Feminist critics have demonstrated double standards in criticism of male and female writing going well back into the nineteenth century.[61] It seems that in the case of 1970s feminist novels, some critics still treated novels by women differently. Some male reviewers, perhaps not wanting to seem sexist, treated these novels very favorably. Such criticism usually begins by remarking on the writer's sex: "Now here is an excellent book by a woman." Mary Ellmann says that woman's femininity imposes an "erogenic form" upon all aspects of her work.[62] For example, John Updike commends Erica Jong's *Fear of Flying* for the same qualities that past women's writing has been praised: her eye for detail and her ability to express the female point of view.[63]

However, this preoccupation with the writer's femaleness can cause the "unease" documented by Levy in her survey of reviews of women's novels. Some male critics chastise writers for speaking frankly of sexuality. Paul Gray remarks that *Kinflicks* only proves that women can write about sex as raunchily as men: "the organs are different, but the scoring is the same." Others say that the sexual explicitness of Jong is vulgar and foolish, since she is obviously just trying to shock.[64] In 1982, writing for the *Times Literary Supplement*, Roger Scruton grumbled about "gynaecological novels" and longed wistfully for the "golden age (presumably the nineteenth century) when women writers kept silent about such matters."[65] If such comments would not be made of male writers, then this sort of criticism smacks strongly of a double standard.

Female critical reaction to the contemporary feminist novel has been complex. Some women reviewers were delighted with these attempts to represent the experiences of female maturation, a type of novel conspicuously absent in earlier American literature. For example, Doris Grumbach hailed *Kinflicks* as a kind of female *Tom Jones*, comparing Ginny Babcock to Huck Finn and Holden Caulfield.[66] In some ways, however, these novels disappointed women reviewers by not providing stronger, more idealized heroines. Since the beginnings of feminist criticism, many feminist critics have expressed a desire for strong, achieving, self-actualizing heroines; for example, Mary Allen called for "an expanded woman, if not an ennobled one, . . . essential to a truthful portrayal of the times."[67] More recently, Gayle Greene dismissed the majority of 1970s feminist novels, saying that the writers take too few chances with their plots, fearing to suggest radical changes in women's working out their destinies. Citing the example of Isadora returning to her husband, Greene says most of the protagonists do not break out of the "closed circle" of femininity; though they ruminate ceaselessly on the past, they show little ability to apply its lessons to themselves or to women in general. In short, though they show some feminist insights, they fail to draw larger conclusions or change their behavior (86-91).

For that reason, Greene chooses to focus her study of feminism in contemporary women's literature on two British writers, Doris Lessing and Margaret Drabble, and two Canadians, Margaret Atwood and Margaret Laurence. Her feeling is that the American myth of individualism makes it difficult for American writers to conceive of their characters as "enmeshed within and formed by social relations" (23). Their feminist critiques do not go far enough, unlike the *Kunstlerromanes* (metafiction) of Greene's four writers, whose protagonists themselves are writers able "to write beyond the ending," and envision new endings for the old plots about women.[68]

Some women critics, perhaps hoping for these sorts of plots and protagonists, have been extremely harsh on feminist novels, calling their portraits degrading to women. Jane Larkin Crain castigates feminist writers for creating weak, dependent, one-dimensional heroines who patiently suffer unbelievable indignities at the hands of stereotypical males who are cads, tyrants, snobs, and philanderers. She cannot understand why writers who must place a high value on self-determination would create such demeaning women characters: "Whatever the motive there is something repugnant in all this celebration of cowards, cripples, and losers; . . . it reeks of the hatred of women."[69] Sara Sanborn finds the passivity of Marilyn French's characters deplorable.[70] Even a sympathetic critic like Mickelson notes that Jong's Isadora, though spunky, never really flies; she ultimately remains grounded by her femininity (48).

Some of the criticism of feminist novels sounds much like previous attitudes toward women's writing. It is said that such writing fails because it is about domesticity and emotional lives as women struggle with romance and marriage. We have already seen Arlyn Diamond's comments about feminist heroines who are too concerned about men and not enough about significant work in the outside world. Again, however, there appear to be double standards at work here. Novels about male experience—experience outside the confines of the home—are somehow superior to those about the human experience that takes place in the home.

Some feminist critics have cautioned that not all novels which *claim* allegiance to the women's movement can rightly be termed "feminist." Rosalind Coward says that women's novels, even if they purport to be feminist, can actually be subversive of feminist values. Like Diamond, Coward believes that feminist novels are about what women's novels have always been about: romance and family. Their popularity is due not to their feminist ideology but to the fact that they correspond "closely to the structures of popular fiction."[71] The implication is that the feminist writer, if she is concerned with advancing the political movement called feminism, should create protagonists and plots that are truly unique and provide different role models for women readers. Similarly, June Sochen dismisses the 1970s novels as old formula fiction tailored for the market: heroine meets lover, rejects him, seeks experience, and returns to him. These novels only seem to be new.[72]

I find such arguments only partially persuasive. While it is true that the popularity of such novels as *Kinflicks* and *Fear of Flying* is due in part to their frankness about sex (a quality that often puts a novel on the best-seller list) and their interest in a woman's reaction to family life, it seems blatantly elitist to suggest that readers are so obtuse that they do not identify with the feminist ideas in the works, that women read *The Women's Room* for the same reason they read romance novels. There seems to be more than a whiff of contempt for women's values in such criticism. Doris Lessing, Margaret Atwood, Margaret Drabble, and Margaret Laurence may indeed be better writers than most of those I have discussed in this chapter, but not because they portray feminist values more effectively.

If we assume that one function of the novel is to give narrative structure to human experience, the novels that I have discussed are a truthful representation of the inner and outer lives of many women during this period. This is why much of this criticism of the 1970s feminist novel seems to miss the point. If women writers of this period hoped to portray the conflicts in the lives of American women, then these novels needed to be written. They told their version of the truth to millions of women during the 1970s. Above all, they said that "liberation" is elusive. Despite the opportunities opened up by the Women's Movement, it is hard to reject years of socialization. As some writers said, in some ways women are the agents of their own oppression, as Stephanie thinks in *Lovers and Tyrants*: "Woman as angel, woman as beast, the ancient divisions.... Our enslavers segregate us into zoos, with our full consent. Never let the blame fall on the enslavers only" (123).

Not only does society segregate women into "zoos" with their consent, but women in their inner lives restrict themselves. Although by the middle of the 1970s many women had achieved a certain amount of self-realization in their outer lives (the women who could seemingly "do it all"), insecurities remained; these successful women authors are writing of their own lives as well as of the lives of many other women. This paradox of life for contemporary women, still a problem in the 1990s for the next generation of women—the conflict between biological, social, and economic freedom and society's traditional values—does much to explain the lack of completely free, confident, and "actualized" heroines in the fiction of the period. Given the continued presence of traditional values, critics should not be surprised that early feminist fiction gave us few heroines who, as Ellen Morgan says, "show us what it is like to live as free and fully human beings in patriarchal society."[73] These novels show that the same existential problems that affect the contemporary hero affect women, too. The problem of "creating oneself" amid the pressures and restrictions of society are as great for women as for men, or greater for women than for men.

Like Nora Johnson, and unlike some of the critics mentioned above, after reexamining these novels twenty years later, I find them remarkably hopeful and affirming. With the exception of *The Women's Room* and a few of the "mad housewife" novels, at stories' end protagonists *have* achieved some measure of understanding of their pasts and hope for their futures. Though they lack a specific direction, their odysseys have given them knowledge both of self and of the workings of society. Not every protagonist has developed a "feminist critique" that goes beyond the personal, but a number have; and certainly the reader has been aided in developing her own critique. I agree with Johnson that as literature, some have worn well and others have not. I still find *Kinflicks* delightfully funny and insightful, and at least the first half of *Lovers and Tyrants* brilliant.

One final point: all of the novels discussed in this chapter are about white, middle-class women, and I believe that has sometimes affected their critical reception. Many critics find it difficult to accept a novel of protest about such a group, the attitude being "What do these women have to complain about anyway?"[74] This could be a reason for the more positive critical reception granted recent protest novels by black women. Implicit here is an issue that feminists have had to contend with since the beginnings of the movement—that feminism is confined to upper-middle-class white women who are already in privileged positions in our society. This makes their movement as well as their literature suspect by some critics. It has also made it difficult for some Afro-American women writers, who are deeply interested in women, to identify as feminists. I will examine this situation in Chapter 6 on Toni Morrison.

CONCLUSION

In summary, feminism influenced American women writers during the 1970s in a number of ways. Writers explored the socialization of women and their roles in society, showing the negative, restricting aspects of "growing up female" and being female. In their novels traditional marriage was the arena where patriarchal values operate on a personal level. In addition, radical writers such as Marilyn French gave grim examples of male domination in public life as well as in private, illustrating the feminist concept of "patriarchy." Some of this writing succeeded as art, painting complex, truthful pictures of the lives of contemporary women and men. Even those works which succeed mostly as powerful polemics provide useful indicators of writers' and readers' feelings and beliefs about women and their position in society. They can, and should, be studied as examples of how art is used to promote political beliefs.

As the historian Carol Ruth Berkin has said, the 1970s was the era of "naming the oppressor."[75] Most of the feminist-influenced novels of that decade concentrated on the problems of being a woman. It was not until the 1980s that women writers began exploring and even celebrating positive aspects of womanhood, ideas that reflect the views of cultural feminism. In particular, in the 1980s we find a turning away from struggles with men—"sexual politics"—and toward bonding with other women.

NOTES

1. Some feminist scholars declare that a similar phenomenon is happening today. See Gayle Greene, *Changing the Story: Feminist Fiction and the Tradition* (Bloomington: Indiana University Press, 1991), 39.

2. According to Greene, feminist movements are always associated with increased opportunities for education for women. In the 1960s more women began to attend college than in the 1950s (47).

3. For example, the commission did not endorse an Equal Rights Amendment.

4. Lois W. Banner, *Women in Modern America: A Brief History*, 2nd ed. (New York: Harcourt Brace Jovanovich, 1984), 253.

5. Carol Hymowitz and Michaele Weissman, *A History of Women in America* (New York: Bantam, 1978), 344.

6. Radical feminists sometimes refer to this group of feminists as "liberal." Such labels, occasionally confusing, are useful in identifying different strains within feminism.

7. This division of feminists into moderate and radical groups dates well back into the nineteenth century, and arguments among Elizabeth Cady Stanton, Susan B. Anthony, and their followers about the relative importance of the vote and woman's emancipation in the family.

8. Josephine Donovan, *Feminist Theory: The Intellectual Traditions of American Feminism* (New York: Frederick Ungar, 1985). Another useful work on the factions in early feminism is Ginette Castro's *American Feminism: A Contemporary History*, trans. Elizabeth Loverde-Bagwell (New York: New York University Press, 1990).

9. Greene describes the effect of *The Feminine Mystique* as a "nuclear chain

reaction," in Friedan's own words (33), but my own recollection is that the ideas of the work did not come into wide circulation until the late 1960s.

10. Even those feminist thinkers who give credence to Freud's theories, for example, "penis envy," believe Freudian thought is more useful to describe processes of socioacculturation. The psychologist Karen Horney agrees that many little girls do wish to be boys because they see that boys are more valued.

11. Not all feminists have agreed that sex differences are entirely socially determined, rather than inherent in biology, and do not agree that the sexes are equal biologically. Shulamith Firestone argued that woman's position as childbearer will always doom her to less achievement in the public world. Thus she advocated modification of biological reproduction.

12. Elizabeth Janeway's *Man's World, Woman's Place: A Study in Social Mythology* (New York: William Morrow, 1971) is an example of an early feminist work examining the cultural mythology establishing woman's position in the private sphere as opposed to man's in the public sphere.

13. The term "patriarchy" to denote male domination in all aspects of society did not come into wide use until the 1980s. It is imprecise because feminist theorists mean different things by it, but is useful in discussing the literature.

14. Simone de Beauvior, *The Second Sex*, trans. and ed. H. M. Parshley (New York: Vintage, 1952, 1989). Throughout *The Second Sex* de Beauvoir uses the terms "transcendence" and "immanence" to suggest the difference between the way men and women relate to their environments. She sees this situation as partly originating in biology, but certainly susceptible to change.

15. Rather than listing numerous radical feminist writers and their writing, I direct the reader to Chapter 6 in Donovan's *Feminist Theory*.

16. Gerda Lerner, *The Creation of Patriarchy* (New York. Oxford University Press, 1986), believes that the origin of sexual division of labor lies in biology, that is, the female's restriction to tasks that permitted her to remain close to her infant. However, this biological explanation holds true only for the earliest stages of human development and "does not mean that a later sexual division of labor based on women's mothering is 'natural' " (43).

17. Susan Brownmiller, *Against Our Will: Men, Women, and Rape* (New York: Simon and Schuster, 1975).

18. For these ideas on early novels of development I am indebted to Elizabeth Boyd Jordan's "The Evolution of the Domestic *Bildungsroman*: Fairy Tale Ending to Domestic Disenchantment" (unpub. MS, Purdue University, 1985).

19. See Hardy's *The Mayor of Casterbridge* (1886), *Tess of the D'Urbervilles* (1891), and *Jude the Obscure* (1895).

20. Patricia Meyer Spacks, *The Female Imagination* (New York: Knopf, 1975), 113-158.

21. *The Voyage In: Fictions of Female Development*, ed. Elizabeth Abel, Marianne Hirsch, and Elizabeth Langland (Hanover, NH., and London: University Press of New England, 1983), 8.

22. Greene, 52.

23. Sylvia Plath, *The Bell Jar* (New York: Harper & Row, 1971), 76.

24. Elin Schoen, "Kiss, Kiss, Kvetch, Kvetch: What's Ailing the New Belles of Letters?" *New York*, 10 (23 May 1977), 59-67. In "Housewives and Prom Queens, 25 Years Later," *New York Times Book Review* (20 March 1988), 32, Nora Johnson

says, "All the housewives are mad"; in *Changing the Story* Gayle Greene includes a chapter (3) on "mad housewife" novels.

25. Sue Kaufman, *Diary of a Mad Housewife* (New York: Bantam, 1967).

26. Barbara White, *Growing up Female: Adolescent Girlhood in American Fiction* (Westport, CT: Greenwood, 1985), 195.

27. See Phyllis Chesler, *Women and Madness* (New York: Doubleday, 1972).

28. Alix Kates Shulman, *Diary of an Ex-Prom Queen* (New York: Bantam Books, 1972), 19.

29. David Lynn, "Determinants of Intellectual Growth in Women," *School Review* 80 (1972), 241-260; Thomas L. Good, J. Neville Sikes, and Jere E. Brophy, "Effects of Teacher Sex and Student Sex on Classroom Interaction," *Journal of Educational Psychology* 65 (1973), 74-87. Georgia Sasson has challenged such studies, showing that when girls are given female-specific tasks, they can be very achievement oriented. "Success Anxiety in Women: A Constructionist Interpretation of Its Source and Its Significance, *Harvard Educational Review* 50 (1980), 13-24.

30. Lisa Alther, *Kinflicks* (New York: New American Library, 1975), 46.

31. Louise Bernikow, *Among Women* (New York: Harper & Row, 1980), 57-58.

32. De Beauvoir, *The Second Sex*, 451-455.

33. In the first two chapters of her *Women in Modern America*, Banner explains that the predicament of the middle-class housewife was already noticeable by the late 1800s.

34. Erica Jong, *Fear of Flying* (New York: Holt, Rinehart, and Winston, 1973), 277-278.

35. Hester Eisenstein, *Contemporary Feminist Thought* (Boston: G. K. Hall, 1983), provides a good account of early feminism's views of motherhood.

36. Anne Richardson Roiphe, *Up the Sandbox!* (New York: Simon and Schuster, 1970), 13.

37. See Susan Griffin, *Pornography and Silence: Culture's Revenge Against Nature* (New York: Harper & Row, 1981).

38. Anne Mickelson, *Reaching Out: Sensitivity and Order in Recent American Fiction by Women* (Metuchen, NJ: Scarecrow, 1979), 37.

39. In *Sexual Politics* Kate Millett wrote about sexual intercourse as a major site of male-female struggle; another important work dealing with this theme is Anne Koedt's "The Myth of Vaginal Orgasm," in *Radical Feminism*, ed. Anne Koedt, Ellen Levine, and Anita Rapone (New York: Quadrangle Books, 1973), 198-207. Koedt argues that men control sexual knowledge and have withheld from women the fact that female orgasm is located in the clitoris. This withholding of sexual knowledge perpetuates the idea that female sexual pleasure depends on heterosexual intercourse.

40. Nancy Regan, "A Home of One's Own: Women's Bodies in Recent Women's Fiction," *Journal of Popular Culture* 11 (Spring 1978), 778-779.

41. Molly Hite, "Writing—and Reading—The Body: Female Sexuality and Recent Feminist Fiction," *Feminist Studies* 14 (Spring 1988), 121-122.

42. Sheila Ballantyne, *Norma Jean, the Termite Queen* (New York: Bantam, 1975), 17.

43. Millett, Firestone, and others have written extensively on this idea.

44. Arlyn Diamond, "Flying from Work," *Frontiers* 2 (1977), 18.

45. Pauline Palmer, *Contemporary Women's Fiction: Narrative Practice and Feminist Theory* (Jackson, MS: University Press of Mississippi, 1989), 116.

46. Nancy Chodorow, *The Reproduction of Mothering: Psychoanalysis and the Sociology of Gender* (Berkeley: University of California Press, 1978), 200.

47. De Beauvoir, *The Second Sex*, xxii-xxxv.

48. Mary Daly, for example, says that femininity requires acting out a part. *Gyn/Ecology: The Metaethics of Radical Feminism* (Boston: Beacon Press, 1978), 56-57.

49. Palmer, 72.

50. Judi Roller, *The Politics of the Feminist Novel* (Westport, CT: Greenwood, 1986), 149. This idea that male behavior on a personal level finds its counterpart in the behavior of an entire society or nation is a common one in some feminist thinking.

51. Marilyn French, *The Women's Room* (New York: Jove Publications, 1978), 268. Feminists sometimes reflect Freudian thinking more than they would like to admit. Freud felt that man's achievement in the world beyond the home was in part a displacement of his libido. *Civilization and Its Discontents* (1930), rev. and ed. James Strachey (London: Hogarth, 1963), 40.

52. Three examples are Julian Monihan, "Adventures of Stephanie," review of *Lovers and Tyrants* by Francine du Plessix Gray, *New York Times Book Review* (17 October 1976), 7; Michael Wood, "Endangered Species," *New York Review of Books* (11 November 1976), 23; and Peter Prescott, "Two Women on the Edge," *Newsweek* 88 (11 October 1976), 107. All three reviewers had high praise for earlier sections of the novel but felt the ending detracted from Gray's achievements.

53. Bonnie Hoover Braendlin, "Alther, Atwood, Ballantyne, and Gray: "Secular Salvation in the Contemporary Feminist *Bildungsroman*," *Frontiers* 4 (1979), 20.

54. Jonathan Raban, "Lullabies for a Sleeping Giant," *Encounter* 43 (July 1974), 76.

55. Jane Miller, *Women Writing About Men* (New York: Pantheon Books, 1986), 12.

56. In *Contemporary Authors: New Revised Series*, ed. Ann Emory, 3 (Detroit: Gale Research, 1980), 241.

57. Nina Auerbach, *Communities of Women: An Idea in Fiction* (Cambridge, MA: Harvard University Press, 1978), 191.

58. Patrocinio Schweikart, "Reading Ourselves: Toward a Feminist Theory of Reading," in *Contemporary Literary Criticism: Literary and Cultural Studies*, ed. Robert Con Davis and Ronald Schleifer (New York: Longman, 1989), 135.

59. Brigitte Weeks, "Separating the Women from the Men," review of *The Women's Room* by Marilyn French, *The Washington Post Book World* (9 October 1977), E1-2.

60. Christopher Lehmann-Haupt, "Books of the Times," *New York Times* (27 October 1977), sec. 3, 20.

61. See, for example, Dale Spender, *The Writing or the Sex?* (Elmsford, NY: Pergamon, 1989). Spender argues that not only do male critics belittle women's writing, they often do not even read it. See also Elaine Showalter, "Women Writers and the Double Standard," in *Woman in Sexist Society*, ed. Vivian Gornick and Barbara K. Moran (New York: Basic Books, 1971), 323-343.

62. Mary Ellmann, *Thinking About Women* (New York: Harcourt Brace Jovanovich, 1968), 31.

63. John Updike, "Jong Love, " *The New Yorker* 49 (17 December 1973), 149-151.

64. Paul Gray, "Blue Genes," review of *Kinflicks* by Lisa Alther, *Time* 107 (22 March 1976), 80; and Paul Theroux, "Hapless Organ," review of *Fear of Flying* by Erica Jong, *New Statesman* 87 (19 April 1974), 554.

65. Quoted in Molly Hite, "Writing—and Reading—The Body," 121.

66. Doris Grumbach, "A Classic Outsider," review of *Kinflicks* by Lisa Alther, *Saturday Review* 3 (20 March 1976), 22-23.

67. Mary Allen, *The Necessary Blankness: Women in Major American Fiction of the Sixties* (Urbana: University of Illinois Press, 1976), 12.

68. Rachel Blau DuPlessis's *Writing Beyond the Ending: Narrative Strategies of Twentieth-Century Women Writers* (Bloomington: Indiana University Press, 1985) is another study of how women writers invent strategies "that sever the narrative from formerly conventional structures of fiction and consciousness about women ... "(x). DuPlessis does not focus exclusively on contemporary writers, however.

69. Jane Larkin Crain, "Feminist Fiction," *Commentary* 58 (December 1974), 62.

70. Sara Sanborn, "A Feminist Jacqueline Susann," *Ms.* 6 (January 1978), 30, 34.

71. Rosalind Coward, "Are Women's Novels Feminist Novels?" in *The New Feminist Criticism: Essays on Women, Literature, Theory,* ed. Elaine Showalter (New York: Pantheon, 1985), 232.

72. June Sochen, *Enduring Values: Women in Popular Culture* (New York: Praeger, 1987), 20.

73. Ellen Morgan, "Humanbecoming: Form and Focus in the Neo Feminist Novel," in *Images of Women in Fiction: Feminist Perspectives,* ed. Susan Koppelman Cornillon (Bowling Green, OH: Bowling Green State University Press, 1972), 204.

74. Audrey Foote, review of *Lovers and Tyrants* by Francine du Plessix Gray, *The Washington Post Book World* (August 29, 1976). Foote asks what Stephanie, with an affluent life, rewarding career, and a loving husband and children, could possibly want.

75. Carol Ruth Berkin, "Clio in Search of Her Daughters/Women in Search of Their Past," *Liberal Education* 71 (Fall 1985), 206.

3

New Developments in the 1980s: Bonds Between Women

The 1980s, especially the first half of the decade, were a hard time for feminists. The election of Ronald Reagan in 1980 marked the beginning of the new political conservatism that would slow the progress of movements for social change such as minority rights and the Women's Movement. This new conservatism was already on the way in the 1970s with the rise of antifeminist backlash in groups like the Moral Majority. Composed of evangelical Christians and other conservatives, the Moral Majority proclaimed traditional family values, declaring that feminism meant the doom of the American family. Antifeminist leader Phyllis Schlafly warned that passage of the Equal Rights Amendment (ERA) would make women eligible for the draft, invalidate laws protecting women in the home, and bring about unisex toilets.

Another sign of the growing conservatism was the popularity of books like Marabel Morgan's *Total Womanhood* (1978). Quoting Scripture, Morgan advised housewives how to keep their husbands interested, pointing out that St. Paul's admonition to wives to submit produced the happiest homes. The popularity of ideas such as Morgan's and Schlafly's showed how threatening the Women's Movement was and how much work had to be done to change such traditional ideas. In the heady excitement of the early 1970s, feminists had not realized how difficult it would be to gain acceptance for their ideas.

As Susan Faludi has shown in her book *Backlash: The Undeclared War on American Women* (1991), throughout the 1980s the mass media promoted the idea that feminism was passé and discredited. A number of popular books and prominent newspaper articles stated that younger women were rejecting feminist ideas and that feminism had caused more problems for women than it had solved. For example, an influential *New York Times*

article by Susan Bolotin used the term "post-feminist" to describe the attitudes of the younger generation of women.[1]

A particular blow to the movement was the defeat of the ERA in 1982. Though feminist organizations put up a valiant push, membership in the National Organization for Women (NOW) nearly quadrupling from 1977 to 1982, it was too little, too late. Since in 1982 a Lou Harris poll showed 63 percent support for the ERA, most feminists blamed the defeat on complacency and a lack of careful political planning. However, some suggested that fragmentation and a too-radical image had hurt the Women's Movement.[2] In 1980 Betty Friedan had stated in *The Second Stage* that feminism had lost adherents because it appeared to denigrate woman's role as wife and mother.[3]

Certainly by the late 1970s feminism had splintered into myriad groups and ideologies. Most of these strains of feminism, cited in Chapter 2, were well in place by the late 1970s and there are many variations within them. In a time of retrenchment and reevaluation this fragmentation undoubtedly made for political difficulties, but it did produce a rich outpouring of feminist theories that found their way into the fiction of the 1980s.

Feminism did not die in the 1980s, despite gloomy or ecstatic predictions of its demise; rather, it continued to evolve. Older women within the movement reassessed their values and concerns, and although not rejecting feminist ideas or their new lifestyles, they became less interested in how they had been oppressed by patriarchy and more in what it meant to be a woman in a positive sense. The idea of "sisterhood," early recognized as a concept necessary for the political unity of women, suggested many questions for feminist thinkers to explore. Were there special, positive experiences in "growing up female," and living as a women in contemporary society, and if so, what were they? Is motherhood, seen as a hindrance to personal growth by many feminists in the 1970s, actually an asset to woman's development of full humanity? What is the importance of women to each other as mothers, daughters, sisters, and friends? How do women help and sometimes hinder each other as they attempt to realize themselves? All of these topics received extensive treatment in feminist theoretical writing; in developing their new ideas, scholars drew on the research and writing of previous generations of feminist thinkers, as well as on more recent ideas of psychoanalysis.

In examining how feminist values are expressed in the literature of the 1980s, it is easy to see these changes and new attitudes. There is less emphasis on the *bildungsroman*, centering on the protagonist's search for identity in patriarchy. Writers did not abandon interest in women's socialization and male/female relations, but definitely shifted toward same-sex relationships. When one considers the central thrust of feminism in the 1970s, it is easy to see why writers focused on female/male relations. Since writers and readers were interested in the negative effects of patriarchy on women's lives, they focused on this theme in the lives of the protagonists—their struggles for freedom and self-definition in courtship and marriage.

Perhaps, too, it was difficult for women novelists to let go of the idea that novels, at least novels about women, are about the relations between women and men. This is the problem of Joanne Frye's "prescripted text" mentioned in Chapter 1. The *bildungsromans* of the 1970s stressed the disillusionment experienced by women who come to see how confining those male/female relationships are, but the focus is still women interacting with men. In 1990 Elayne Rapping cited the preoccupation with male/female power structures of "upscale" white protagonists as *the* major weakness of earlier feminist fiction, and called for writing "that deals with women's lives in terms of larger, more vital and dynamic social and political contexts."[4]

In the 1980s the ideas that Josephine Donovan calls "cultural feminism" were popularized and found their way into novels by women writers. As was stated in Chapter 2, cultural feminists suggest that women's "differences"—their ability to nurture life, care for others, reverence the earth, and see all of creation as an organic whole—are enhanced by their life experiences of birth, caregiving, and domesticity. Though cultural feminists sidestep the issue of "nature or nurture," believing it dangerous to concede that women's differences may be biologically based, they agree there *are* important sexual differences that, if allowed to flourish in the public sphere as well as the private, would have much to offer all humanity.[5] They argue that men, too, suffer from patriarchy—in the atrophying of feeling, in the constant need to appear strong and competitive, and in the lack of close relationship to their children. The larger society suffers from patriarchal thinking in the continual pressure for more military spending, and the consequent neglect of the poor, minorities, and the aged, as well as of the environment. In the 1980s these concerns found their way into mainstream women's fiction in several ways: the exploration and celebration of female relationships; a celebration of feminine values of interconnection and harmony—what one could call domestic virtues; and the creation of more sympathetic male characters, even by the more radical writers.

MOTHERHOOD/MOTHERS AND DAUGHTERS IN THE 1970s

As we have seen, early feminist thinking, though it grudgingly acknowledged the pleasures of motherhood, tended to portray it as an institution from which women needed to be liberated. Theorists also suggested that a mother could be a negative force in a daughter's life by inculcating patriarchal values in her and limiting her sense of her own possibilities. In keeping with these theories, most of the novels of the 1970s gave little attention to the relationships of mothers and daughters or made the protagonist's mother one of her problems. These mothers, traditional women of the 1940s and 1950s, are poor role models in the eyes of their daughters. As "castrated"

representatives of the patriarchy, they are the socializers, the "corset tighteners" and "foot binders." Louise Bernikow says: "To 'socialize' a ram-
bunctious ... tense, intellectual, turbulent daughter—this was the task, to
tame, train her to be 'woman' at the same time retaining love between them
and looking good in the eyes of the world. A link in the chain of women
binding each other's feet."[6] This view of the mother is a small step from
the "monster mother" who devours the lives of her children because she
has no life of her own.[7]

In *Lovers and Tyrants* Stephanie's mother is one of the "tyrants" in her
life; her concern for social status precludes her taking much interest in her
daughter's development. Sasha's mother, in *Memoirs of an Ex-Prom Queen*,
"as clever and ambitious" as her father, focuses all her ambitions on Sasha,
whom she encourages to achieve by "marrying well" (73). In *Fear of Flying*
Isadora's mother is a frustrated artist who believes she might have been
successful if it had not been for her children. At the same time, she tells
Isadora that a woman cannot both achieve in a career and be a successful
wife and mother (40). All these women are jealous of their daughters'
expanded opportunities, and this jealousy combines with sincere fear for
their daughters' happiness, which might be sacrificed if the daughter attempts to transcend a traditional role.

One of the most complex and atypical portraits of a mother-daughter
relationship in the novels of the 1970s is that of Ginny Babcock and her
mother in Lisa Alther's *Kinflicks*. Alther alternates between Ginny's consciousness and her mother's, letting us see how each reacts to the relationship
that they are facing for the first time. As she lies dying, Mrs. Babcock is
trying to justify and understand the meaning of her life. She hopes that it
had some meaning, for she had spent most of her time nurturing others,
perhaps more so than some women because she always felt that her own
mother had neglected her. For her part, Ginny would like to blame her
unhappy predicament on her mother, who raised her to fulfill a traditional
female role.

As if anticipating the ideas of psychologist Nancy Chodorow, Alther
suggests that this chain of "frustrated nurturing" needs to be broken so
that daughters can lead lives different from those of their mothers. To do
this, mothers need to let go and not reproduce the chain. As Mrs. Babcock
approaches death, Ginny asks her if she should return home to her family.
Mrs. Babcock is torn: she would like to nurture Ginny, to tell her everything
will be all right; she would also like to tell her to "Do her duty," as she
was told by her own mother. However, recognizing that Ginny's duty to
herself might conflict with her role as wife and mother, she breaks the
"generational spell," what Chodorow calls the "reproduction of mothering." "I don't know what you should do, Ginny. You must do as you think
best" (431). Soon Mrs. Babcock turns to the wall and asks to be alone.

Ginny's existential crisis that follows, her futile attempt at suicide, is precipitated by her anger at her mother's leaving *her* alone. As Ginny rails at being left without answers, she is clear about one thing: we each die alone. A woman does *not* gain immortality through her children; one day Ginny will face death alone, without the help of her daughter, whom she will leave alone. Nonetheless, a mother can give her child autonomy, as Mrs. Babcock does in her final words to Ginny: "Look after yourself." Mary Anne Ferguson compares Alther's story to the Psyche/Cupid myth, in which Psyche (Soul) searches for Cupid (Love), aided or hindered by a powerful mother figure, Venus. As Ferguson says, Ginny's mother gives the greatest gift of any parent: "acceptance of one's mortality accompanied by the determination to fight it."[8]

However, this portrait of a mother/daughter relationship that brings strength and insight to the protagonist seems unusual in the 1970s. Margaret Drabble, a British writer whose novels from 1962 to 1980 depict very few "good" mothers, has remarked on her own inability to create mothers who enhance their children's growth.[9] Well-groomed, proper, caring for their husbands and children with impeccable concern, they lack "self-awareness, imagination, and humor," and seem unable to recognize who their children are. As Earlene Hawley says, "They are in stunning contrast to the individuation which daughters and sons are attempting in their ardent struggle from intelligence to wisdom."[10] With few exceptions, the same can be said of the mothers of women protagonists in American novels of the 1970s.

MOTHERHOOD/MOTHERS AND DAUGHTERS IN THE 1980s

By the late 1970s we begin to see a different view of motherhood and mother/daughter relationships emerging in feminist nonfiction and in the literature as well. Opposite the view of "monster mother" is the view of the mother as muse, as a source of encouragement and inspiration. Louise Bernikow called on the new generation of daughters to view mothers this way, as well as to recognize how they may have harmed their daughters' development, in order to understand how female connections create and strengthen women, propelling them into the future (69). Similarly, writers like Kathryn Allen Rabuzzi and Carolyn Heilbrun urged women to reinvent the old myths, such as that of Demeter and her daughter Persephone, to see how our links with our female ancestors provide gifts and strengths to use in our heroic quests.[11] One could say that the theorists of the 1970s deconstructed the traditional myths of motherhood, but by the 1980s they were creating new myths that would be more useful to contemporary women.

One of the most influential cultural feminist studies of motherhood was Adrienne Rich's *Of Woman Born: Motherhood as Experience and Institution* (1977). Calling on her own experiences, Rich acknowledged the frustrating, limiting aspects of being a mother, due to the institution of motherhood as it has developed in patriarchal society. With cultural changes, motherhood would not have this effect on women's lives. Rich asserted motherhood's potential for developing valuable characteristics of strength and concern for others. This understanding of the paradoxical nature of motherhood—that in patriarchal society it limits a woman's growth and at the same time provides a source of pleasure and even power— was a growing understanding in the fiction of the period as well.

Besides Rich's and Chodorow's studies, remarkable adaptations of Freudian thought to a feminist perspective, cultural feminist thinkers explored motherhood and mother/daughter relationships in the late 1970s and 1980s. In 1980 Sara Ruddick suggested that maternal, nurturing activities foster a mode of living which promotes growth and preservation. Since the caregiver is aware that she cannot control the Other, she adopts a waiting attitude more likely to enhance life than questing male activities that seek to change the environment. Similarly, speaking of traditional female activities such as caregiving and housekeeping, Nancy Harstock in 1983 argued that woman's perspective creates a life-enhancing mode of thinking that sees all reality in context. Women's experience is of continuity and harmony that integrate mind and body; such ways of thinking can provide a way out of the mind/ body split that is at the heart of much masculine ideology.[12] And, of course, in addition to the work of American feminist thinkers, French scholars such as Hélène Cixous, Luce Irigaray, and Julia Kristeva contributed profound insights into the mother-child relationship. According to Kristeva in her adaptation of Freudian-Lacanian thought, the mother-child bond prefigures the symbolism of all that we know as civilization; it erases subject-object polarity and is that against which the child must struggle as it emerges into the symbolic.

Though it is difficult to tell how much of this theory directly influenced fiction writers during the 1980s, we see unmistakable resonances of the theoretical ideas in the fiction. Some novelists, echoing ideas of the cultural feminists, celebrated the pleasures of domesticity and mothering young children. One of these is Mary Gordon in *Men and Angels* (to be discussed in Chapter 5). Perhaps the most popular treatment of motherhood in 1980s fiction is Sue Miller's *The Good Mother* (1986). This highly touted first novel recounts a bitter custody battle between Anna Dunlop, mother of little Molly, and her ex-husband, Brian, who believes (wrongly) that Anna's lover, Leo, has sexually abused Molly. In this novel Miller skillfully combines a critique of the patriarchal leanings of our legal system with a celebration of the passion of maternal love, in Anna's case a love partaking of and surpassing the erotic.

Recent divorcée Anna (several critics have noticed the resemblance to Anna Karenina) is not a stereotypical feminist protagonist.[13] Unambitious, she supports herself by working as a lab assistant and piano teacher rather than pursuing a career that would take her away from Molly. She is also passive, preferring to say what the system wants to hear—that she will give up Leo to get Molly back. As she tells her feminist friend Ursula, "I don't care about *dignity* or *pride* or any of that stuff."[14] All she wants is Molly. Though some reviewers were annoyed at Anna's passivity, Diane Cole felt that it is Anna's lack of heroism, her humanity, that makes the novel so powerful.[15] Roberta White agrees, saying that Miller is "affirming the superior value of the inner life over the outer life and of the private over the public good."[16] In this novel a mother's love for her child supersedes any abstract notions of public justice.

Miller's skill as a writer makes the reader care passionately about Anna's predicament. More than any other novelist I discuss here, Miller makes a little child a real person, a person we ourselves would not want to lose. In the early sections of the novel she celebrates the profound beauty of the domestic life Anna and Molly have together:

I carried her wrapped in a towel down the long hallway to our bedrooms, and dressed her for the night. Mosquitoes and moths danced outside the screens on bedroom windows, tapping them lightly over and over as I read her a story. She leaned against my breast while I read, and her head moved slightly with my every breath, as though she were still part of my body. With one tiny forefinger she rhythmically flicked at the button eye of her stuffed bear (8).

The early parts of *The Good Mother* are filled with such scenes that make the subsequent events of the novel harder to bear, for we know what Anna must give up. Linda Wolfe, the reviewer for the *New York Times*, suggests that no one has done the beauty "of the commonplaces of motherhood and ordinary life better" (40). Scenes like this sanctify domesticity, confirming cultural feminist Kathryn Rabuzzi's belief that there is a "natural luxury" to being a woman that allows her to take joy in the private sphere, perhaps in a way that men have been prevented from doing.[17] Some feminist critics have suggested that such scenes "sentimentalize" domesticity and distract women from their fight for public justice, but cultural feminists might retort that we need to remember equally important values, that fiction which invests traditional female activities with dignity and worth can only enhance women's struggle for public justice.[18]

Miller emphasizes the passionate nature of Anna and Molly's relationship through flashback scenes showing Anna's own childhood in a cold, unloving home. Because Anna was unloved by her own mother and had a distant relationship with her husband, Molly's is really the first love in her life. Anna's mother, functioning as the representative of patriarchy, has taught her to be uncomfortable with her body. In a scene where the adolescent Anna is dancing sensuously to rock and roll, watching her new body in the mirror, her mother tells her, "I hate to see you move like that" (33). The warm preoedipal physical pleasure of the mother-child bond comes into Anna's life only when she has her own child.

The novel illustrates a deep conflict between society's expectations of mothers and erotic love—Anna's passionate bond with Molly versus her bond with Leo. As Josephine Humphreys says, Miller asks whether maternal and erotic love can coexist. When wild, bohemian Leo enters Anna's life, her life at first expands; sexually awakened for the first time, she now has adult eroticism to add to maternal eroticism. However, when society, in the form of her ex-husband and the court, intrudes, Anna must choose, and her bond with Molly wins out. Anna does not chastise patriarchy for what has happened; but rather she chastises herself for "having succumbed to a euphoric forgetfulness of all the rules" (280). She has forgotten to protect her child. Meredith Powers defends Anna by pointing out that this mother/child bond is "the elemental root of all sociality. Hers [Anna's] is a preverbal compulsion expressed by a centrality of focus which is unshaken by distractions of either orthodox culture or overt rebellion."[19] These maternal attachments, expressed in narrative form as early as the myth of Demeter and Persephone, are deep and cannot be brushed aside. Like Demeter, Anna must compromise to retain her tie with her daughter; but, as Powers suggests, after losing custody and a brief flirtation with suicide (a sort of descent to the Underworld?) Anna emerges a wiser and stronger woman.

Feminist critics have found fault with this novel. Mary Gordon has stated that part of its popularity may be due not to its sensitive portrayal of motherhood but to the passionate romance between Anna and Leo.[20] It does seem as if Anna's newfound freedom comes in the traditional way—through a man. Nevertheless, I decided that my own criticism of Anna's lack of a career commitment may be an imposition of society's male-oriented standards on her quirky independence. At one point Leo chastises Anna for not having a serious commitment to a vocation. She testily defends herself, however, saying she has a commitment to Molly and "to doing carefully and well what I do." When Leo presses her further, Anna retorts:

"It used to be that men would say, 'I want a woman who' and the list would be different. 'Who cooks, who sews, who can entertain my friends.' But it's the same impulse.... It's still *your* judgment, *your* list, your game.... You're still saying I'm just an extension of you, that I'd better look good to the world so I make you look good. That's all it is." (118)

Though she may not describe this as cultural feminism, Sue Miller certainly echoes cultural feminist ideas in *The Good Mother*.

Another novel of the early 1980s concerned with motherhood, as well as with relationships between sisters, is Gail Godwin's *A Mother and Two Daughters* (1982). Godwin's first two novels, *The Odd Woman* (1974) and *Violet Clay* (1978), were more in the *bildungsroman* mode and dealt with lone women protagonists, with relatively little attention paid to familial relationships. In *A Mother and Two Daughters*, she continued her interest in intelligent, sensitive middle-class professional women who are struggling to achieve their aspirations in the face of self-imposed and cultural restraints.[21] Instead of portraying one woman's struggle, however, Godwin focuses on a community of women. The story concerns the dynamics between mother Nell and two daughters, Cate and Lydia, who must readjust after their underpinning—the husband and father of the family—has died. Three women alone, they must find themselves in relationship, as well as in connection with others around them. Godwin has said that she was interested in how each character "had shaped and been shaped by the other two heroines."[22] The novel also contains a number of other women characters who illustrate various types of contemporary women's problems.

In its concentration on a loving network of women of different generations who help each other through various crises, A Mother and Two Daughters reflects the ideas of nineteenth-century cultural feminists who lived within such networks and celebrated them in their thinking and writing. Probably the first promoters of "sisterhood" in history, women such as Elizabeth Cady Stanton, Charlotte Perkins Gilman, and Jane Addams continually affirmed their love for women, declared that feminine virtues would reform society, and urged that women work together to effect such reforms.

Like many feminist scholars, A Mother and Two Daughters says that the terrible responsibilities of motherhood never end, for even when our children are adults, we cannot psychically free ourselves from them. As Nell has recently lost her role as a wife, she must now begin to reevaluate her role as a mother. Nell loves her daughters but finds them tiring and sometimes annoying; she is proud of the achievements of the flamboyant Cate, a feminist college professor, yet troubled by her inability to achieve a fulfilling personal life: "Nell felt a strong but utterly impractical urge to seize control of Cate's life. She wished she could pick her up, figuratively, and clean off the spoilage."[23] Later, Nell speculates on the helplessness of the mother in the face of her firstborn's pain. There is so much a mother wishes to do for her child and so little she really *can* do to shield her. With the second child, Lydia, it was easier, and yet Nell feels she failed with her, too, because although she now had the knowledge, she did not have the energy to use it. As feminist theorists have suggested, it is the nature of motherhood to feel powerless.[24]

Nell's reevaluation of motherhood, something she never thought about while she was being a mother, affects her decision making in other areas of her life. Near the end of the novel Nell decides to nurse a dying woman friend. This is a difficult decision because she has adjusted to her single life, feels she is becoming more "self-contained" and happy with herself. Should Nell abandon this free life for one of traditional female nurturance, self-denying service, in a sense continuing to mother? Telling herself, "You can be self-contained in the coffin" (454), she nurses her friend, which leads her to further self-discoveries, including the desire to return to her pre-marriage career of nursing. This is certainly a different message from the *bildungs-roman* of the 1970s, whose protagonist found her "self-actualization" in solitary flight from her society.

Though Godwin is not often discussed as a feminist writer, all of her works deal with women's issues, as well as other issues affecting American society. In *A Mother and Two Daughters* we see women responding to many social forces and problems; some of the other issues the novel treats are abortion, mastectomies, unwed mothers, older women, women divorcing and entering college, and women in relation to men—lovers and husbands—as well as displacement of rural people by urban sprawl and environmental destruction. In the setting of the story, a small town in the North Carolina mountains, this network of women characters gives all members warm support in their various problems, as well as a sense of community. Like cultural feminists, Godwin suggests that female unity and helpfulness, how we treat our families and friends, can be a paradigm for how we treat each other in the larger fabric of the amorphous thing called "society." As the quote by Montaigne that opens the novel states: "To storm a breach, conduct an embassy, govern a people, those are brilliant actions. . . . to deal justly with one's family . . . that is something rarer, more difficult, and less noticed in the world" (17).

Actually, as Marianne Hirsch points out in *The Mother/Daughter Plot*, most of the "mother plot" writing of the 1980s focuses on motherhood not from the mother's point of view but from the daughter's. Feminists are uncomfortable with motherhood for a number of reasons, and have chosen to deal with it through the back door, so to speak. Hirsch believes the reasons for the discomfort with motherhood lie in the identification with the mother as victim of patriarchy (she is the victim we fear in ourselves), because she represents vulnerability, lack of control, and fear and discomfort with the body, and because we are angry at the power of the mother.[25] According to Brenda Daly and Maureen Reddy in their anthology of essays on literature from the mother's point of view, another reason there is little of this writing is that all women are daughters but not all are mothers. According to Daly and Reddy, literature in the daughter's voice is a logical step in the political analysis of motherhood, and as time passes, we should have more writing from the mother's point of view.[26]

The period since the mid-1970s has seen an outpouring of scholarship on mother-daughter relations, very recently including mother-daughter relations in literature. Though it would be impossible to summarize all this theory here, several ideas emerge that are reflected in the literature. First, the mother-daughter bond is fraught with paradox or antithesis. As Adrienne Rich says, the daughter views her mother both as Herself and as the Other from whom she must split to define her own sense of self. Because the mother usually represents and inculcates patriarchal values, the daughter senses that to imitate her is to lose independence.[27] Despite this antipathy for her mother, though, the strong preoedipal bonds, her need for nurture, draw the daughter to her mother, making it much more difficult for her to break away than for the son. The result is a lifelong tension, a shifting back and forth from love to "matrophobia," a rejection of the mother (238). Theorists disagree about the source of the conflict; Chodorow locates it in patriarchal family relations, while Jane Gallop feels it is an "inevitable component of the growth of both mother and daughter"; nevertheless, this tension is the guiding dynamic in all mother-daughter relations.[28]

Though in *A Mother and Two Daughters* Godwin gives a positive portrait of mother-daughter relationships, her treatment of such relationships in her next novel, *A Southern Family* (1987), is more problematic, reflecting the tension outlined above. Autobiographical and again set in North Carolina, it recounts the story of successful novelist Claire Quick, who once a year returns home to her "escaped" roots and becomes enmeshed again in the lies and evasions of her mother Lily's life. Lily Quick was a journalist and fiction writer of questionable talent who married beneath herself, as Kim Lacy Rogers says, making the "classic female trade-off of independence for economic security and social mobility," and a family.[29] She now spends her time attending the Episcopal Church, visiting nursing homes, and musing sadly about her lost Art.

The lies Lily tells herself about her past have negatively affected the whole family, all of whom are neurotic in some way. The novel focuses on the suicide of Theo, one of Lily's sons; through working out her own guilt for her brother's death, Claire is able to break away from the family pattern. She comes to realize that her mother's lies have affected her self-esteem and her work. Critics accuse her (as they have accused Godwin) of writing quaint, charming Southern stories in which plots are resolved happily, with everyone getting her heart's desire—and Claire fears they may be right. By the end of the novel, Claire accepts whatever guilt she may have for Theo's death, throws away a manuscript she has been working on, and finally sees the web of illusions of her family's life together. Rogers suggests that the realizations Godwin expresses in this novel will enable her to "move beyond this kind of family romance—which is essentially a daughter's story—and on to a woman's story, free of a mother's powerful charm and feminine delusions" (68).

Another novel that focuses on the theme of facing the lies and silences of a mother's life in order to have one's own life is Marilyn French's *Her Mother's Daughter* (1987). Here French departs from the sexual politics featured in *The Women's Room* and her novel that followed, *The Bleeding Heart* (1980), and turns toward relations between women. Of all the works I discuss here, *Her Mother's Daughter* reflects most strongly the ideas of the cultural feminists. Like Rich, French stresses the powerful bonds between mother and child and the wonderful, almost erotic pleasures of nurturing. She then contrasts them with the severe limitations patriarchal society places on mothers, who come to feel profound anger toward their children. Also like Rich, French emphasizes the importance of daughters' understanding and coming to terms with their mothers' lives. Rich warns daughters that "matrophobia"—a rebellion against the imposed female role in an attempt to be "individuated" and "free"—can produce a "splitting," a harmful denial of self that can create a person with no sense of roots or of herself (238).[30] If a woman can accept her mother's life and at the same time be confident that she need not repeat it, her relationship with her mother can provide a source of strength.

In *Her Mother's Daughter*, French concentrates on the relationships between four generations. The narrator, Anastasia, a liberated career woman, tells us the story of Frances, her Polish immigrant grandmother, and her own mother, Belle, who is modeled after French's mother, Isabelle. Anastasia has her own daughter, Arden. The joy and pain of these intertwined relations form the novel's plot. For French the joy and pain of motherhood are the most authentic work a woman ever does. Though Anastasia's adventuresome career as a professional photographer takes her all over the world, it is her relationship with her mother and daughter that occupies her inner life.[31]

Her Mother's Daughter is a large and complex novel, with many subplots, but certain generalizations can be made about French's themes. First, French says that within the nuclear family, motherhood is a much more difficult task than in earlier centuries, when children were raised in an extended family. A mother is expected to supply her children's every physical and emotional need; she is also held responsible, not only by the society but also by the children themselves, for how they turn out as adults. This responsibility puts severe pressure on mothers to sacrifice themselves and limit their own development. They martyr themselves, resent their children as a consequence, and yet never feel they have really measured up. They can never give enough love or nurturing:

Mother love. There is supposed to be no room in it for coldness of heart, for a private cell for oneself, with doors that sometimes clank shut. And the more you love your children, the more shocked they are to discover that you possess a single strand of ambivalent—or negative—feeling. Insatiable for this love we expect to be absolute, we cannot forgive its mere humanness.[32]

Anastasia has been raised by a cold Belle, and into her fifties is still seeking a warmth and approval that is never enough when it is grudgingly given. In turn Belle was deprived of love by her own mother, Frances, when her other three children were taken from her after Belle's father died. Guilty at having chosen Belle, her heart broken by losing her children, Frances never expressed much love for Belle, who was raised in abject poverty. Later, when Belle and her husband pull themselves into the middle class, she gives her children everything that she had not had—music lessons, nice clothes, a pleasant home. However, Belle can not supply the warmth that Anastasia continually longs for, for she is a bitter, silent woman (except when she complains of her lot), who is angry at how she has lost her life to her children.

French uses the metaphor of the "midge" mother to illustrate the hollowing effect of too much mothering. The insect midge hatches her eggs inside herself, and the hatchlings then eat the mother's body away. The difference with humans, Anastasia thinks, is that the midge babies do not have to listen to their mother complaining. Anastasia tries to break this chain of frustrated mothering by never being a midge mother. She will "have it all"; as Belle later says, she will live like a man. Her name, which means "resurrection," suggests that she will be a new version of Belle, liberated from the agonies of poverty and sexist oppression. However, all her successes in creating herself—two husbands, three lovely children, an exciting career, and sexual pleasure with both men and women—do not break the chain. In middle age she finds herself depressed and having difficulties with her daughter Arden, who has rejected her mother's lifestyle and has joined a commune, where traditional sex roles are practiced. Arden will not be a neglectful mother like Anastasia, who finds herself more and more retreating into the bitter silences of Belle, truly becoming "her mother's daughter."

Ultimately, the way out of this frustrating cycle of mothering and its angers is to break the silence, as so many feminist thinkers have said: to speak the unspeakable.[33] Mary Rose Sullivan points out that by Anastasia's telling her story, acknowledging her similarities to Belle in personality and behavior (like Belle, Anastasia was forced to marry too young and pregnant), and by owning up to the "deep ambivalence" she feels over the terrible burdens of mothering, she can break away.[34] A woman can take pleasure in her life and in her children, and can reconcile her relationship with her own mother by telling her story, as French has done here.

As in The Women's Room, in Her Mother's Daughter French also depicts the intense pleasure of motherhood, perhaps the answer to the question "Why do we keep on doing it?" (47). This oneness, a kind of primal pleasure of physical and emotional connection written of by feminist theorists like Julia Kristeva, dissolves the subject-object separation of civilized culture.[35] For example, Anastasia watches her sleeping children:

Arden with her eyes open just a crack, so you couldn't be sure she was sleeping, and Billy with his thumb in his mouth—clear through until he was ten years old. They would be pink and sweet-smelling from their baths and their sweat, and warm with sleep, and my heart would roll over as I looked at them and often I'd kneel down by the side of the bed and lay my face on their cheeks. (92)

According to thinkers of Kristeva's bent, this kind of primal precultural experience is something denied men, a situation that engenders fear of women (and thus compensating contempt for them). Whatever the pleasures of this basic female experience, French's warning is clear: motherhood can be women's ruin, if they allow themselves to be consumed by it as the society has said they should. On the other hand, it can be women's greatest source of strength, what makes them morally superior to men: "women *are* more selfless, more sympathetic, more empathetic, more sensitive, more fun—all the things you have to be to raise kids" (565).

Near the end of the novel, Anastasia tells Arden, with whom she is renegotiating a relationship, that she has come to believe that freedom, "self-actualization," has not brought her the happiness she has sought. In her effort not to be like Belle, she has neglected an important part of herself. As Gail Godwin said in *A Mother and Two Daughters*, Anastasia believes it is in relationship that we find not only each other but ourselves:

I believed freedom was independence, needing no one, having your work and doing what you damn well wanted to do. And that this was what the heroic man—or woman—did, . . . being with people was a compromise, a deference, a dependency. . . . That's what I felt. Until very recently." (674)

For some women making those compromises is very difficult: How much can we give up and still be ourselves? When Arden asks if she should stay in her troubled relationship with her husband, Anastasia replies, "I can only tell you what I know." Like the scene in *Kinflicks* when Mrs. Babcock grants autonomy to Ginny, Anastasia gives the gift of her own experience, here suggesting that some compromise for those we love can be a source of a woman's meaning and strength. The tricky thing is not to end up like Belle, a "midge mother." This grudging admittance of Anastasia (Marilyn) that women find meaning in sacrifice and some giving up of autonomy seems a different sort of conclusion than that found in *The Women's Room*, perhaps warranted in part by the changing times and changes in French's own thinking about women.

French also illustrates the ties of love and loyalty between mother and daughter that are impossible to assess (as theorists say, because they prefigure speech). Though Anastasia never felt that Belle loved her, as a child she often brooded about how she would seek revenge on a teacher who hurt Belle's feelings. Similarly, at age fourteen Arden writes a defensive letter to a male critic who panned Anastasia's first book of photographs. In a very real sense our mothers are ourselves.[36]

In *Her Mother's Daughter* French gives us not only a sensitive account of the universality of mother-daughter relationships but also some perceptive insights into the differences between the last three generations of American women. For many older women who entered the middle class relatively late in life, pleasure in their hard-won affluence is difficult. Like Belle, they are afraid of change. In some cases they have difficulty finding pleasure in sex because of their own mothers' teaching. They accepted the traditional woman's role and have sacrificed their own development for their children's, but resent their children's successes, particularly their daughters'.

Anastasia's successes show us that life is measurably better for younger women, those who came of age in the 1950s and 1960s. In many cases, they have experienced sexual freedom, they have realized themselves in creative work outside the home, and in most cases they have had husbands, children, and lovers. They are more confident than their mothers and find much pleasure and variety in life. However, their circumstances are difficult, too. They have had to juggle careers and children, and because of society's pressures, often feel inadequate as mothers. They are sometimes alienated from their own mothers and have problems with their daughters, who secretly long for the traditional mother who stayed at home and gave them milk and cookies after school. These women have paid a price for their freedom, in that many of them are now divorced and alone.

It may appear that *Her Mother's Daughter* has a theme similar to that of *The Women's Room*, the depressing message that both the traditional and the liberated woman are bound to be unhappy, given the constraints of patriarchal society. However, such is not the case. Marilyn French has acknowledged that the circumstances for women had improved in the ten years between the two books. Yes, women continue to have serious problems; society expects too much of mothers, and the "free" woman can sometimes be lonely. Yet there is no doubt that Anastasia's life has been better than Belle's. This novel of the 1980s is considerably more optimistic about the possibilities for women.

Some authors have completely avoided the myth of mother as "monster," instead stressing the new myth of the mother as muse, as a source of inspiration. One such example is Erica Jong's *Fanny: Being the True History of the Adventures of Fanny Hackabout-Jones* (1980). After *Fear of Flying* Jong published two sequels to the adventures of Isadora: *How to Save Your Own Life* (1977) and *Parachutes and Kisses* (1984). With *Fanny*, however, Jong left the picaresque quest of the late-twentieth-century woman and turned to the beginning of the novel with a female eighteenth-century novel in the manner of Fielding. One of Jong's premises is that had Tom Jones been female, she would have had a more difficult time.

Though *Fanny* is certainly a *bildungsroman* like those of the 1970s, being a woman's quest for identity in a patriarchal world, certain themes show it to be a transitional novel. For example, *Fanny* clearly reflects the budding feminist interest in the myth, lore, and magic of ancient female culture. Although much of the novel concerns Fanny's relationships with men—her rapist foster father who later turns out to be her real father, an evil doctor who denies her a cesarean section, pompous aristocrats who want her for their pleasure, and her lover Lancelot—equally important are her relationships with women, especially her daughter, Belinda, and her mother, Isobel.

This makes *Fanny* much different from Jong's earlier novels, which, as many critics pointed out, were centered on Isadora's relationships with men.

As with *Kinflicks*, Mary Ann Ferguson equates the novel's theme with the Psyche/Cupid myth, but this time the influence of the mother is wholly beneficent. Fanny begins her tale as a motherless foundling. As part of her adventures, she finds herself under the protection of a group of witches who embody all the benevolent female virtues. (By the beginning of the 1980s cultural feminists were beginning to examine the heritage of ancient female lore, including witchcraft.) Isobel, the leader of this coven, gives Fanny a red garter on which is written "My Heart is fixt, It will not range, I like my Choyce too well to change."[37] Later Isobel, seemingly killed by a cruel band of ruffians, reappears to serve as the midwife for the birth of Fanny's daughter, Belinda. The idea of female-centered birth was another prominent feminist concern during the 1980s. Isobel and the other witches' kind counsel and love, the gift of a motto by which she can live her life, and the female lore they teach Fanny contrast with the pain Fanny experiences from most of the males she encounters. This myth "of female power separate from the prevailing male dominance" gives Fanny the strength not to be a victim, no matter how she suffers.[38]

The conclusion of the novel, with three generations of women united, along with Lancelot, who has experienced his own quest, portrays a cultural feminist vision of a loving and harmonious world where the wisdom of women is valued, where strong women achieve selfhood alongside men, and where female values offer a basis for rebuilding the world. Though this vision is far from the realities for women in the eighteenth century, it certainly reflects the direction of feminist thinking in the early 1980s. In this novel traditional feminine "weaknesses" are seen as strengths to bring about a better world.

One of the most popular of the mother-daughter novels of the 1980s is Amy Tan's critically praised best-seller *The Joy Luck Club* (1989), a book that certainly answers feminist theorists' call for writing which celebrates the gifts of mothers to daughters. In many ways, it makes the same points about mother-daughter relationships as *Her Mother's Daughter*. Though French's novel features European immigrants and Tan's Chinese immigrants, the feelings of mothers and daughters are much the same. Though a mother can have a negative effect on her daughter's development, on balance a mother can be a primary source of inspiration, if the daughter knows her story.

Set in pre-World War II China and California of the 1950s and 1980s, *The Joy Luck Club* explores the antagonistic, yet achingly tender, feelings of Chinese-American mothers and daughters for each other. On the one hand, it deals with immigrant women who must struggle to understand their daughters' new language, who fear for their girls' freedom, and who live through their daughters' accomplishments. It shows equal sympathy with their Americanized daughters, who struggle to understand their connection to China, a country they never saw. Their struggles to break away from their mothers are complicated by the fact that if they reject their mothers, they reject their Chinese heritage, an important component of who they are. Though the novel is particularly meaningful to readers of first-generation immigrant parentage, Tan speaks to all contemporary women struggling for understanding with mothers who have lived such different lives from themselves.

The Joy Luck Club is a revolving mah jong party held in the homes of the four mothers, feisty "aunties" who meet regularly to cook competitively for each other, gossip, and brag about their children. The party began during World War II, when Suyuan Woo gathered a group of her friends to feast and celebrate in the face of disaster: "What was worse, we asked among ourselves, to sit and wait for our own deaths... Or to choose our own happiness?"[39] The party gave them the chance for "joy" and "luck" amid life's pain. This theme becomes central to the lives of these women, women who have never had any lives in America other than home and family, and so with "honey voiced, dragon-hearted competitiveness" compete fiercely through their children.[40] Says June Woo, who tells her mother's story first:

Auntie Lin and my mother were both best friends and arch enemies who spent a lifetime comparing their children. I was one month older than Waverly Jong, Auntie Lin's prized daughter. From the time we were babies, our mothers compared the creases in our belly buttons, how shapely our earlobes were,... how smart Waverly was at playing chess. (37)

Tan shows how this rivalry between the mothers, produced by their strong need to achieve through their children, can create immense pressures on the daughters. For example, June recounts the struggle between her mother and her over piano lessons. Suyuan hopes to make June into a concert pianist to top the achievements of Waverly, the neighborhood chess champion, but clever June resists her mother's ambitions and fools the deaf piano teacher, disgracing the family at her recital. Tan ends the conflict by emphasizing the stark gulf between the mother's and the daughter's experience. When Suyuan drags June to the piano, shouting that there are "only two kinds of daughters, those who are obedient and those who follow their own mind! Only one kind of daughter can live in this house," June shouts back that she wishes she were dead, like her two half sisters abandoned in wartime China: "It was as if I had said the magic words. Alakazam!—and her face went blank, her mouth closed, her arms went slack, and she backed out of the room, stunned, as if she were blowing away like a small brown leaf, thin, brittle, lifeless" (142). Tan's juxtaposition of these two events, one humorous and the other tragic, clearly shows the division between mother and daughter. How can June ever hope to know her mother's life and world of such unimaginable suffering? How can she understand her mother's desire not only to live through her daughter but also to have her daughter live for the lost sisters?

Tan illustrates again and again the power Chinese mothers and American daughters have over each other. Long into adult life, Suyuan is able to anger June by calling her a college "drop off"; June's inability to finish college is a subconscious lashing out at her mother. Nine-year-old Waverly resents her mother's glorying in her chess accomplishments: "My mother would join the crowds during these outdoor exhibition games. She sat proudly on the bench, telling my admirers with proper Chinese humility, 'Is luck.' . . . At the next tournament, I won again, but it was my mother who wore the triumphant grin" (96–97). Waverly retaliates by reminding Lindo that she cannot do the things Waverly can: "Why do you have to use me to show off? If you want to show off, then why don't you learn to play chess?" (99). Later, when Lindo withdraws support for her chess playing, Waverly stops winning. Such is the power of a Chinese mother. Later in life Lindo is able to depreciate Rich, Waverly's Caucasian boyfriend, by criticizing a mink jacket he bought her: "This is not so good. It is just leftover strips." Looking at the jacket, Waverly knows her mother is right: "I couldn't fend off the strength of her will anymore, her ability to make me see black where there was once white. . . . The coat looked shabby, an imitation of romance" (169).

The vehicle Tan uses to bring together mothers and daughters is the mothers' stories of the hardship of being female in old China. Stories of sadness and suffering, of joy and pleasure, sometimes of weakness as well as strength, in every case they show the resiliency of the traditional Chinese woman. As the grandmother says to the Queen Mother (really her baby granddaughter) in the folk tale that begins the last section, " . . . you must teach my daughter. . . . How to lose your innocence but not your hope. How to laugh forever" (213).

For example, in one anecdote we learn of the sad life of Chinese concubines. This section of the novel shows the pain of all the wives in polygamous marriages who struggle to wrest dignity and security from a situation where their existence depends on their relation to one man. An-Mei, daughter of a disgraced rich man's concubine, is raised by her grandmother, Popo, who tells An-Mei her mother is a ghost. When Popo is dying, however, An-Mei's mother comes back, and in an attempt to save Popo, cuts a small bit of flesh from her arm and feeds it to her. An-Mei, who loves this new mother and forgives her for marrying the rich man "to exchange one unhappiness for another," sees the worth of this pain:

This is how a daughter honors her mother. It is *shou* so deep it is in your bones. The pain of the flesh is nothing. The pain you must forget. Because sometimes that is the only way to remember what is in your bones. You must peel off your skin, and that of your mother, and her mother before her. (48)

One could say that this entire novel is an attempt to peel back that skin to get to those "bones" one has in common with one's mother. Later, An-Mei's mother takes her own life, but not before she engineers a safe future for her daughter.

In the story of Lindo's arranged marriage, called by one critic a combination of "feminism and fairy tale,"[41] we see how such marriages sometimes were circumvented by wily girls who were unwilling to lose themselves. Tan shows us the pain of twelve-year-old Lindo and her mother when Lindo is forced to leave home to serve her rich, bossy mother-in-law. Discussions of arranged marriages often forget the pain of the bride's mother in a patrilocal society; she must give up her child. Lindo learns to find meaning in her servitude, later comparing herself to an American housewife:

How much happier could I be after seeing Tyan-yu [her future husband] eat a whole bowl of noodles without once complaining about its taste or my looks? It's like those ladies you see on American TV these days, the ones who are so happy they have washed out a stain so the clothes look better. (56)

However, a small part of her former self is left intact, and on her wedding day she plots to let no one take her identity away:

I had on a beautiful red dress, but what I saw was even more valuable. I was strong. I was pure. I had genuine thoughts inside that no one could see, that no one could ever take away from me.... I made a promise to myself: I would always remember my parents' wishes, but I would never forget myself. (58)

After the wedding Lindo manages to extricate herself from the marriage without disgracing her family, ending up with money for passage to America.

This story of a young girl who succeeds in preserving herself even in a society where a girl child is given little value is truly a gift to the next generation. Though one might question its credibility—surely few girls escaped a hated marriage so easily—many must have used their wits to make the best out of bad situations. The figure of the mother-in-law is stereotypical, yet stereotypes do contain truth. We are told that in India, for example, the woman torn from her home and forced to serve a mother-in-law looks forward to the day when she has a daughter-in-law to serve her: such are the compensations whereby patriarchy secures women's complicity in their own oppression.

The worst problem these mothers and daughters face is poor communication, caused by traditional Chinese values. All the mothers have been raised to efface themselves and be silent, a silence contributing to misunderstandings between mothers and daughters. As An-Mei says, "I was taught to desire nothing, to swallow other people's misery, to eat my own bitterness" (215). Little Ying-ying was told by her *amah*: "It is wrong to think of your own needs. A girl can never ask, only listen" (70). Ying-ying feels that because she has kept silent so long, her daughter, Lena, does not see her: "We are lost, she and I, unseen and not seeing, unheard and not hearing" (67). For her part, Lena recalls a period in her life when her mother, depressed at the loss of a valued boy baby, stayed "resting" in her bedroom for days. Not understanding her mother's pain and loneliness—Ying-ying's Caucasian husband has isolated her in an Italian neighborhood—Lena longs to be the daughter in the noisy Italian family in the next apartment. Lena fantasizes a girl who feels the unbearable pain of "not being seen," and kills her mother with "the death of a thousand cuts" (115), in order to be seen by her.

Tan emphasizes that submissive Chinese female traits are learned *despite* the best intentions of the mothers, who are aware of how they have been raised and of American ideas about women's behavior. Wanting to be modern and good Americans, they try to raise their daughters in the new ways, yet are frustrated. Thinks An-Mei:

> . . . though I taught my daughter the opposite, still she came out the same way! Maybe it is because she was born to me and she was born a girl. And I was born to my mother and I was born a girl. All of us are like stairs, one step after another, going up and down, but all going the same way. (215)

According to Amy Ling, An-mei realizes that the fate of women has not changed. Despite cultural, geographical, and chronological changes, it is "inevitably tragic."[42] The daughters also wonder if Chinese female passivity is hereditary. Well-educated and talented, tax attorneys, architects, and copywriters, in one way or another they defer to their husbands. Rose cannot make decisions and refuses to take responsibility in her marriage, to the point where her husband, Ted, demands a divorce, telling her she must accept a $10,000 settlement. Lena divides household expenses with her husband, Harold, even though he makes seven times more than she does in the joint business she created and he manages.

Ironically, it is Rose's mother who jolts her out of her depression, asking, "Why do you not speak up for yourself?" (193). An-mei has always told Rose she is weak (born without the element of wood) because she listens to too many people, including "psyche-atricks." Her mother's advice gives Rose the "wood" to tell Ted that she will not sign the settlement. Similarly, the "tiger" Ying-ying vows to cherish her pain and use it to penetrate her daughter's skin, and cut her tiger spirit loose. In *The Joy Luck Club* the mother/daughter relationship is a painful one, an overt "battle between two equally strong forces in which the mother uses the pain of her past experience both to 'cut loose' the spirit of her daughter and to instill in the daughter the mother's own spirit."[43]

In large part, *The Joy Luck Club* is about cross-cultural conflicts and the difficulty of assimilation:

I saw myself transforming like a werewolf, a mutant tag of DNA suddenly triggered, replicating itself insidiously into a *syndrome*, a cluster of telltale Chinese behaviors, all those things my mother did to embarrass me—haggling with store owners, pecking her mouth with a toothpick in public, being color-blind to the fact that lemon yellow and pale pink are not good combinations for winter clothes. (307)

But finally, and most important, the novel is about discovering one's identity through knowledge of one's mother. Yes, there is a "social construction of femininity," even stronger with Chinese women, but it can be overcome if one realizes the victories and pains of female ancestors. When the Joy Luck aunties give Jing-mei (June) a plane ticket to China to visit her lost sisters and tell them about their now-dead mother, she is afraid. What does she really know about her mother? One never thinks about the importance of one's mother until she is gone, but Tan clearly implies that one should. As the scandalized aunties ask, "How can one not know one's mother?"

Ying-ying tells Jing-mei, "Tell them stories she told you, lessons she taught, what you know about her mind that has become your mind" (40). Amazingly, after the stories are told, when Jing-mei enters China, she feels different: she is "becoming Chinese" (267). Though she is still American, she is Chinese and Suyaun's daughter in a way she was not before. Says Ling:

... to be truly mature, to achieve a balance in the between-world condition ... one cannot cling solely to the new American ways and reject the old Chinese ways, for that is the way of the child.... If the old ways cannot be incorporated into the new life, if they do not "mix" ... then they must nonetheless be respected and preserved in the pictures on one's walls, in the memories in one's head, in the stories one writes down. (141)

When Jing-mei meets her sisters and they weep over the "Mama" that all three never fully knew, they see her in each others' faces. They are their mother. Thus, the novel ends on a note of reconciliation and understanding.

This novel speaks not only of immigrant experience but also of mothers and daughters who hope to know each other and themselves. As feminist critics and scholars have said, we must know not only our mothers' sufferings and the ways they were limited, but also the ways they overcame those limitations. We cannot form images of heroism for ourselves if we lack knowledge and respect for our foremothers. *The Joy Luck Club* also illuminates the psychological bonds and separations between mother and daughter. It does not take Freudian-Lacanian theory to tell us of a mother's difficulty in seeing her children as separate people. As Lindo says of Waverly, "How can she be her own person? When did I give her up?" 256). Likewise, it is difficult for an adult daughter to conceive of her mother as a person with a past, with thoughts of her own. As my mother has told me, "You don't *really* know me."

These mother-daughter relationships in literature certainly confirm Nancy Chodorow's ideas about the difficulties women have in separating themselves from their mothers, and their tendency to see themselves in webs of relationships rather than as autonomous individuals. Because women mother children, Chodorow says:

> ... growing girls come to define and experience themselves as continuous with others; their experience of self contains more flexible or permeable ego boundaries. Boys comes to define themselves as more separate and distinct, with a greater sense of rigid ego boundaries and differentiation. The basic feminine sense of self is connected to the world, the basic masculine sense of self is separate.[44]

Such studies suggest that women are considerably older than men before they successfully separate from their mothers. Another psychologist, Carol Gilligan, says that woman's moral sense is based on a feeling of responsibility within a framework of relationships that presumes people are connected rather than autonomous individuals.[45] One certainly can see this connectedness in all these novels. As Joan Lidoff states, "Whether imaged as nested dolls and reversible wombs, or as tangled vines, the embeddedness and mirroring entanglement of maternal and filial identity rests at the heart of personality and literary style."[46]

Despite these sensitive portrayals of motherly love and the attention to mother-daughter relations, Louise Bernikow's call for fiction showing the mother's gifts to the daughter has not yet been fully answered. Mickey Pearlman points out in her anthology of essays on mothers and daughters in fiction that at best these mother-daughter relationships are "puzzling" and contradictory (2). And, as I have stated, these contradictions are also revealed in the nonfiction studies of mother-daughter relations which show that although despite their closeness to their mothers, most daughters wish to be different from them and express ambivalence about their closeness. For their part, mothers, who are often jealous of their daughters' opportunities, perpetuate the "Big Lie" by failing to tell their daughters the truth about motherhood, and inculcate patriarchal attitudes by teaching them to fear their sexuality.[47] Even in *The Joy Luck Club*, the most positive of all these novels, the Chinese mothers' inspiring tales of survival are balanced with the submissive traits that the daughters find burdensome.

OTHER FEMALE RELATIVES

As Toni McNaron states in the 1985 collection *The Sister Bond*, there is little in feminist theory or literary criticism on relationships between female relatives other than the mother-daughter bond. Louise Bernikow suggests that sisterly bonding is partly a myth (in the sense of a myth being a distortion of reality), and partly true. Sisters often feel intense sibling rivalry, especially if there are two and one is prettier than the other. They will often develop in seemingly opposing ways, choosing different paths; however, the bonds are strong, bringing them together at various points in their lives, where they nurture each other in difficult times. McNaron believes that sisters bond intensely (as with mother-daughter bonds, these bonds are preverbal and inexpressible) and, as with mothers and daughters, tension is a continual component of the relationship.

According to McNaron, sisters may be rivals, not so much for the attention of men, including their father, as for the love of their mother. The contrast between sisters can be attributed to their desire for differentiation: "... a sister can be seen as someone who is both ourselves and very much not ourselves—a special kind of double." Having a sister gives one the opportunity *not* to develop certain aspects of one's personality. If one sister is a traditional stay-at-home, the other can roam the world. For that reason a sister may find it frightening if her sibling makes radical changes in her life. The balance between them is upset, so to speak.[48] Despite these tensions, though, the desire for union is strong.

Certainly these ideas are reflected in many of the novels I discuss here. In *Her Mother's Daughter*, Joy, Anastasia's sister, is a traditional nonrebel, in contrast with her sister. Celie and Nettie, in the yet-to-be discussed *The Color Purple*, contrast in many ways. Of all the novels discussed here, however, in Godwin's *A Mother and Two Daughters* the relationship between Cate and Lydia develops this pattern most deeply. Cate is a free-spirited feminist, English professor, and socialist, twice married, and childless by choice. Emotional, disorganized, thoughtful, ironic, and often angry at the injustices of her society, she is an activist who once lost her job over an antiwar protest. A complete contrast with Cate, the pretty Lydia is just separated from a conventional marriage. With two children, she has never worked outside the home, is exceedingly organized and efficient, controls her emotions, and hates labels like "feminist."

Godwin obviously has more than one purpose here. In the two sisters, she illustrates the sisterly conflict we so often see: the "good," sometimes beautiful, dutiful sister and the rebellious, "bad" sister who drives her parents to distraction and yet gets all the attention. According to Bernikow, sisters are often "deep in antagonism," and this novel is no exception (76). Also, in creating such different women, Godwin contrasts how women respond differently to the social forces affecting them. While Lydia would like to go beyond her previously conventional role, Cate is questioning the rootlessness and lack of human connection in her life.

Jealousy and rivalry for parental, especially maternal, attention is at the root of the conflict between Cate and Lydia. Cate is the superior student and the more creative and clever of the two, yet seems unable to hold a job or succeed in a woman's role. Lydia covets her sister's intellectual achievements, at the same time smugly congratulating herself on her fine sons and successful marriage. Lydia has left this supposedly happy marriage by choice—unlike Cate, whose marriages ended messily, as have many ventures in her life. However, it is clear that Lydia is motivated partly by a desire to emulate Cate, who is contemptuous of Lydia's conventionality and, unfairly, her desire to obtain the same degrees and status that Cate has achieved. Here we can see that the Women's Movement produces new rivalries between sisters; the sister who chooses a traditional role may feel inferior to the one who rejects the traditional route of development. By novel's end Cate and Lydia are still sparring with each other, despite the ties of love that draw them together.

Joan Chase's very fine first novel, *During the Reign of the Queen of Persia* (1983), also demonstrates an interest in the bonding between female relatives: five sisters, their mother, and four girl cousins. Set in the 1950s in a rural community in Ohio, *Queen* has a unique vehicle as narrator(s): the collective vision of four adolescent cousins who live together in this extended female family. Like the 1970s novels discussed in Chapter 2, *Queen* is a novel of initiation wherein the four girls confront nearly every aspect of human experience: sexual awakening, relationships between adults, and finally the death of one of their mothers. Through it all, strong bonds between the girls and their aunts and mothers (all of whom live on the farm some of the time) provide the glue holding the family together.

This extended female network is dominated by the grandmother, called the Queen of Persia because she owns a Persian rug and acts like a queen. A rough, capable, yet sensitive farm girl, Gram married for security and hoped for something more. After she bears five girls for her taciturn husband, and in middle age inherits some property to give her security, she spends the rest of her life going to bingo parties and the movies. Life in the big farmhouse revolves around her because she owns the house and controls the money. To some degree, Gram has withdrawn from nurturing, and her daughters fill the void for each other that she filled when they were younger.

Gram's five very different daughters provide the cousins with different patterns for female development. Aunt Elinor is a stylish New York career woman who descends on the farm with flashy clothes and later becomes converted to an optimistic Christian Science faith that Gram scorns. Aunt Rachel cracks dirty jokes and rides her horse across the fields. Aunt May mothers them all while soft Aunt Grace dies of cancer with dignity. Aunt Libby cautions the girls to "marry a man who loves you more than you love him." "Don't give it away," she says, like generations of mothers, teaching the girls to fear their sexuality:

"There's nothing to be done about it," Aunt Libby said. . . . She meant us . . . being female. She referred to it as . . . if it were both a miracle and a calamity, that vein of fertility, that mother lode of passion buried within us, for joy and ruin. "None of us can no more than look at a man and we're having his baby."[49]

As we have seen, not all female influence is beneficial, due to the socialization function played by older women. Still, the girls are fascinated by sex and introduced to its allures together. When the oldest, Celia, turns at fourteen into a ripe, blossoming beauty, the girls watch her necking with her duck-tailed boyfriend:

Tasting instead Corley's mouth on ours, its burning wild lathering sweetness. In the shaft of light we saw them pressed together, rolling in each other's arms, Celia's flowered skirt pulled up around her thighs. His hand moving there.... Our hearts plunged and thudded. At that moment we were freed from Aunt Libby. We didn't care what it was called or the price to be paid; someday we would have it. (26)

Try as they may, older women are often unable to convince teenage girls to give up sexual pleasure. Much later, the wild, beautiful Celia, left by her fiancé, sells herself lightly and at eighteen marries the next boy who comes along. Later we learn that Celia becomes pregnant and, depressed, attempts suicide, one of the many casualties of the limited options the 1950s held for young women. The other girls learn from Celia's experience that a woman's beauty can be her doom.

The relationships between the family women are not always warm and peaceful; mother-daughter and sister-sister tension abounds. Hostilities break out between Gram and Aunt Elinor, who persists in believing that Grace will be saved from cancer by a miracle. "Sometimes," Gram says, "there ain't no hope." Nevertheless, despite the shouting and accusations, the closeness between these women is palpable, just as it is between the girls, who are also sometimes rivals. It is a closeness that the men in the story envy. Neil, Aunt Grace's husband, remarks that the trees in the orchard remind him of the family:

some a little apart, on the fringes, a few little tots here and there, the gnarled old crone [Gram] in the center, and then the five sisters, close together, their slender branches intertwined thrashing in any wind at all, making much ado about nothing. The sawn-off waterlogged stumps he compared to the few men who ever dared approach. (130)

According to Chase, the traditional patriarchy was hard on men, too, because in their shared oppression and lack of power, women often grouped together to exclude men, who found themselves on the fringes of the family unit. Mostly, though, in this house full of women, men are simply unimportant. This is a story about female relationships, and the men occupy only the background. As we shall see, Alice Walker makes this point a central theme of *The Color Purple*.

FRIENDSHIPS BETWEEN WOMEN

Related to bonding between female relatives, an equally important theme in the novels of the 1980s has been the role of female friendship. The importance of male friendship to the growth and development of heroes has been a cultural myth since preclassical times. We all know the story of David and Jonathan, whose love for each other "passed the love of women."[50] However, until recently little has been said in literature about friendship between women.

In a 1986 article Margaret Atwood gives a capsule history of friendship between women in literature. She states that despite the historical evidence of deep friendship between women gleaned from letters and autobiographies, literature by both men and women has neglected "that certain thing called the girlfriend." This is not the case in novels for adolescent girls but, says Atwood, in literature, once girls become women, they put away such pursuits and turn to the real business of life, romances with men. Thus Jane Eyre moves from her love for Helen Burns, from whom she learns much at Lowood School, to her love for Rochester. Part of the reason for this, Atwood speculates, is that the perceived subject of the novel had always been heterosexual romance; further, it might have been partly dictated by the demands of a female audience: "friendships with women were real life, romance was escape."[51] This tradition of ignoring relationships between women persisted into twentieth-century literature. When shown, female friendships were portrayed as catty rivalries. The popular culture reinforced these attitudes, telling women that their friendships with women were not to be taken seriously. Any girlfriend would understand if her chum broke a date with her to be with a man.

As with relations between female relatives, the women's movement has produced new interest in the bonds of friendship between women. Early in the movement Juliet Mitchell wrote of the difficulty women had during the 1960s in maintaining friendships. Encouraged to think of each other as trivial, and flattered when men wanted to be their friends, many women were embarrassed to admit they had close women friends.[52] Other theorists suggested that the hostility women sometimes express for each other is based on self-contempt. As the 1970s progressed, and even more in the 1980s, feminist thinkers stressed the importance of women forming bonds with each other and recognizing the strong female bonds in their lives.[53] This idea of cherishing female friendships relates to the more abstract idea of "sisterhood," the solidarity among women based on shared experience and essential to progress in changing women's status.

Until recently, because of a dearth of subject matter to study, there has been little critical work done on women's friendship in literature. However, this situation is now being remedied. For example, Janet Todd has studied female friendship in eighteenth-century fiction; Elizabeth Abel has pointed out that late-nineteenth-century women writers, such as Kate Chopin in *The Awakening*, often used the friends of the protagonist to illustrate optional lifestyles for the heroine.[54] In her study of radical feminist novels, Paulina Palmer discusses a number of works that feature lesbian friendships or set female friendship in the context of feminist collective work projects. Through their concentration on feminist action in the political arena, women forge bonds of love and solidarity.[55] Even popular culture is now examining women's friendship in women's "buddy" films such as *Thelma and Louise* and *Fried Green Tomatoes*.

According to Abel, contemporary novels suggest that the dynamic of female friendship is "commonality" (415). Women are drawn together because of similar interests and values, and in some cases, as will be shown with Toni Morrison's *Sula*, recognize that despite surface differences, they are much the same. Judith Kegan Gardiner, on the other hand, feels that "commonality/complementarity alternate in many of these novels as a 'fluid process,' whereby the narrator can differentiate herself from her friend and identify with her at other times in the story."[56] In any case, whether they are similar or different in character, their friendship is a major vehicle for their self-definition.

Friendship in the 1970s Novel

In most of the novels of the 1970s, female friendship, when it appeared as a theme, illustrated how patriarchy induces female rivalry or suggested various options for the heroine. In *Memoirs of an Ex-Prom Queen*, Sasha learns her commonality with other girls when the boys band together to pick on them; later this commonality turns to rivalry in her high school sorority, when the girls gather for Round Table, an exercise in which, in the guise of helping each other, each girl is criticized by her sisters. (My own high school clique did a similar thing called, less euphemistically, "cutdown session.") Later Sasha has a close friendship with the career woman Roxanne, but its importance seems to be the options Roxanne's lifestyle presents for Sasha. Similarly, we will see that in Mary Gordon's *Final Payments*, Isabel's two friends function partly as alternatives in lifestyles.

In *Kinflicks* the mentorship of Ginny by her spinster philosophy professor, Miss Head, shows Ginny what she does not want to become. A life with no passion holds little allure. After leaving college and Miss Head, Ginny lives with a female lover, Eddie, in a radical feminist commune. Here she learns that a life lived almost entirely at the level of the body does not suit her either. In both cases the women in Ginny's life seem to function as symbols rather than as people with whom she shares intimacy. (This is not the case with her mother, as we have already seen.)

In other 1970s novels, female friendship takes varied roles but is usually secondary to other plot concerns. In *Fear of Flying*, friendship has almost no importance, the main theme being Isadora's rejection of her need for men. Stephanie of *Lovers and Tyrants* has a close friend, Claire, whose free lifestyle she envies, and to whom she is vaguely sexually attracted. However, she finally acknowledges that relationships with women lack the force and excitement of those with men. Though female friendship in *The Women's Room* is certainly an important theme, Mira's relationships with her sub-urban housewife and college friends being central to her growth as a feminist, the focus still is on sexual politics—the oppressive institutions of patriarchy. Many of the women in the story seem to function more as representatives of certain types or problems: the lesbian, the rape victim, the black woman.

Friendship in the 1980s

In the 1980s we move into new territory, and female friendship becomes a central theme. No novel of the 1980s features this theme more prominently than Alice Walker's *The Color Purple* (1982). A novel of development set in the rural South from around 1916 to 1942, it has female friendship as its central theme—indeed as its "primary agent of redemption."[57] The pro-tagonist, Celie, whom we follow in her letters to God and her sister from age fourteen to middle age, finds independence, hope, and finally transcen-dence through her love of women. Though the novel is certainly concerned with the oppression of women by men and of blacks by whites, Walker's main theme concerns how black women comfort and help each other to grow in a world where they are not valued. Thus, even though it is a *bildungsroman* showing a woman's growth to maturity in patriarchy, the stress on the power of female friendship makes this novel quite different from those of the 1970s.

Starting at a very young age, Celie is abused by nearly every male in her life. Raped at fourteen by the man she believes to be her father (later we find he is her stepfather), she has two babies by him, quickly given away by the stepfather to a childless couple. Always told she is ugly and stupid ("you black, you pore, you ugly, you a woman, you nothing at all"),[58] she is married off to Albert, a widower with four children who sees her as a sexual convenience and drudge. The only way Celie can endure her bleak situation is to numb herself to feeling: "You a tree," Celie says to herself as Albert beats her, "That's how I know trees fear men" (30).

Celie finds her way out of this brutalized existence through female bonds, first with Sofia, a feisty girl who marries Harpo, Albert's son. Harpo has been imbued with the idea that a husband should beat a disobedient wife, but Sofia refuses to bend to Harpo's will; Celie looks with wonderment at the unthinkable—a woman who fights back. Sofia and Celie form a close friendship as they work together on the farm, exchanging ideas about mar-riage and the lot of women. Celie begins to believe that she need not accept her fate with such resignation. It is important to note here that Celie's relationships to other women, even those her own age, resemble mentorship or the relationship of an older woman to one younger and less experienced. Some psychoanalytic feminist critics have pointed out that female friendship may involve an attempt to replace the warm ties of the preoedipal mother-daughter bond.[59] Certainly Celie never had a relationship with her own mother or was given the coping skills such a relationship would teach her.

Celie's most important mentor is Shug (Sugar) Avery, a local blues singer and lover of Albert. Celie is first Shug's nurse for "a nasty woman's disease," but slowly a friendship grows between them, completely shutting out Albert. Like Sofia, Shug is a strong women who chooses her men and never lets them "mess with her." She teaches Celie to love and respect herself, and introduces her to sexuality, a feeling unknown to Celie. Eventually they become occasional lovers, although the sexual relationship means more to Celie than it does to Shug. Celie's lesbianism reflects radical lesbian feminist views that sexual relationships between women are a way to avoid demeaning, brutalizing encounters with men; indeed, Linda Abbandonato argues that Celie's choice of lesbianism is politically charged.[60] Through Shug's encouragement, Celie musters the will to tell Albert off: "You a lowdown dog.... It's time to leave you and enter into the Creation. And your dead body just the welcome mat I need" (181).

Walker shows the reader that cultural feminist values lead to new spiritual values. Shug not only protects and nurtures Celie, she also is her priest. To Shug, God is all that is lovely and fun in life. When Celie says God is an old white man, reflecting traditional patriarchal views, Shug replies that God is everything, and God loves all human feelings that are joyful, including the sexual. "God loves admiration," Shug says, meaning admiration for his creation. "I think it pisses God off if you walk by the color purple in a field somewhere and don't notice it" (178). Celie begins to notice the color purple. According to Olga Kenyon, this "respect for the life and power of the spirit" is an important feature in female novels of the 1980s.[61]

Equally important as her relationship with Shug Avery is Celie's tie with her contrasting sister, Nettie, who disappeared in Celie's childhood and eventually becomes a missionary in Africa. Through Nettie's letters to Celie and Celie's replies, we can see the growth in Celie's strength. These letters reinforce the cultural feminist theme of female bonding. Walker tells us that African women are also devalued in their culture, and that to compensate, the women find love in their relationships with each other. Their shared work, and sometimes shared husbands, are important sources of warmth and social contact.

For Walker, these close friendships of black rural Southern women—and indeed of women around the world—are nothing short of redemptive. Through her closeness with other women, Celie learns to feel love, to sense beauty, and even to forgive Albert, who also becomes humanized in the process. As in Jong's *Fanny*, the expansive ending reveals a feminist utopia, where men have adopted more humane values and the future stretches ahead for humankind with harmony and peace. Though a number of critics felt that this departure from the realism of the earlier parts of the novel weakened Walker's achievement—the sight of Albert in an apron doing the dishes—others defend this "mythmaking" as essential to Walker's theme. As Lauren Berlant states, Celie's final letter, which she addresses "Dear God. Dear stars, dear trees, dear sky, dear peoples. Dear everything" (249), shows us the "fulfillment of the womanist promise, as the community turns toward the future in expectation of more profit, pleasure, and satisfaction from their labor and from each other."[62]

Another novel, which has received little attention but gives a sensitive portrayal of friendship between adolescent girls, is Ella Leffland's *Rumors of Peace* (1979). Though published at the end of the 1970s, it anticipates some of the themes explored in the 1980s. *Rumors* treats a theme seldom tackled by women writers—war. Set in northern California from Pearl Harbor to Hiroshima, the novel focuses on the years from eleven to fourteen in the life of its protagonist, Suse. Suse confronts all the dilemmas of growing up—boys, awakening sexuality, introduction to intellectual ideas and artistic beauty, and death, along with the faraway drama of World War II. Central to her maturation is her friendship with two sisters, Peggy and Helena Maria, one an anti-role model and the other a mentor.

Suse is linked to the war through an older brother in the service and her hometown's having a sizable Japanese-American population. Suse hates the Japanese, she discovers. At first she finds it difficult to believe the gentle Nagais, who own the town's flower shop, are spies, but soon she becomes infected with the hatred sweeping the community. When she hears the Japanese are being herded into detention centers, she feels such measures are justified: "They had stuffed their wireless sets in the false bottoms of suitcases and baby buggies. They would escape from the camps and spread into the countryside to work from there. It was a measly, pointless move. those who tried to kill you should be killed."[63]

Through the two sisters, Leffland shows us how girls use their peers as guides to their own social and intellectual growth. Suse becomes close to Peggy, her childhood playmate, first; but as they enter junior high, Peggy becomes socially conscious and disinterested in schoolwork. Peggy is one of the TOWKs (Those Who Count), as independent Suse calls them, and Suse rejects their values. The friendship dissolves as Peggy becomes what Suse decides she does not want to be. Peggy's older sister, Helena Maria, on the other hand, is a bright young woman who encourages Suse to read and explore ideas. Scornfully rejecting the values of the TOWKs, she points out to Suse the irrationality of her hatred for the Japanese. Helena Maria tells Suse that hatred induced by war is "a scabby hysteria that attacks inferior souls" (141). She gets Suse to admit that the California Japanese are not really such bad people, saying, "... you can't hate nations, they're only people" (142).

Another important agent of Suse's growth is her first crush on a young man, who, not coincidentally, is dating Helena Maria. Egon Krawitz is a mysterious, dark German boy, a Jewish refugee. Suse knows little of Jews: "... what was a Jew? From Sunday school they were mixed up with bulrushes and date palms, and that's where they were, the Bible" (192). On the advice of Helena Maria, she does some research on Judaism, which spurs an interest in history and social questions. Near the end of the war Suse sees some disturbing pictures of concentration camps: "... on the front page was a mass of white tangled worms, extremely large, with a couple of people standing in them knee deep, each pulling a worm out. Then I saw it wasn't worms they were pulling, but a pair of long arms" (344). Suse now realizes the result of racial hatred, and at war's end she no longer gloats over thousands of enemy dead. She welcomes the formation of the United Nations but realizes that such an organization "smacked of good faith, hard work, and nothing more. But it was the spirit behind those things [the United Nations] that counted, and that was what we must put our hope in" (356). Though she does not yet realize it, Suse has forged ties with humanity and has come to reject racist ideologies that debase human beings. In large part these changes have come through her friendship with Helena Maria. Like *The Color Purple*, *Rumors of Peace* says that love redeems and hatred kills, and the love and guidance young women give each other can provide that redemption.

A myth about female friendship is that it is based mostly on exchanging confidences about boyfriends, husbands, and children. As we shall see in Chapter 5, Mary Gordon often stresses friendships that have an intellectual as well as an emotional dimension. Similarly, in Gail Godwin's *A Southern Family* an important theme of the story is the deep friendship between Claire and her friend Julia.

Like many women's friendships in literature that I have already discussed, the women contrast with each other: Claire, the dark one of the strange Quick family, has fled her North Carolina mountain home; Julia, the fair one, has returned to nurse her dying mother and then care for her widower father. The never-married Claire has a live-in lover and the more glamorous job; she is a writer of novels about quirky Southern families. The divorced Julia teaches history at the unprestigious local college. Claire is more ambitious but is insecure, while Julia has an inner security that makes her content without the comparative fame Claire has won from her writing. Nevertheless, the friends have much in common: both forty-two years old, both Southern and sharing a common past at private Catholic schools, both intellectuals.

Godwin captures the closeness of this thirty-five-year friendship and perceptively describes the way it functions. The women discuss not only their families but also their careers and accumulated wisdom. Julia tends to be the supportive one, relieving Claire's insecurities about her writing; Julia enjoys Claire's insights into life and sense of humor. The two women are aging together and together explore the meaning of this universal experience, an experience that can be traumatic for women, even those with full lives and careers. They usually greet each other after periods of separation with "You're looking great." Though they can see the signs of aging on each other, which confirm their own aging, they are reassured in each other's presence because, in fact, they *are* still each other and offer the same pleasures they always have. Godwin here suggests that an important component of women's friendships is the vehicle they provide to evaluate and cope with the life stages each woman passes through.

Whenever Claire comes back to North Carolina, Julia takes her to a new lovely spot in the mountains as a gift, and also perhaps to remind "her old friend that there were rewards for those who returned to live in the place where they were born" (45). Julia feels just a little defensive about the less exciting life she has chosen, as does Claire about her rejection of her roots. As the two women sit and reminisce on the top of Pinnacle Old Bald, they agree that one must have a position on aging. Should one strive to be a dramatic old witch, one who is feared or admired? Claire feels women must have a power base of wealth or fame to do that. Julia complains that when she goes to the health spa, the young people don't see *her* anymore, only a middle-aged woman; Claire points out that they never saw her when she was young either: they just saw "a really pretty tulip in this year's garden."[64] One could compare some of their conversations to consciousness-raising sessions.

Godwin shows that friendship need not be based on total agreement, even on basic issues of life. For example, the women do not agree on the pleasure of intimacy with men. Julia admits she will enjoy not having to "date" anymore, to get to an age when she can just be herself in a way that one never can with men, even men with whom one is very intimate. On the other hand, Claire enjoys her relationship with her lover. Both agree that it will be somewhat of a relief to get to the age where they will not care what people think.

At one point in the conversation Claire thinks, "The more I contemplate it...the more astonishing it seems: I have liked this other person, not a member of my family, and exactly my own age...for almost my whole lifetime" (52). She realizes that Julia provides a "healthy contrast" to her own values and needs, plus a way to think about herself. Sometimes the contrast makes her uncomfortable; she doubts she would have given up a good job in New York to nurse an ailing mother. Finally, though, she is relieved not to have to be Julia: "But I don't want to be put to her tests. I don't want to trade places with her, or be like her. I just want her to go on being herself so I can watch her fine moral nature in action" (58). In *A Southern Family*, Judith Kegan Gardiner's theory of commonality/complementarity is clearly at work. Besides providing love and support, friends are a sounding board to bounce off and a mirror to step into. And, as Toni McNaron suggests in her theories about sisters, the lives of friends may provide outlets for vicarious aspects of our own personalities. Godwin is also right that same-sex friendship is often more restful, precisely because one can be oneself.

In *The Mother/Daughter Plot*, Marianne Hirsch suggests that some of the interest in female friendship in recent women's literature may be due to the power of the "fantasy of sisterhood." Whether real sisters or friends, the pair may nurture each other in a maternal sense and yet provide the reciprocity and equality not found in the mother/daughter relationship, which is always distorted by the anger of the mother at her powerlessness and the resentment of the daughter at the mother's power. Friendship—"sisterhood"—fulfills the fantasy of the mother/daughter relationship we all long for—the mother who nurtures and is a friend whom we can also mother, but without the power struggles between actual mothers and daughters. Though calling sisterhood a "fantasy," Hirsch believes, and I agree from experience, that it is both an ideal and actual practice within the feminist movement that has been very powerful in the lives of women (164).[65] According to Hirsch, one negative effect of the idea of "sisterhood" has been to silence the voices of mothers. If we have "sisters," then we don't need mothers.

Whatever its possible negative effects on ideas concerning motherhood, women writers during the 1970s and 1980s have revealed the centrality of women's friendships to women's lives. I believe this is a phenomenon that women come to understand later in their lives, as Julia and Claire come to understand it in their forties. I sometimes hear younger women say that they don't like women, that they have few women friends; but I hear few older women say that. By naming the experience, writers have made an important contribution to understanding the nature and importance of female friendship, and have invested it with meaning and value.

CONCLUSION

Although I have concentrated in this chapter on female relationships, I need to cite one more major difference between the feminist-influenced popular fiction of the 1970s and the 1980s—the portrayal of males. As I pointed out in Chapter 2, even the finest *bildungsromans* of the 1970s gave short shrift to the men, particularly if they were "sexed" males, that is, male characters who play a sexual role in the lives of protagonists.[66] Conversely,, writers in the 1980s, perhaps aware of the criticisms of earlier feminist male characters and more willing to admit that masculinity is a social construct, have created male characters of sympathy and complexity. This greater attention to and sympathy for male characters is clearly seen in most of the novels I have discussed here, even those by more radical writers such as Marilyn French. Godwin in both *A Mother and Two Daughters* and *A Southern Family* has produced some fine portraits of men. Though there was much criticism about the bastardly men in *The Color Purple*, for the most part, the men change when exposed to the humanizing force of Celie and Shug.[67]

I intend to reserve my larger conclusions for Chapter 7, but this discussion of selected mainstream women's novels from the 1980s shows a number of themes that relate to feminist politics. First, it is clear that in the 1980s there is less emphasis on sexual politics and the oppressive effects of "growing up female." Writers established the "social construction of femininity" in the 1970s and by the 1980s were exploring female bonds as a prime area of interest. This interest in female bonding and community reflects a growing awareness in women committed to feminist values that our salvation lies not only in "naming the oppressor" but also in realizing our strengths and our gifts to each other. Novelists' treatment of these bonds suggests some interesting questions: Are women able to be better friends to each other than men are to each other because of their close relationship and longer bonding to their mothers? And, now that we have had literature that exposes the role of mother as "tool of the patriarchy," is there a need for fiction creating more positive images of mother-daughter relations? Can the discoveries of theorists about mother/daughter relationships ultimately lead to greater understanding between the generations of women? Finally, how can women translate their powerful private bonds with each other into public commitment to actions that will benefit all women? Unlike the radical feminist novels, these mainstream popular American novels of the 1980s do not show women engaging in public feminist action. Their personal quests are exclusively private, and their bonds with other women are personal as well.

In 1984 Elinor Langer expressed some regret for the passing of feminist fiction, "the partisans of yesteryear," the questing heroines of the 1970s, struggling in patriarchal society. Though she believed the accomplishments of 1980s women writers in rendering female experience, especially female relationships, were truly impressive, she saw a danger that such "excavations in female memory" may neglect larger moral concerns.[68] In a similar vein Gayle Greene more recently depreciated much of the women's fiction of the 1980s, saying its focus on the personal, the family, and the nostalgic expresses resignation and depoliticization. Even the writers she admires, such as Margaret Atwood and Doris Lessing, have abandoned the struggle for change (200).

I believe I have shown that Langer's and Greene's concerns may not be warranted, that women writers of the 1980s have been freed by the work of feminist scholars and fiction writers of the 1970s to continue to examine important moral questions in the light of female experience. In assessing the accomplishments of women writers, we must not fall back into the habit of pigeonholing fiction dealing with traditional female experiences into the "domestic" slot, thus not giving these writers praise justly due them. There should be room for the exploration of varied themes in women's writing, from the traditional to the visionary; all adds to our understandings of who we are.

Literary decades do not end, of course, when the decade concludes on the calendar. It remains to be seen if the trends I have discussed here will continue in the 1990s. What is astounding is the number of novels women writers produced in the 1980s, and how many of them treated the subjects of mothers, daughters, sisters, friends, as well as male characters who are more complex and sympathetic. Most important is how writers have used these subjects not only to document women's oppression but also to celebrate women's lives and gifts to their female relatives, friends, and all humanity. In the next three chapters, we will see how these trends are illustrated in the careers of three very different women writers.

The work of all these writers, as well as of many others, is bringing to fruition the vision of a women's fiction that reflects the variety and complexity of the new ideas about women. In Chapter 7 I will try to reach some tentative conclusions about the general effects the feminist movement has had on twenty years of popular fiction by American women, and will suggest some possibilities of what we may expect in the next decade.

NOTES

1. Susan Bolotin, "Voices from the Post-Feminist Generation," *New York Times Magazine* (17 October, 1982), 28ff.

2. Lois Banner, *Women in Modern America: A Brief History*, 2nd ed. (New York: Harcourt Brace Jovanovich, 1984), 265.

3. Betty Friedan, *The Second Stage* (New York: Summit Books, 1980). Friedan's suggestions were harshly received by some feminists, who attacked Friedan as a traitor, saying she was misrepresenting feminist ideas and playing into the hands of opponents.

4. Elayne Rapping, "A Novelist's Career," *The Women's Review of Books* 7 (February 1990), 13.

5. Josephine Donovan, *Feminist Theory: The Intellectual Traditions of American Feminism* (New York: Frederick Ungar, 1985), 62.

6. Louise Bernikow, *Among Women* (New York: Harper & Row, 1980), 56.

7. In the 1950s Philip Wylie wrote an influential best-seller on the American mother called *A Generation of Vipers*. According to Wylie, a generation of men had been emasculated by possessive and conniving mothers.

8. Mary Ann Ferguson, "The Female Novel of Development and the Myth of Psyche," in *The Voyage In: Fictions of Female Development*, ed. Elizabeth Abel, Marianne Hirsch, and Elizabeth Langland (Hanover, NH, and London: University Press of New England, 1983), 237.

9. Barbara Milton, "Margaret Drabble, The Art of Fiction," *Paris Review* 70 (Fall-Winter 1979), 55.

10. Earlene Hawley, "The Older Mothers in Margaret Drabble's Novels," unpublished MS (Waverly, LA, 1982), 1–2.

11. Kathryn Allen Rabuzzi, *Motherself: A Mythic Analysis of Motherhood* (Bloomington: Indiana University Press, 1988); Carolyn G. Heilbrun, *Reinventing Womanhood* (New York: W. W. Norton, 1979).

12. Sara Ruddick, "Maternal Thinking," *Feminist Studies* 6 (Summer 1980), 348–350; Nancy Harstock, *Money, Sex and Power: Toward a Feminist Historical Materialism* (New York: Longman, 1983), 246.

13. For example, Linda Wolfe, "Men, Women, and Children First," review of *The Good Mother* by Sue Miller, *New York Times Book Review* (27 April 1986), 1; Josephine Humphreys, "Private Matters," *Nation* 242 (10 May 1986), 648–650.

14. Sue Miller, *The Good Mother* (New York: Harper & Row, 1986), 218.

15. Diane Cole, "Catch Up Time," review of *The Good Mother* by Sue Miller, *Ms.* 14 (June 1986), 32–34; Humphreys, "*Private Matters,*" 650.

16. Robert White, "Anna's Quotidian Love: Sue Miller's *The Good Mother*," in *Mother Puzzles: Daughters and Mothers in Contemporary American Literature*, ed. Mickey Pearlman (Westport, CT: Greenwood, 1989), 11.

17. Rabuzzi, *Motherself*, 5.

18. See Gayle Greene, *Changing the Story: Feminist Fiction and the Tradition* (Bloomington: Indiana University Press, 1991), 200; and Paulina Palmer, *Contemporary Women's Fiction: Narrative Practice and Feminist Theory* (Jackson: University Press of Mississippi, 1989), 165.

19. Meredith Powers, *The Heroine in Western Literature: The Archetype and Her Reemergence in Modern Prose* (New York: McFarland, 1991), 176.

20. M. Deiter Keyishian, "Radical Damage: An Interview with Mary Gordon," *The Literary Review* 32 (Fall 1988), 71.

21. *Contemporary Literary Criticism*, ed. Jean Stine and Daniel G. Marowski, 31 (Detroit: Gale Research, 1985), 194.

22. Gail Godwin, "Becoming the Characters in Your Novel," *The Writer* 95 (June 1982), 12.

23. Gail Godwin, *A Mother and Two Daughters* (New York: Viking, 1982), 347.

24. Nancy Chodorow and Susan W. Contratto, "The Fantasy of the Perfect Mother," in *Rethinking the Family*, ed. Barrie Thorne and Marilyn Yalom (New York: Longman, 1982), suggest that feminist theoretical writing is full of anger and maternal powerlessness.

25. Marianne Hirsch, *The Mother/Daughter Plot: Narrative, Psychoanalysis, Feminism* (Bloomington: Indiana University Press, 1989), 164–167.

26. Brenda Daly and Maureen T. Reddy, eds., *Narrating Mothers: Theorizing Maternal Subjectivities* (Knoxville: University of Tennessee Press, 1991), 1–3.

27. Adrienne Rich, *Of Woman Born: Motherhood as Experience and Institution* (New York: Bantam, 1977), 236.

28. Helena Michie, "Mother, Sister, Other: The 'Other Woman' in Feminist Theory," *Literature and Psychology* 32 (1986), 2; Jane Gallop, *The Daughter's Seduction* (Ithaca, NY: Cornell University Press, 1982).

29. Kim Lacy Rogers, "A Mother's Story in a Daughter's Life: Gail Godwin's *A Southern Family*," in *Mother Puzzles*, ed. Mickey Pearlman, 60.

30. See also these recent works on motherhood: Susan Cahill, ed., *Mothers: Memories, Dreams and Reflections by Literary Daughters* (New York: Mentor, 1988); Rabuzzi, *Motherself*; and Paula Kaplan, *Don't Blame Mother: Mending the Mother-Daughter Relationship* (New York: Harper & Row, 1989). Though most of these studies postdate the novels I will discuss, my point is that the late 1970s and 1980s provided a climate of interest in motherhood and mother-daughter relationships.

31. Alice Hoffman, "Momma Never Said Goodnight," review of *Her Mother's Daughter* by Marilyn French, *New York Times Book Review* (25 October 1987), 7.

32. Marilyn French, *Her Mother's Daughter* (New York: Summit Books, 1987), 71–72.

33. See Marianne Hirsch, *The Mother/Daughter Plot*, 1–27.

34. Mary Rose Sullivan, "Breaking the Silence: Marilyn French's *Her Mother's Daughter*," in *Mother Puzzles*, ed. Mickey Pearlman, 41–47.

35. Julia Kristeva, "Oscillation between Power and Denial," in *New French Feminisms*, ed. Elaine Marks and Isabell de Courtivron (New York: Schocken, 1981). Kristeva bases many of her ideas on the thinking of French psychoanalyst Jacques Lacan.

36. See Nancy Friday, *My Mother/My Self: The Daughter's Search for Identity* (New York: Delacorte Press, 1977), for a pop culture approach to the mother-daughter bond.

37. Erica Jong, *Fanny: Being the True History of the Adventures of Fanny Hackabout-Jones* (New York: New American Library, 1980), 80.

38. Ferguson, 241.

39. Amy Tan, *The Joy Luck Club* (New York: G. P. Putnam's, 1989), 25.

40. Rhoda Koenig, "Heirloom China," *New York* 22 (22 March 1989), 82.

41. Ibid.

42. Amy Ling, *Between Worlds: Women Writers of Chinese Ancestry* (New York: Pergamon, 1990), 140.

43. Ibid., 139.

44. Nancy Chodorow, *The Reproduction of Mothering: Psychoanalysis and the Sociology of Gender* (Berkeley: University of California Press, 1978), 169.

45. Carol Gilligan, *In a Different Voice: Psychological Theory and Women's Development* (Cambridge, MA: Harvard University Press, 1982).

46. Joan Lidoff, "Tangled Vines: Mothers and Daughters in Women's Writing," *Women's Studies Quarterly* 11 (Winter 1983), 16.

47. Abby H. P. Werlock, in "A Profusion of Women's Voices: Mothers and Daughters Redefining the Myths," in *Mother Puzzles*, ed. Mickey Pearlman, provides an excellent summary of recent nonfiction writing on motherhood.

48. Toni A.H. McNaron, ed., *The Sister Bond: A Feminist View of a Timeless Connection* (New York: Pergamon, 1985), 8.

49. Joan Chase, *During the Reign of the Queen of Persia* (New York: Harper & Row, 1983), 35.

50. The centrality of male bonding to the male novel of development has often been noted. See Leslie Fiedler, *Love and Death in the American Novel* (New York: Criterion Books, 1960). Fiedler says that male friendship in literature is often a device for breaking away from the constraining bonds of domesticity woven by women.

51. Margaret Atwood, "That Certain Thing Called the Girlfriend," *New York Times Book Review* (11 May 1986), 39.

52. Juliet Mitchell, *Women's Estate* (New York: Pantheon, 1971), 57.

53. Chodorow has said that women need a "network" of female kin to develop their sense of self (*Reproduction*, 198); Heilbrun believes that without female bonding, a woman who moves outside the home enters the limbo world of the "honorary male" (*Reinventing*, 89).

54. Janet Todd, *Women's Friendship in Literature* (New York: Columbia University Press, 1980); Elizabeth Abel, "'(E)Merging Identities: The Dynamics of Female Friendship in Contemporary Fiction by Women," *Signs* 6 (Spring 1981), 414.

55. See Palmer, *Contemporary Women's Fiction*, ch. 6.

56. Judith Kegan Gardiner, "The (US)es of (I)dentity: A Response to Abel on '(E)Merging Identities,' "*Signs* 6 (Spring 1981), 436–437.

57. Peter S. Prescott, "A Long Road to Liberation," *Newsweek* (21 June 1982), 67.

58. Alice Walker, *The Color Purple* (New York: Washington Square Press, 1982), 187.

59. Palmer states that many women are reluctant to view their friendship with women in this way, especially lesbians, who dislike the idea of their relationship being a kind of "incest with the mother." McNaron, on the other hand, frankly acknowledges this may be a factor in lesbian relations; although it gives the relationship tension, it adds deeper intimacy (6).

60. Linda Abbandonato, " 'A View from Elsewhere' ": Subversive Sexuality and the Rewriting of the Heroine's Story in *The Color Purple*," *PMLA* 106 (October 1991), 1108. As Abbandonato says, Celie does not find her way out of her predicament by finding the right man but by finding the right woman.

61. Olga Kenyon, *Writing Women: Contemporary Women Novelists* (Concord, MA: Pluto Press, 1991), 69.

62. Lauren Berlant, "Race, Gender, and Nation in *The Color Purple*," *Critical Inquiry* 14 (Summer 1988), 854.

63. Ella Leffland, *Rumors of Peace* (New York: Harper & Row, 1979), 38.

64. Gail Godwin, *A Southern Family* (New York: William Morrow, 1987), 55.

65. Hirsch cites Bell Gale Chevigny's "Daughters Writing: Toward a Theory of Women's Biography," *Feminist Studies* 9 (Spring 1983), 95–96, which discusses the fantasy of reciprocity in "sisterhood."

66. Peter Prescott, "Living Sacrifices," review of *Final Payments* by Mary Gordon, *Newsweek* (10 April 1978), 92.

67. A number of other critics have praised Walker for dealing with the touchy issue of abuse of black women by black men. See, for example, Olga Kenyon in *Writing Women*, 79.

68. Elinor Langer, "Whatever Happened to Feminist Fiction?" *New York Times Book Review* (4 March 1984), 35.

4

Marge Piercy: The Radical Tradition

The first writer I have chosen to examine in detail is Marge Piercy. Piercy is an unusual phenomenon in American writing—a radical feminist who has achieved wide readership. A fair number of critics have disparaged her work, saying it is polemical and clumsy; even a feminist critic has called her approach as heavy-handed as a "meat cleaver."[1] Nevertheless, Piercy has acquired legions of die-hard fans who look forward to her novels, despite their radical ideas about women, men, and society.

Deborah Silverton Rosenfelt places Piercy within a socialist feminist tradition in women's writing that goes back to the nineteenth century. This tradition questions institutions of capitalist society, especially as they impinge on women, and advocates sweeping social and political change, although it differs in the various "aspects of the private sphere—sexuality, reproduction and motherhood"—that should be changed.[2] This fiction, unlike some of the work discussed in earlier chapters, directly advocates radical solutions to the problems of women and men. Because it promotes social/political change, and in fact uses art to advance this change, such writing has been labeled "polemical" and "propagandistic." More than other writers influenced by the feminist movement, these writers have found it difficult to achieve critical acceptance.[3]

Besides being successful and well known, Piercy is also one of the most prolific of the feminist novelists. Between 1969 and 1991 she has written eleven novels, as well as a number of volumes of poetry. She is equally famous for her poetry, in which she addresses not only subjects relating to women but also other concerns of the Left, including capitalism's oppression of all people, the destruction of the environment, and the impoverishment of urban life.

Piercy came of age in the 1950s and 1960s, and her experiences "growing up female" in the 1950s, her involvement in the New Left of the 1960s, and then the Women's Movement have provided a source of material and insight into her subjects. All of her novels reflect these experiences, and some of her protagonists' lives are quite similar to Piercy's. A chronological study of the novels from the first, *Going Down Fast* (1969), to the latest at this writing, *He, She and It* (1991), illustrates the growth of Piercy's feminist consciousness, rising out of the New Left of the 1960s, her gradual disillusionment with the male Left, and then the development of a feminist critique of the society, which would demand profound changes in the lives and even basic thought processes of individuals.

Piercy was born in 1936 in Detroit, a violent place with "an excessive amount of cruelty," and grew up in a multiracial, working-class neighborhood that "formed and deformed her."[4] Half-Jewish, she always felt like an outsider among the other white children. In Detroit and later in Chicago, where she went to graduate school, Piercy gained her respect for the working class and eventually her drive to speak for "those largely unspoken for" (*PCB* 168). A bright student, Piercy received a scholarship to the University of Michigan, where she vastly expanded herself, but not without a sense of class betrayal. Though at this point in her life she lacked a vocabulary to express it, she felt there was something wrong about the relations between the sexes and the role of women in society. As she later put it, "I cared about women's issues before I could understand them" (*PCB* 143). Women were never mentioned by the male professors who taught her, and when she wrote poetry dealing with women's subjects, she was told such topics were inferior to the "universal" experiences of men. In the *Partisan Review* (1974) Piercy described her feelings of alienation in the conformist environment of the 1950s.[5] During these college years she began her political activism, though she says she has identified with the Left since she was fifteen years old.

After Michigan, Piercy attended Northwestern University, living in a gritty working-class neighborhood of Chicago where she was again exposed to the oppression of different races and ethnic groups by the urban establishment. Here working-class neighborhoods were "razed" in order to construct high rises for the wealthy. Believing that she would never become a writer if she stayed in the university, Piercy left graduate school and supported herself with odd jobs. Other experiences, like marriage to a graduate student whom she supported, contributed to her developing ideas about the role of women. During these years she gained the experiences that are most directly reflected in *Going Down Fast*. Since leaving academe, Piercy has supported herself by writing and lecturing, and has elected not to remain part of an academic environment, unlike many other writers I discuss here. She has married Ira Wood, who assists in reading her manuscripts, and lives on Cape Cod, where she writes, gardens, cooks, and revels in the natural environment.

As with many young women of the time, Piercy's involvement in the New

Left in the late 1960s and early 1970s led her to believe that traditional radical solutions did not get at the heart of society's ills. Her discovery in Students for a Democratic Society that radical men were as traditional in their attitudes toward women as bourgeois businessmen, set her on the path toward a feminist solution to the problems of capitalist society.[6] These discoveries are best detailed in the experiences of the protagonists of *Small Changes* (1972), probably the best-known and most influential of Piercy's novels, and *Vida* (1979).

In her novels, especially those written from 1970 to 1982, Piercy subscribes to most of the radical feminist ideas that I described in Chapter 2. Though she is a socialist and believes that women should work with oppressed people of both sexes, she believes women's status needs to change before other changes can occur. She feels that many traditional heterosexual relationships are exploitative, that the primacy of male attitudes of rationality and order has caused much damage in the world, and that both men and women need to change the way they think about their relations to each other.

EARLY NOVELS

Piercy's first published novel, *Going Down Fast*, has a male protagonist, to which she attributes its publication. Written between 1965 and 1967, Piercy feels that it has the "least feminist consciousness" of any of her novels—not surprising, since she had little at the time. Described as her "love-hate musing on Chicago," *Going Down Fast* is actually written from two viewpoints, both male, and concerns the efforts by wealthy property developers to gentrify urban neighborhoods.[7] It pits the poor black and ethnic residents of the neighborhood and some leftist middle-class organizers against the rapacious landlords and city bosses who care nothing for the lives they are disrupting—the exercise of "power and powerlessness," as Piercy calls it. Later, Piercy seemed to not like *Going Down Fast* very much, calling it "literary" and a little overwritten (*PCB* 192).

Her next novel, *Dance the Eagle to Sleep* (1970), concerns the youth-oriented New Left movement of the late 1960s and says more about the counterculture than it does about women's issues. The novel contains many of the standard counterculture criticisms of the deadening values of the Establishment. Piercy steps into the near future to show a group of young people pitted against a power elite, who in order to contain the reformist elements of the youths, have required each nineteen-year-old to serve the nation for one year in the armed forces, in conservation projects, or teaching the underprivileged. The sinister purpose of the government is to diffuse the impulse for social change and prepare each youth to marry, reproduce, and become an eager, uncritical consumer. *Dance the Eagle* tells the reader that liberal solutions to society's problems do not get to the root of the evil that lurks in the capitalist system, implying that radical surgery is needed.

Dance the Eagle cannot be called a feminist novel in the same way that some of Piercy's later works can. Clearly, when she was working on the book, Piercy was moving from a leftist to a feminist consciousness. Of her half-dozen protagonists, the two most important are male, Shawn and Corey. Within the "tribe" of radical youth (they model themselves after Native Americans), feminist issues do arise and are debated. Most of the males, even the heroes, use women sexually and at first view them mainly as nurturers for themselves and the children. As a rock singer, Shawn exploits his sexuality to attract groupies and impress other males. In reviewing *Dance the Eagle*, Elizabeth Hardwick accused Piercy of "phallic obsession," apparently not realizing that she was criticizing such an attitude.[8]

Piercy shows the reader the difficulty of changing gender roles, even among radical people, and how such roles are deeply rooted in female lack of self-esteem and male egos. In *Dance the Eagle* the youths in the commune follow traditional patterns. The women seldom are allowed to serve the group as "warriors"; only the most aggressive can join the men in the street actions, and when they do, they pridefully scorn the women who remain in the traditional roles:

Whatever the rhetoric, in tribe after tribe women mostly end up running the kitchen, taking care of housework and babies, running the mimeograph machine, serving as bodies in demonstrations ... doing all the tedious daily tasks that made tribal life possible. The women who made it into more effective and interesting roles did not think of themselves as representing a constituency of downtrodden women, but hung out with the male warriors and acted as much like them as possible.[9]

Piercy obviously sees the traditional female role as less desirable but is critical of those women who have "made it" in the male culture and scorn their sisters left behind. Cultural feminist theorists might argue, however, that lack of value for traditional female activities causes such attitudes of superiority. These diverging attitudes reveal a basic split in feminist thinking: Are traditional female activities, such as mothering, mostly tedious and therefore to be shared by both sexes, or do they provide opportunities for enrichment and growth denied the warrior males? Are there not aspects of being a warrior that are terrifying or even tedious? One can see that in 1991, in *He, She and It*, Piercy is still grappling with these fundamental questions.

Despite the considerable attention Piercy pays to feminist issues in *Dance the Eagle*, the novel's themes are more broadly focused, with sexism being one aspect of a larger problem. The chief culprit is not patriarchy as such, but the capitalistic system that lets a few powerful, greedy companies tyrannize the Third World peoples, rape the environment, and encourage the working-class police and public school teachers to hate and fear those lower than they—youths, blacks, and the poor. Unlike the radical males in Piercy's later novels, these young men become aware of their sexism and try to change. For example, Corey struggles against the sexual double standard that will not allow his girlfriend Joanna sexual freedom while he sleeps with many girls. Here Piercy reveals a radical feminist belief—that male sexual possessiveness is based on ego and rivalry with other males, in this case Corey's friend Shawn. We do see the two most important young women of the group, Joanna and Ginny, achieve a clearer understanding of themselves as separate from the males in their lives. They come to realize that the male/female relationship is perhaps the most basic of the dominant/submissive relationships of our culture.

FEMINISM IN FULL FLOWER: *SMALL CHANGES*

Whereas in her first two novels Piercy's feminist consciousness was just coming to bud, *Small Changes* represents its full flowering. Here she concentrates on the big changes young women went through in the late 1960s and early 1970s, as they moved from the New Left and into the feminist movement. Though not as well known as French's *The Women's Room*, *Small Changes* sold very well and in the 1970s became equally instrumental in the lives of many women as a vehicle for raising feminist consciousness. Indeed, Piercy has said the novel is "an attempt to produce in fiction the equivalent of a full experience in a consciousness-raising group for many women who would never go through the experience."[10]

Conceived as a "very full novel that would be long, almost Victorian in its scope and detail" (PCB 92), *Small Changes* contains many characters but focuses on two women, Beth and Miriam, one working class and one middle class, whose lives intersect, thus illustrating many differences and similarities of women's problems. Piercy alternates between Beth's and Miriam's stories, with the ironic chapter titles telling us her approach, "debunking of traditional women's pablum": "The Happiest Day of a Woman's Life," the tale of Beth's miserable wedding day; "Come Live with Me and Be My Love," Beth's affair with the male chauvinist Tom Ryan; "You Ain't Pretty So You May as Well Be Smart," Miriam's high school days; and "Love Is a Woman's Whole Existence," Miriam's unhappy affairs with Phil and Jackson.[11]

In *Small Changes* Piercy gives the reader two feminist *bildungsromans*. Beth's and Miriam's backgrounds are different but what happens to them is similar, emphasizing the idea that women's oppression is no respecter of class. Beth is small, quiet, unobtrusive, always the good daughter to whom parents and teachers pay little attention. (When reading of Beth, I thought of the many obedient and unexciting young women I have taught, whom I hardly noticed because they so well fit the mold they were encouraged into.)

Beth marries young because she has no education or skills, and because she hopes her marriage to Jim will give her "a life, where she would be loved."[12] And, of course, books and magazines, her entire culture, have told her that marriage will be an ending and the source of her happiness. But unlike earlier novels of development, marriage does not provide closure.

As all feminists warn, marriage does not give a woman a life if she has no self-esteem to begin with. Marriage is a bitter disappointment for Beth, who chafes for "something, something [that] hung out there in music and birds wheeling against the dusk and crickets chirping in the weeds" (39). Jim refuses to see her as an adult, calling her his "Little Girl," and believes the solution to her discontent is pregnancy. Recognizing that she will be trapped by children, she flushes her birth control pills down the toilet. Jim has all the characteristics of the stereotypical 1970s feminist male: he is brutal (at one point he rapes Beth to assert his dominance), he cannot show feelings, and he objectifies women. Piercy shows the rape as not primarily a sexual act but, as Susan Brownmiller says, a male attempt to control and assert property rights through intimidation and fear.

Unlike some 1970s heroines, mousy Beth resists victimization in the captivity of marriage. She compares herself to a turtle she had captured as a child. The animal had been miserable in its captivity, and finally, in pity, she freed it. As Beth ponders her situation, she comes to some important realizations: like a turtle she is not brave and glamorous, but she is dogged and perhaps, eventually, she will get where she wants to be and "she can carry with her what she needs" (39). She determines to steal his property from Jim and "belong to no one but herself" (45). With this insight Beth's *bildungsroman* really begins. Piercy's description of Beth's emotions as her plane takes off for Boston must be one of feminist fiction's most joyful portraits of a woman emerging from her shackles: "She clasped her hands and joy pierced her. She was wiry with joy and tingling. How beautiful to be up here! How beautiful was flight and how free (even though it cost money). She was the only flying turtle under the sun" (46).

Beth's salvation comes through sisterhood, close female friendships in a women's commune, and a love affair with an older woman mentor. In this treatment of the importance of women's friendships, *Small Changes* anticipates a theme most writers did not stress until the 1980s. However, because Piercy concentrates on male brutality in the novel, it is easy to overlook the importance of women's bonds to the characters' emancipation. After some lonely times and a dismal relationship with a man in a coed halfway house where men talk to each other and women do the dishes, Beth finds her way to the women's commune. Here the women help each other in their struggles toward individuation. For example, Beth says to Dorine, the "house whore" of the halfway house, "You're not a dog. Why do you want to be owned?" (88).

In this section of the novel, Piercy shows how lesbianism can develop naturally from women's brutalization by men. Some radical feminists believe that heterosexuality is learned, not innate, and that therefore it can be unlearned. If women realize how they are sexually exploited by men, they can learn to find sexual pleasure with women. Eventually Beth settles into a lesbian relationship with Wanda, an older feminist activist. As well as being her lover, Wanda teaches Beth, explaining how their feminist rituals give each other power and a sense of personal beauty. Beth tries to mythologize Wanda for a time, to make her into an earth mother, but Wanda rejects this role, pointing out that she suffers from loneliness, too, that she needs the others as much as they need her (*RO* 187).

In her depiction of the warmly supportive women's commune, Piercy shows us some of the same radical feminist ideas seen in her next novel, *Woman on the Edge of Time* (1976): children are nurtured better by several people at one time, relations between people are more harmonious without the competition of patriarchy, and polymorphous sexuality is more health-enhancing than the heterosexual monogamy of patriarchal society. In *Small Changes* Piercy seems to have moved away somewhat from the more hopeful attitudes of *Dance the Eagle to Sleep*; radical men are just as patriarchal and domineering as bourgeois men.

Miriam's story forms the bulk of the novel, and most critics have found her a more interesting character than Beth, perhaps because she is more robust and flamboyant. At first, we expect that Miriam, rather than Beth, will effect the most changes in her life and will emerge as a truly free woman. Miriam, a large, voluptuous Jewish girl from Brooklyn, has always thought of herself as homely: "You're not pretty, Miriam mine, so you better be smart" (95). She is the "unloved," unpretty daughter who compensates by being a math whiz, supposedly an unusual talent even in bright females.

As with Beth, Piercy takes pains with Miriam's story to show us the "social construction of femininity" and the dangers of the myth of romantic love. Miriam is raised by an indifferent father and a smothering mother, but begins to open up in college, where she does well in her studies. However, she has thoroughly absorbed her society's ideas about romantic love and finding a life with a man, attitudes that prove to be her downfall. Her first affair, with Phil, shows Miriam's self-deception at work. A poet, Phil is more sensitive and playful than most men (some feminists believe that characteristics associated with the arts are regarded as feminine), but he sees women as extensions of his ego and as representatives of the mysterious powers of womanhood. When he meets Miriam, he tells Jackson, his best friend, that he has found his own Jewish princess. "And she's mine. . . . the pot of gold, the end of the rainbow. The poet's delight!" (102).

From time to time Miriam's good sense rebels against his abstracted view of her: "I won't represent the world. Or physical being. Or procreation. Or spring. I'm a person just as much you are" (149). But to her own detriment Miriam buys into his picture: "She was born to herself. She had become beautiful and a woman and the Queen of Sheba and Merciful Mary and Holy Aphrodite" (103). The awkward "ugly duckling" now feels like what society says she should be, a beautiful woman finding herself in sexual love with a mate. At this point in her life, Miriam is seemingly a free woman, sensual, "wearing her body like a flag," a woman who looks forward to a rewarding career in a nontraditional field for a woman, computer science, and a woman who does not ever want to be married, fearing she will end up like her own mother, "Krechtzing" and washing floors. However, the reader can see that Miriam has made the typical female mistake, trying to find self through "love."

In order to show us the effects of patriarchal values, Piercy carefully develops the characters of Phil and his friend Jackson, an Establishment dropout, who is even more constrained in his feelings than Phil. Both Jackson and Phil, though railing against the values of the System, the oppression of the Third World, and the poor, treat the women in their lives as warm bodies to be used and discarded. Believing that showing emotion is weak, Phil and Jackson can express their love only through the locker room camaraderie of punching each other. When Miriam comments on this to Phil, he replies, "That's just fooling around. What do you want us to do, kiss each other? He's my old buddy, Jackson. We both know where the other one's at" (182).

Part of their relationship involves edgy competition, the competition they despise in the "straight" world. Sometimes their punches are angry and their words insulting. Inevitably, Miriam becomes a part of their rivalry, an intolerable situation that indirectly leads to her total annihilation as a person, when Jackson "steals" her away from Phil. Piercy masterfully sets this seduction in the context of a protracted chess game between Miriam and Jackson, in which the female desire for connection and approval is set against the fierce male will to win a prize:

She could feel his intense will to beat her flowing over the table. She did not have an enormous counterweight to that will.... She did not want to win nearly that much.... She tasted again her curiosity. What would she ask for if she won? She would ask him for less uptightness, more acceptance. (186–187)

As Miriam lies with Jackson, after their tempestuous sex, she "briefly remembered then that she had wanted him to like her, not to want her." In the final words of the scene Piercy perhaps goes too far, telling us that Miriam "felt lost, battered. Yet something in her stretched and purred: see, he wanted me, he did. And called that reality" (188). Despite this didacticism the message is powerful: women confuse desire for possession with desire for themselves as persons. As the following events show, Jackson no more regards her as Miriam, herself, than does Phil.

In Jackson and Phil, Piercy shows the contradictions inherent in the Left's program for social change. These men cannot change society when in their personal relations with women and other men they are acting out the qualities they hate in the Establishment: dominance and competition. The accumulated stories of all the characters in *Small Changes* confirm a basic feminist belief: "the personal is political." These happenings, which Piercy repeats to show their pervasiveness, are not isolated incidents; they are part of a larger problem based on the sexual domination of women by men that can be changed only through radical reforms.

Miriam's tale ends in total defeat for this promising young women. After several years of continued injury by Phil and Jackson, she retreats into the security of marriage with Neil Stone, a cold, rational, and cautious computer scientist. Neil (his last name is instructive) represents all the hated qualities of the patriarchy. Her career ended, Miriam becomes a nonperson, dedicating her life to her husband and children and fearing Neil's interest in younger, more attractive women. It is the less-educated Beth who instructs her that no one should be responsible for making a life for another person. This part of the novel—the spiritual death of the richly endowed, wonderfully loving, giving, and brilliant Miriam—is frightening.

Thus, the woman with such exciting potential who seems to be making great changes falls victim to the "frightening power of the status quo." As Carol Burr Megibow perceptively points out, Piercy shows that it is partly Miriam's intense femaleness that seals her doom.[13] As a male mentor tells her, "You have an unusual intuitive mind—the best thing one can say about any scientist. But you're attractive.... So you'll do nothing" (37). He goes on to tell her that she would do better as a "grand courtesan" than as a systems analyst.

In *Small Changes* Piercy tells us that it is the "ancient patriarchal myths" that do women in. According to Megibow, the novel says that since women "have no stories of their own," they have little choice but to opt for doing what women have always done. The changes they can make are only "small" (201). Anne Mickelson, however, disagrees, believing that the novel shows that: "Women's lives can change if women are honest and willing to risk change from the traditional pattern of dependency on men" (*RO* 187). Although Beth has been forced to go underground after her lover, Wanda, goes to prison, we feel that eventually she will be able to continue her growth and to work in the feminist movement toward a better community. Dorine, a minor character, finally enters into an equal relationship with Phil, who makes sincere attempts to change his sexism. I believe that the novel's conclusion, where the defeated Miriam frets about Neil's affair with a younger woman, clearly shows the hopelessness of traditional heterosexual relationships. Like *The Women's Room*, *Small Changes* paints a gloomy picture of the possibilities of good relations between the sexes, given present social arrangements.

Although I intend to reserve most of my critical evaluation of Piercy's work for this chapter's conclusion, I would like to respond here to a general criticism of her work, especially in the early years: her tendency to create bastardly males. Besides Phil, Jackson, Jim, and Neil, there are any number of other exploiting, unfeeling, mechanical male chauvinists trooping through *Small Changes*, including fathers, coworkers, and professors. Typical of reviewers' comments is that of Margaret Ferrari:

Aside from the novel's bulk and humor and its frequently marvelous poetic imagery, hateful men are its most viable commodity.... This elimination of the male half of the human race as real, with real, deeply civilized feelings for women, is the single most disturbing factor in the novel because it seems so blatantly untrue and destroys some of the novel's deserved credibility. (507)

First, Piercy's characters, though often bastardly, are very real and vital. True, their vitality, when directed toward women, is destructive, but Piercy's careful attention to detail—for example, Jackson's constant habit of scratching himself, showing his inability to get beneath his surface—makes these men come alive (*RO* 180). Second, not all remain unchanged in their dealing with women. There is evidence that Phil changes in his new relationship with Dorine—too late to change the damage done to Miriam.

Third, and most important, says Mickelson, Piercy makes it clear that it is the system that is at fault, not individual men:

The treatment of women by men is seen as the result of society's emphasis on the separation of male and female roles, and the perversion of all natural feelings between men and women.... Society is the villain because of its stress on manhood as equated with competitiveness for money and wealth, and its clinging to a narrow dogmatism which refuses to view woman in any way except as inferior.... [Piercy] is adamant about the reconstitution of individual man and woman which she believes can only come from a break with established societal patterns.... (*RO*182–183)

In fact, the problem is not just patriarchal values but the entire Western capitalistic system based on private property, economic competition, and denial of the body. Thus, feminists must not separate themselves from the struggles of other oppressed people including men, as some cultural feminists have suggested. Wanda explains this to Beth when Wanda decides she must go to prison rather than testify to the grand jury about the doings of the Movement. Though many of these people are men, Wanda says:

The corporations that poison the rivers and make war profitable and the state that makes war—those are my enemies.... I believe in a separate women's movement so we can be in control of our own political destiny, and our own struggle.... But I have to believe in making alliance with other groups who are fighting too, because we do want to win. (490, 493)

Nevertheless, despite these defenses—characterization is believable in *Small Changes* and Piercy does show that individual men are not to blame— I have to agree with Margaret Ferrari's central premise. If one knows men who treat women decently and try to live with them in respect, then the credibility of Piercy's powerful novel is somewhat weakened. Finally, all this blaming the system aside, if one believes in individual responsibility, and I suspect Piercy does, then the individual men do become culpable for their actions. She certainly seems angry enough at them to indicate she blames them. In Chapter 2 I suggested that the "social construction of masculinity" was not a prominent idea in the literature of the 1970s. Though in *Small Changes* Piercy does explain *why* her men are so cruel, the general effect on the reader is to suggest that all men are cruel exploiters.

Though male-female relations are the focus of this novel, as in most fiction of the 1970s, Piercy also anticipates another 1980s theme besides female friendship—the relations of mothers and daughters. However, like many 1970s novels, the mother's influence seems mostly negative. Beth's mother restricts her growth in any way she can. Miriam, like other protagonists we have seen, feels unloved by her mother, Sonia, the chief socializing force in her life, who constantly tells her how important it is to catch a man ("have prospects") and behave properly. Sonia is literally the "corset tightener," scolding Miriam for not wearing a bra: "It isn't like you're a little girl anymore, nobody would mind. You're big as a horse and you want to go around hanging out like a bum!... How can you run around with people looking?" (118–119)

Though Miriam lacks respect for Sonia, she longs to express her love to her:

There was a law in operation that mothers and daughters could not teach each other, could not inherit, could not relate. They must continually react against each other, generation after generation.... (138)

She could remember Sonia as the sun that warmed her world from the center, the milky heart, the lap of roundness and comfort. (158)

Piercy shows us how Nancy Chodorow's "reproduction of mothering" (see Chapter 3) keeps daughters living their mother's lives. Though Miriam vowed she would never be like her mother, living only for her family, she does the same thing, partly out of guilt. Clearly, it is the traditional stories that are at fault. Since Miriam lacks any way to pattern her life other than her mother's, when faced by an exploitative society, she retreats into what she feels will be the safety of marriage. As we have seen, these themes are quite similar to those in Marilyn French's 1987 novel *Her Mother's Daughter*.

A FEMINIST UTOPIA: *WOMAN ON THE EDGE OF TIME*

Like *Dance the Eagle to Sleep*, *Woman on the Edge of Time* (1976) is another projection into the future, this time a utopia where feminist values have triumphed. If *Small Changes* concentrates on the problem, *Woman on the Edge of Time* gives us the solution. Because of the current interest in feminist science fiction, especially feminist utopias, *Woman on the Edge of Time* is Piercy's most studied novel, most feminist critics placing it among the best feminist utopian writing.[14]

Piercy says that *Woman* is one of her favorite novels and Consuelo (Connie) Ramos is the best character she has ever created. She describes her intention in this way: "My first intent was to create an image of a good society, one that was *not* sexist, racist, or imperialist: one that was cooperative, respectful of all living beings, gentle, responsible, loving, and playful. The result of a full feminist revolution" (*PCB* 215). Connie Ramos is one of "those unspoken for," a poor Chicana, aging (thirty-seven), formerly an abused wife now single, and incarcerated in a mental institution. She has lost custody of her child, Angie, because she injured her during a particularly difficult time after her lover's death. Her life a litany of trouble—neglected by a harassed mother who had too many children, abused by men, lacking an education (even though she has shown cleverness in college courses she has taken)—Connie is unable to get any work that will decently support her. Not a complete victim, she is rebellious, having come to the point where the system cannot hurt her any more. Connie understands that in the guise of trying to help her, "they" are trying to take away her personhood: "They trapped you into saying something and then they'd bring out their interpretations that made your life over."[15]

Connie escapes her bleak situation by time traveling to the "edge of time" in 2137, to Mattapoisett with a strange asexual person named Luciente. In this world sexual distinctions are small, women appearing more like men because they do not have to wear confining clothes and are encouraged to exercise. This is a world of joy, harmony, peace (for the most part), and personal fulfillment. People live in villages close to nature; high-level technology exists to serve humans, and all signs of the urban nightmare of late-twentieth-century America have disappeared. Extreme care is taken with the land, so that the people live in symbiosis with the environment. Luciente is scandalized when she hears that people in Connie's time put their wastes into the water.

All creators of utopias must confront the question of the family, that unit of society where the human psyche is formed.[16] In this feminist utopia, to free women to use their creative potential, the function of childbearing has been deconstructed "as an essential source of women's private satisfaction and public virtue."[17] As Shulamith Firestone suggested, babies are grown outside the female body and cared for by the community (although each child knows who its three mothers are), reflecting the idea that society cannot change if men remain the chief controllers of the public sphere and women the chief controllers of the private. In fact, *Woman on the Edge of Time* is predicated on the New Left belief that the division of industrialized society into public and private spheres has done great damage to human beings. Relevant here are earlier counterculture critiques such as those by Paul Goodman (*Growing up Absurd*, 1960) and Herbert Marcuse (*One Dimensional Man*, 1964; *Eros and Civilization*, 1966). As Frances Bartkowski has pointed out, what Piercy has done is graft onto this thinking, which wholly left out woman's point of view, the feminist insights of Millett, Firestone, Phyllis Chesler, and Dorothy Dinnerstein (63-64).

In Mattapoisett each child has three mothers, including men, who even have the opportunity to breast-feed infants (because of hormone dosages). Luciente explains it all to Connie:

There was that one thing we had to give up too, the only power we ever had, in return for no more power for anyone. The original production: the power to give birth. 'Cause as long as we were biologically enchained, we'd never be equal. And males never would be humanized to be loving and tender. (105)

There is some nostalgia expressed here for this loss of women's exclusive power, but since women have gained so much, the benefits outweigh the regrets. Adult sexual relationships are also radically altered. People love others of the opposite and same sex, and monogamous unions that last a lifetime are unknown, though promiscuity is not the result. Jackrabbit, one of the other characters, calls the one man-one woman bonding of our time "unstable dyads, fierce and greedy, trying to body the original mother-child bonding" (125). This is another feminist idea relating to Freudian-Lacanian thought: that adult sexuality is closely related to preoedipal feelings. *Woman on the Edge of Time*, however, like most feminist thought, is based on the premise that human behavior, even behavior thought to be innate and inevitable, is malleable. For real change to occur, as Dorothy Dinnerstein has suggested, bonds to a past symbiosis between men and women must be altered.[18]

This is a society without evil, but not without conflict or war, which comes from battle with the enemy—the remnants of the evil, masculine, authoritarian society of Connie's time. Sexual jealousy does exist, but not to the murderous degree it does in our culture. When someone's lover goes to another person, feelings are hurt, but the individual tries to realize that "person must not do what person cannot do" (101). Anyway, people's self-esteem in this society is high, so jealousy is a fleeting emotion. Language, too, has been altered to eliminate sexist usage and different pronouns for the sexes, reflecting the hopeful feminist view that although langauge is resistant to change and can be a repository of oppressive values, it is also malleable and useful for social change.

Throughout the novel Piercy alternates scenes from this world with the evil patriarchal world tormenting Connie. At first, we are unsure whether the new world is real or only in Connie's imagination. In the words of Luciente, Piercy reminds the reader of the ambiguous nature of the future: "We're struggling to exist" (197). Finally, we come to understand that this world is one of only several possibilities. Says Luciente to Connie: "Those of your time who fought hard for change, often they had myths that a revolution was inevitable. But nothing is!" (177). In case we lack the imagination to envision it, Connie time travels to an alternative, horrible future where patriarchal values have been led to their ultimate conclusion. In this world, the rich live long lives, the poor are used for expendable "organ banks," and bioengineered males employ female prostitutes as sexual slaves and housekeepers. This world somewhat resembles the dystopia of Canadian novelist Margaret Atwood in *The Handmaid's Tale* (1986).

Does this feminist vision of a brave new future work? As I have stated, many feminist critics have praised the novel for its visionary themes, insights into present social arrangements, and ingenious social innovations. Bartkowksi finds it innovatively takes feminist ideas further than earlier utopias, such as Charlotte Perkins Gilman's *Herland* (1911), since Piercy had the thinking of the feminist writing of the 1970s to draw upon (66). Carol Kessler believes that its focus on a poor Chicana affirms with sympathy the variety of women's experience, and its radicalism "unashamedly" acknowledges the important social function that fiction *should* have. To the accusation that the novel does not provide usable solutions, Kessler replies that utopias need not provide solutions but, rather, values and guidelines. This *Woman* certainly does (311).

Judith Kegan Gardiner, however, though finding Piercy's novel sometimes "moving and persuasive," feels that she has not adequately bridged the gap that often exists in radical feminist thinking between the evil, public male world and the good, private female world. In this public world men are "evil, nasty dominators." In contrast, women, like Connie's niece Dolly, do evil things only when duped by a male. As complete victims, women thus seem unable to take control of their fate and create this new world. Though Connie does achieve a limited amount of vengeance at the end of her story, this could not lead to a revolution. The novel exhorts us to "midwife" the new age, but gives no clue as to how women will begin these changes; to long for political power is dangerous because in a patriarchy "power is intrinsically corrupting."[19] So, says Gardiner, this good alternative world emerges as a private female fantasy, and that of a "crazy" woman as well, whose reactions to the public, bureaucratic world "mimic the mad privacy of paranoia" (75).

Gardiner suggests that Piercy and other feminist writers need to stop viewing evil as something outside the protagonist and the other female characters; in other words, if we really are to build a better future, we must reject double standards of morality (men are bad; women are good) and turn to the standard of individual moral responsibility. My own feeling is that the complexity Gardiner demands would have produced a different kind of novel than the didactic work of social protest that Piercy creates here. Other writers may give us more ambiguity and complexity, but there also should be a place in feminist writing for the outcry against dehumanization and abuse that we see in Piercy.

THE HIGH COST OF LIVING: LESBIANISM

Piercy's next novel, *The High Cost of Living* (1978) explores a number of themes: the "price of moving from the working class to the college-educated working class. . . . the limitations of cultural feminism and separatism," why Piercy does not believe that feminism works without an economic and class analysis.[20] It also provides a thoughtful analysis of some of the problems faced by lesbians both in their sexual relationships and in relations with the larger society. Of Piercy's later novels, it has received the least attention, which is hard to understand because it is as good a read as any of her works and contains interesting ideas.

Through her protagonist, Leslie, a lesbian graduate student in history, Piercy sympathetically shows the conflicts of a lesbian lifestyle in society's mainstream and also how a separatist lifestyle, urged by some radical lesbians, is not always an attractive option. Leslie feels that she has to compromise her values in order to work in the male-oriented hierarchies of the university, but she enjoys her work and is ambitious. Although she feels guilty for compromising, she finds the separatist rural life (some lesbian friends are living on a dilapidated farm) lacks contact with the "real world" and with the amenities of pleasant living. Leslie admires her friends for living their principles, but does not feel such a life is for her; she hopes she is accomplishing more by working within the system. She maintains her contact with the feminist community and assuages her guilt by working for a rape hotline and taking karate lessons. Telling herself she is comfortable with her gayness, she still conceals it from most people, which causes her to feel emotionally constricted, lonely, and anxious most of the time, a problem that numerous gay people have written of.

Through Leslie's relationship with the lesbian community, Piercy illustrates the complexities of lesbian relationships, factions within the community, and problems in a gay lifestyle. Recently Leslie has been left by her lover, Val, who has become involved with a boutique owner, definitely a member of the establishment. In effect, Val has become a wife, living off her lover and taking "enrichment" classes at the local university. Val's situation shows that sexual relationships with women are not the answer to women's oppression if they simply substitute a woman for a man care-taker. Without a total social revolution, such changes are only cosmetic. This is the "class analysis" that Piercy says is necessary to understand women's predicament. Piercy is vague about the changes needed in the economic system to ensure more equality, but she clearly shows that simply allowing some women to become capitalists does not get at the deeper ills.

The High Cost of Living could be faulted for some of the same problems as Piercy's other novels. All the heterosexual males are women-abusers. Particularly obnoxious is George, Leslie's boss, who sexually exploits his women students but becomes enraged when his wife has an affair. The only decent male is Bernie, a sensitive, working-class gay man, who forms one corner of a love triangle involving himself, Leslie, and Honor, the beautiful seventeen-year-old sister of a colleague of Leslie's. Leslie is attracted to Honor, as is Bernie, which is difficult to understand in Leslie's case since Honor is so naive, in many ways a typical seventeen-year-old. Piercy did not make me accept this attraction.[21] Another problem is the glorification of the working class: bourgeois people, like Val's lover and George, are shallow and distorted by the system's values. Working-class Honor, Leslie, and Bernie are uncomfortable with their backgrounds but are the most sensitive and real people in the story.

Lesbianism in Mainstream Novels by Women

As we have seen, several of Piercy's novels feature lesbian relationships, and they illustrate how feminist writers of mainstream popular novels tend to treat this issue. First of all, lesbian issues have been prominent in theory and politics since the beginning of the Women's Movement, and writers of a feminist bent have reflected this in their work. Lesbianism is a part of female experience that has been marginalized—indeed, interdicted—for most of history, and the Women's Movement opened up a new freedom to treat it. As Paulina Palmer shows, an entire subgenre of lesbian feminist literature has arisen to deal with issues such as the problems of living within a hostile mainstream, difficulties in sexual relationships, such as problems of dominance (one person becoming the "husband"); problems of lesbian mothers; whether bisexuality is compatible with radical feminist values; and factionalism within the lesbian community. A related development is the study of lesbian literature by feminist critics and lesbian feminist criticism, an attempt to look at all literature, not just literature about lesbians, from a lesbian worldview.[22]

In the mostly mainstream literature I am discussing, I suspect by mostly heterosexual or bisexual writers, although many of these issues are alluded to, lesbianism is seldom a central theme but only one of many issues. When it is treated, even sympathetically, it is seen as an aberration from the norm. In this sense most of these writers could be accused by lesbian critics of being "heterosexist." For example, in *The Color Purple*, Celie's sexual love for Shug is another possibility of love for women: it is not *the* alternative.[23] Even with Piercy, who extensively treats lesbian lifestyles in her work, more than half her protagonists are heterosexual or bisexual. *The High Cost of Living* is the only Piercy novel that deals with a lone lesbian protagonist. Nonetheless, of all the writers I treat in this study, Piercy has gone the farthest, I believe, in sympathetically rendering heterosexual and lesbian viewpoints. Other writers introduce the topic by including a lesbian as a friend of the protagonist, as Mary Gordon does in *Final Payments*, and others, like Lisa Alther in *Kinflicks*, have their protagonist go through a lesbian "phase."

Although most of the novels I discuss could be accused of heterosexism by lesbian critics, in treating lesbianism at all and doing so mostly sympathetically, they *have* assuredly done much to popularize greater tolerance for diverse sexual lifestyles. Certain generalizations can be made about the way these writers treat lesbianism, ideas that can also be found in feminist theory. First, lesbianism *can* be a preferable alternative to brutal sexual relationships with men. Even though women are socialized toward heterosexual behavior, many have the capacity for sexual pleasure with other women. Further, sexual love between women is seen as the end of a chain of bonds between women, an idea that theorists call the "lesbian continuum."[24] Close, "nonsexual" friendship between women is a place that women can be along this continuum which leads gradually to sexual expression in some people. However, unlike some radical lesbians, none of these writers advocates separatism or implies lesbianism is the only way for a feminist to express herself sexually, that is, that lesbianism is the *political* solution to women's problems.[25]

This is not the place to discuss the various theories and positions concerning lesbianism within the Women's Movement, except to say that no issue has been fraught with greater difficulty. Heterosexual women have been made to feel traitors by radical lesbians, that they are "sleeping with the enemy." Lesbians have been told they are a liability to the movement and their problems should be deemphasized. Radical lesbian separatism evolved partly as the result of such rejection, a situation that is obviously damaging to sisterhood and opportunities to work together on issues that affect us all. On the other hand, I know that for some people wavering on the edge of feminist identification, the "radical lesbian" label is deeply threatening. I am not posing any solutions here, only pointing out the seriousness of this division within the movement; it seems to be something we all see but are powerless to remedy.

Though no doubt the writers I deal with in this study can be accused of slighting lesbian themes, I got the opposite reaction from a group of women students in a recent course on the contemporary novel by women. Several of the novels I discuss in this study were on the syllabus, and the students wondered if the authors weren't exaggerating the prevalence of lesbianism. "Why do many of these writers include lesbian characters?" they asked, and suggested that writers were responding to what was now permissible and trendy, rather than reflecting women's actual experience. These attitudes show that one reader may see radical lesbian ideas in a novel, whereas another may see it as reactionary and "heterosexist." Such reactions also show that though mainstream women writers have dealt with the subject of lesbianism more often and more candidly than prior to the 1970s, public attitudes have a way to go to catch up with even the views of popular mainstream writers.

FEMINISM AND THE NEW LEFT: *VIDA*

Piercy's last foray into the 1960s and 1970s counterculture is *Vida* (1979), the story of a political fugitive living in the movement underground of the mid–1970s. Piercy hopes to expose her readers to different sorts of people, those they might never meet in real life, and *Vida* is part of that effort (*PCB* 169). Piercy also wanted to focus on a woman activist, a type prominent in American history but largely missing from fiction.[26] In its focus on the youth movement of the late 1960s, the novel resembles *Dance the Eagle to Sleep* but is more realistic and more feminist, focusing on a lone female protagonist.

Vida explores a number of themes relating to the radical politics of its period; the plot vividly contrasts the movement of the late 1960s, when there was an exciting sense of change in the entire culture, and the grim mid-to-late 1970s. As many critics pointed out, in the sections of the novel dealing with the New Left, Piercy vividly communicates the sense of excitement of that era.[27] With the knowledge of one who has been there, she describes demonstrations and street fairs, communes and women's groups, and brings the times, now sometimes hard to conjure up, to life. For example, Piercy differentiates between the joy of Flower Power in 1967 and the anger after the invasion of Cambodia in 1970:

Some kids were playing with long paper streamers, weaving patterns in and out.... a subversive musical comedy poured out of the streets, bumping in huge good-natured crowds, peaceful as soap bubbles.... Never would the authorities be able to cram the genie back in the bottle: this was a permanent change of the American psyche.[28]

In 1970, after three more years of demonstrations and organizing, the war still raged on, and now Piercy shows us the discouragement and exhaustion:

She was always late now—running, running but never arriving.... From the time she crawled out [of bed] till she collapsed in her clothes.... They had not done enough... because the proof was before her every morning and every evening the war went on. It was raining blood outside... the blood was splattering down, and the hot wind that blew across the city smelled of ashes.... (217-218).

Vida makes a number of perceptive observations about 1960s radicalism. As the activists become more and more violent, they find themselves isolated from the working class. When Vida meets an "ordinary" person, a battered woman named Tara whom she helps drive to a shelter, she finds she does not like her: "...sympathizing with the oppressed from a distance was often easier than dealing with somebody distorted, damaged by oppression" (180). After the Vietnam War is over, the group looks for new issues, coming up with nuclear power, but discards it as being "too bourgeois." All the while the lure of middle-class life and the "Meism" of the 1970s exerts a steady pull. Vida finds she hates the poor food and uncomfortable conditions of life on the run, and wonders if her friends who have chosen to work within the system as radical lawyers and health care workers are accomplishing more. Like Lisa Alther in *Kinflicks*, Piercy shows the failure of the back-to-the-land phase of the movement, where middle-class kids know nothing about farming and the men grab the interesting outside jobs while the women do the housework.

Even more than in her other novels, in *Vida* Piercy skillfully connects feminist ideals and the goals of the New Left. As in *Dance the Eagle to Sleep* and *Small Changes*, the "personal is political," and many of the movement men are incredibly oppressive toward women. Though they battle U.S. imperialism, they make women their colonies. Kevin, for example, an extremely macho occasional lover of Vida, successfully orders one of Vida's friends to have sex with another male in the group to prove her solidarity with the collective. For a time Vida tells herself the "sense of compulsion" of the relationship makes it real (236-237), but later she calls her time with Kevin her period of female masochism. Piercy says that part of the process of liberation for women involves breaking away from these powerfully arousing, yet demeaning, relationships. In a 1991 study Elaine Hoffman Baruch states that one limitation of feminist thought may be its minimizing of the irrational elements in sexual relationships—the fact that, despite its power to erode individuality, sexual surrender to a powerful male involves a voluptuousness that is attractive.[29] In characters like Kevin and Jackson in *Small Changes*, Piercy honestly acknowledges these unconscious drives but urges women to resist them.

Like feminist theorists, Piercy shows that the so-called sexual revolution works to the advantage of men. In the "liberated" sexual environment of *Vida*, women must get illegal abortions, sleep with men they are not attracted to in order to please them, and put up with their mates having affairs while they mind the children. According to Piercy, each woman must work out for herself the place of the "women's question" within the larger movement.

Vida's sister Natalie, herself in a patriarchal marriage that eventually ends, becomes a leader in the women's group that splinters off in the 1970s. Vida, however, finds it difficult to relate to the problems of married women with children, and other women's issues do not seem real to her.

When Natalie shows her a pamphlet on rape, Vida is embarrassed because the issue seems trivial placed alongside the war and the suffering of the Third World people: "It really was about rape.... What a weird subject! Next they'd be doing pamphlets on mugging or toothache." When Natalie talks to her about her own rape by a black man, Vida cautions her not to say the man was black: "He was probably incredibly oppressed" (227, 229). Explaining to Vida Susan Brownmiller's theory that rape is a form of male political terror, Natalie argues that women's issues are of *their* own time, that revolutions between the men and women of today are more meaningful than what happened in China and Cuba years ago. Obviously, liberation of other oppressed groups cannot come if the first, and oldest, oppression of one group by another is not dealt with.

Although Vida does become more knowledgeable about women's issues (being nearly raped by Kevin contributes to this growth), they never have the immediacy of traditional radical issues to her. She remains a man-centered women, which is clearly harmful to her. Though she is able to live for long periods without male companionship, Vida is overly dependent for her self-esteem on her relationship with her husband, Leigh, who has stayed above ground. Leigh treats Vida shabbily, finally divorcing her and marrying another women. Vida's jealousy, which she knows is self-defeating, shows the power of women's traditional attitudes. By the end of the novel Vida is in love with a young draft evader named Joel. Although he does not abuse her, Joel is obsessed by Vida's past relationships and, in fact, is captured because he leaves his cover to confront Leigh. This destructive jealousy, says Piercy, results from male egos, from desire for possession, and from not recognizing the woman's personhood.

Though Piercy gives her main attention to Vida's relationships with men, she devotes a good deal of space to her bonds with women: Natalie, her feminist sister; Ruby, her working-class Jewish mother who still worries about her; and several of her women friends in the movement. Vida loves several women, gaining strength and knowledge from them over the years; she has a few sexual relationships with women friends, partly because doing so seems "politically correct" and partly because she loves them, but in truth men are first in her life. When Vida brags to Natalie that she has a "serious relationship" with a woman lover, Natalie replies: "I have more serious relationships with the women in my consciousness-raising group than you do with any woman.... An orgasm or two doesn't mean you put each other first" (205). As in *The High Cost of Living*, Piercy seems to be suggesting that sex between women per se does not make for sisterhood. Vida's basic problem is that she never seems to understand the importance of these female relationships to her; culturally determined attitudes tell her that men are more important for her self-esteem. At one point Vida reflects that she enjoys being with Natalie more than with men, but she dismisses this gut realization.

Though many critics focused on Piercy's successful handling of the historical material in *Vida*, Jennifer Uglow felt its "strength lies . . . in the power with which the loneliness and desolation of the central characters are portrayed."[30] I tend to agree. Vida is a more complex protagonist than some of Piercy's—not a heroic radical but a confused woman who makes many mistakes and gropes for dignity and understanding of her situation and her world. However, the novel's weakness relates to its success with the historical analysis. *Vida* does render the smug righteousness of the movement people accurately. As Elinor Langer says, these people have not at all altered their thinking, which has led them to such disastrous ends. Because Piercy has made a conscious decision here to sacrifice detachment for commitment, the novel has a "hermetic" quality very like the people in it (36). In *Vida*, Piercy offers more insights into her protagonist's personal mistakes than into her political ones.

SMALL CHANGES REVISITED: BRAIDED LIVES

As we have seen, by the 1980s many feminist writers were moving away from sexual politics toward other themes; however, in *Braided Lives* (1982), Piercy concentrates once again on the oppression of women by men, dealing with many of the themes she treated in *Small Changes*. Some of the feminist issues treated are the "social construction of femininity," male dominance in courtship and marriage, rape, abortion, and educational discrimination against women. *Braided Lives* follows Jill, a young working-class woman, through her adolescence in Detroit and her college years at the University of Michigan in the late 1950s, into her attempts to gain entry into the writing world in New York City. The strands in the "braids" are the lives of Jill and her friends as they weave in and out of each other. Strongly autobiographical, it is narrated by an older Jill who is married to Josh and lives on a freshwater marsh near Cape Cod. Through the story of Jill we get a sense of the alienation Piercy felt growing up in Detroit and attending the University of Michigan during the 1950s.

A *bildungsroman* that seems more a feminist novel of the 1970s than of the 1980s, *Braided Lives* focuses on two characters. Besides Jill, a political activist who refuses to make compromises with her society's traditional expectations of her as a writer and woman, the novel also focuses on Donna, Jill's close friend and cousin, a weaker woman whose compromises lead not only to the death of her spirit but also to her physical death from a botched abortion. In obvious ways, these protagonists compare with Beth and Miriam. Piercy often uses characters for purposes of comparison, Jackson and Phil in *Small Changes* being another example.

Jill, Donna, and their friends endure a staggering amount of cruelty in this novel: indifferent fathers; possessive, stifling mothers; cruel, domineering boyfriends; and intellectual putdowns by male professors and colleagues. The amount of physical suffering is also staggering: three abortions, a rape, a seduction of Donna by her brother-in-law, betrayal by a married man, addiction to prescription tranquilizers, and wife abuse. Theo is raped by her psychiatrist and expelled from college for being a lesbian. It is as if Piercy wants to include *every* possible horror of being a woman, even aspects she may have left out of earlier novels. This technique, which Paulina Palmer calls "accumulation," emphasizes the cultural pattern of male abuse of females, showing us that these problems are not only those of individuals (49). As such, it certainly makes its feminist point, but it also weakens the novel, giving it, as one reviewer said, a "lurid predictability."[31] Piercy may well answer such criticisms by asserting that all these things happened to women she knew: nevertheless, we still do not believe. It may be argued that "fiction of ideas" does not need to be credible, but when a writer adopts a realistic style, as Piercy does, the reader expects that events will conform to her perception of what life is actually like.[32]

Characterization in *Braided Lives* is also not as strong as in *Small Changes* or *Vida*, which contain their share of macho woman-oppressors but also a number of sensitive, multidimensional men. Almost none of the men in *Braided Lives* have anything redeemable about them. Peter, Donna's husband, is especially diabolical; he pokes a hole in her diaphragm, precipitating a pregnancy and subsequent abortion that kills her. This brings to mind Jim flushing Beth's pills away, and Neil making love to Miriam when he knows she is not wearing her diaphragm. Piercy turns around a standard myth: since patriarchy uses motherhood to control women, it is not women who trap men by getting pregnant; rather, men trap women by getting them pregnant!

Jill's boyfriend, Howie, bright and working class, is especially disappointing because at first he seems unusually sensitive, having had to suffer while growing up, unlike the rich kids from Grosse Pointe. However, he eventually becomes bourgeois on his way to medical school, and tells Jill she will have to give up her illegal abortion service if she wants to marry him. The only male to escape most of Piercy's wrath is Kemp, an Ann Arbor "townie" and small-time hoodlum whom Jill dates briefly. His street smarts and joy in common pleasures are preferable to the dry intellectualizing of experience that most of the college men indulge in. With Howie and Kemp, as in previous novels, Piercy shows us what we have to give up to become bourgeois. In sum, though *Braided Lives* is a powerful novel, though it makes us examine our own experience and catch Piercy's fervor, its excesses weaken it considerably. Piercy has not channeled her righteous anger enough to eliminate some of the redundancy, has not given quite the attention to detail of her characters as in *Small Changes*. In fact, she has written a novel too much like *Small Changes*, but without its craft and complexity.

In Chapter 2, I defended some of the 1970s *bildungsromans* against the charge of being too autobiographical, saying that this sort of plot invites confessional material. However, in the case of *Braided Lives*, even though Piercy uses the third person for most of the novel, the resemblances between her life and Jill's are so strong that I became uncomfortable as a reader. Since Jill is so obviously in some sense Marge, and since she is the only strong, fighting, truly admirable character in the book, I begin to detect, perhaps incorrectly, an air of self-righteousness. Is Piercy telling her reader that *she* wasn't a conformist like so many others in the 1950s? This reaction may lie in guilty defensiveness on my part, but it is one experienced by quite a few Piercy readers. I felt harangued when reading *Braided Lives*. At the beginning of the novel, Jill (speaking in the first person), now a successful writer, complains about the many literary workshops she attends where people want to know about the connection between her and the books:

Ah, come off it," I wanted to say. "It's just this person, me. All those years when I made a living at part time secretarial work, people like you wouldn't even say hello to me. What's the fuss?" They think I am the books solidified, but the books are the books.[33]

With such obviously autobiographical material, it is difficult to see the books as separate from the writer.

Despite these faults I have found with *Braided Lives*, it is also deeply engaging fiction. Piercy does speak the truth about women's lives. If she does not, as John Leonard says of *Vida*, tell us "exactly how it was,"[34] she does tell us how *some* of it was. As Jill and her friends struggle with the double standard and the expectations of parents and professors that they follow traditional roles, and as they experience the moral aridity of their literary education, I am cast back to 1961, also at the University of Michigan. If I surely did not experience the suffering and ruined dreams of Piercy's women, I remember some of it—the pregnant girl down the hall who dropped out to disappear into suburbia; the surreptitious visits many of us paid to an elderly Hungarian woman doctor, who in an office above Wool-worth's dispensed birth control pills; my literary education in which women writers were not read or even mentioned. As Jill herself says, she wants to give herself a "long view back," and Piercy certainly gives me that, too.

RECENT WORK: A VARIETY OF THEMES

As I have stated, *Braided Lives* seems to be a novel written in the early 1970s rather than the 1980s. With it, Piercy gave her last blast of feminist rage, and for the rest of the 1980s turned to plots that while certainly revealing her feminist convictions and identification with the Left, seem more conventional. In fact, one could call *Fly Away Home* (1984) a typical "woman's novel" in that it deals primarily with a woman's discovery of self and new love after her marriage falls apart. However, as Ellen Sweet pointed out, Piercy takes this hackneyed plot and with her feminist sensibility makes it fresh.[35]

Fly Away Home sounds a note of caution to the middle-class woman who seemingly "has it all"—a lovely family, career, and home—but in fact is totally dependent on her marriage for her self-esteem. The protagonist, Daria, is a successful, "liberated" woman who writes best-selling cookbooks, appears on talk shows, and travels widely to promote her books. In many ways, however, she is a traditional woman who truly enjoys homemaking, and her career is based on her female talent for preparing food. We soon discover that it is all a sham. In fact, Daria's husband, Ross, is having an affair with a younger woman and is a criminal, joining with other greedy men to buy up old apartments to gentrify them and sometimes to burn them for the insurance. Cold and rational, Ross seems to represent extreme patriarchal values, as does Miriam's Neil Stone.

The plot, as detailed as most of Piercy's novels, concerns Daria's attempts to re-create herself, her values, and her sense of family. She does this by befriending the people who live in the buildings that Ross is burning, and becoming the lover of Tom, an attractive neighborhood organizer. Although by the end of the story Daria's lovely suburban home has been burned, she is living with working-class people. Best yet, she has found herself by herself, and knows she will never again live so totally part of a couple that if the relationships dissolves, she will become half a person: she is now part of a larger family that gives her a sense of belonging:

He [Tom] didn't save me...not even from a burning house. I saved myself. No gratitude other than the daily appreciation of each other's small and middling contributions to the common good and the common pleasure binds us....I have my daughters...I have my work, I have my chosen new community, she realized she was doing it again, counting her blessings, proving to herself that she was happy. But I am...and maybe a better woman finally than I used to be, when I was Ross's before I was my own.[36]

Some of Piercy's other novels have been accused of being too facile in plot development (too many fortuitous coincidences), and although sometimes such criticism seems alleviated by other, strong points, *Fly Away Home* does have some serious fictional weaknesses. The appearance of Tom so soon after Ross leaves is too good to be true. Further, unlike most of the "bad guys" in her other novels, who are complex, believable bastards, Ross is so evil, so diabolical in his cruelty and indifference to others' suffering, that he is not believable. To have him twirl a mustache would not be out of character.[37] At one point Daria wonders how she could ever have loved him, and the reader wonders this through the whole novel. Finally, those in the novel who are working-class are generally more moral than those who are middle-class: more kind, more feeling, more courageous, less materialistic.

The effect is too pat, so much so that a plot summary reads like a parody of a best-selling feminist novel: "so-called liberated woman left by villainous husband makes a new life for herself, in the process discovering community and love with a left-wing, activist hunk." *Fly Away Home* could be accused of being written with an eye on the best-seller lists, a charge made by more than one critic about such novelists as Marilyn French and Erica Jong; as I explained in Chapter 2, these critics assert that their work is really traditional women's fiction in feminist disguise, being mainly about men and children, the perennial topics of women's novels.[38] Such a charge often seems unjust because these topics *are* important in many women's lives; feminist writers, as I have shown, are trying to put that experience in a new light. However, in the case of *Fly Away Home*, the reality is that the majority of middle-aged women left by their husbands are *not* successful cookbook writers and find it considerably more difficult to make new lives. Still, the novel does tell important truths to women who may be too dependent on others for their self-esteem.

Fly Away Home has some elements of a mystery story, and in *Gone to Soldiers* (1987) Piercy successfully adapts feminist ideas to two other popular genres usually associated with male writers, the war novel and the historical epic. Set during World War II, the book has the length and breadth of an epic, being over seven hundred pages long and moving from the home front in Detroit, New York, and Washington to London to wartime France and the concentration camps behind German lines. It also has the large cast of an epic: ten protagonists in all, six women and four men, as well as many important minor characters. Piercy manages to incorporate her feminist themes by concentrating on the home front and the interior lives of characters rather than on the blood of the battlefield. Thus the story seems more intimate than most historical/war novels, which often sacrifice character development for action and breadth. One could call this novel a *Winds of War* with a feminist touch, but that would not do justice to Piercy's effort.

Piercy's technique is to alternate among her ten protagonists, spinning the reader from one disparate setting to another. The most interesting character to me is Ruthie Siegal, a young, working-class Jewish woman employed in the wartime industry of Detroit and attending college part-time to become a social worker. In the story of Ruthie, Piercy shows us the hectic, conflicted life of a woman who is doing something few women of her time and class had to the courage to do. The long-distance romance between Ruthie and her Marine boyfriend, Murray, illustrates another of Piercy's themes—that although we were fighting the racism of the Nazis, our own society was imbued with oppression. As a Jewish Marine, Murray must endure cruel anti-Semitic prejudice.

In general, Piercy shows a great deal more sympathy to her male characters than she does in previous novels, although a few women-exploiters do make their appearance. Ruthie's womanizing brother, Duvey, works on merchant marine ships and dodges German U-boats. His story seems to mesh poorly with the others, perhaps being included for the opportunity to add some traditional combat scenes to the novel. At first we think Duvey, though enjoying women, is not a woman-abuser:

Duvey had figured out while he was still in high school that the only women worth his time wanted it as much as he did, and so it was a matter of settling that you liked each other enough and when and where, and not a matter of begging and arm-twisting and promising what he hadn't the wherewithal to deliver.[39]

However, while home on leave he makes sexual advances to the young Naomi (see below), thereby disappointing us somewhat. Another sexist male is Leib, Ruthie's former boyfriend, who cruelly seduces Naomi. Leib, who seems to have wandered in from *Braided Lives*, is the kind of character feminist readers love to hate.

A second set of characters are Bernice Coates and her brother, Jeff. Bernice is a type whose story has seldom been told in literature—the woman who participated in a direct way in the war, as a pilot for the Women's Air Force. The story of Bernice, who discovers her lesbianism in the course of the war, documents the obstacles and prejudices faced by such women: "In the Soviet Union women were flying in combat.... In England, women were ferrying planes regularly. Here they wouldn't even let women fly domestically.... She longed to use her skill, her strength" (99). Although eventually allowed to ferry planes, these women were never allowed to do as much as they wanted and were capable of; nevertheless they contributed greatly to the war effort, and for their pains were subjected to scorn by their fellow citizens and comrades in arms. Though Mary Biggs felt Piercy stereotyped Bernice as a typical mannish lesbian, she did feel Bernice's story was one that needed to be told.[40]

Jeff Coates, Bernice's artistic brother, becomes involved in intelligence work in southern France and the Resistance movement. Here he meets his lover, Jacqueline, a Jewish Resistance fighter, the favorite character of many reviewers. Jacqueline had begun the war years as an arrogant Parisian teenager who denied her Jewish heritage. The adventures of Jeff and Jacqueline provide exciting action and romance. Their lives intersect with that of Jacqueline's younger sister, Naomi (cousin of Ruthie), who is one of a set of twins; she escapes the Nazis and finds her way to Detroit, where she grows to womanhood as an American teenager. Her *bildungsroman* is haunted by the specter of her twin, Rivka, in Auschwitz, and by her sexual exploitation at the hands of Duvey and Leib. In the parallel tale of Rivka, Piercy departs occasionally from her usual realism by having Naomi dream through Rivka's eyes, thus showing us the harrowing events at Auschwitz. This inclusion of the Holocaust and her creation of Jewish characters show Piercy's increased interest in her own Jewish background, an interest found in her more recent novels.

Piercy uses the life of Louise Kahan, a romance writer who gets a chance to become a serious journalist because of the war, to comment on the nature of propaganda directed toward women. As a writer of women's fiction, Louise is encouraged by government guidelines to break with tradition and depict the working women as eager and competent war workers. Through Louise, Piercy tells us how the "powers that be" perpetuate whatever stereotype is needed to make women effective participants in the capitalist society. When women are needed outside the home, then they are encouraged to move into the wider sphere. True to her radical traditions, Piercy reminds us from time to time that although the Nazis were surely the "shit of the earth" (238), the authorities on our side were power-seeking and sometimes supported the pro-fascist government in Vichy France when it suited them.

Piercy uses the intersected lives of Louise; her lover, Daniel; her husband, Oscar; and his lover, Abra Scott, to show how wartime situations enable women to break away from men and achieve self-esteem. Louise is recently divorced from the philandering Oscar, who loves aristocratic Abra—young, "spirited," and uninterested in marriage. Abra follows Oscar to London, where we have a close-up view of the German blitz. For a time, Louise seeks consolation in the arms of Daniel, a young cryptographer who works for the War Department, and is also a distant relative of the Siegal family. However, eventually both these May-December unions end, with Louise and Oscar reconciling and Abra and Daniel finding each other, both predictable resolutions. Louise and Abra gain strength from their independence from men, and we know their future relationships will be ones of equality.

This plot summary sounds like popular melodrama, and on one level it is. Adventure, action, sex, suffering, and the testing of human beings are combined in a variety of ways. *Gone to Soldiers*' difference from other war epics lies in its emphasis on the folks at home, especially women and working-class people, and the interior lives of the characters as they struggle for sanity and personal integrity. Though Piercy focuses on women and some macho chauvinists make their appearance, even the sexist males change in the course of the novel. This is one of the few Piercy novels where men's stories are their own, not those of the women they are connected with. As such, it represents real growth in Piercy's handling of character.

Gone to Soldiers does have its weaknesses, most of them common to the genre. With this large cast of characters, not all can be rendered equally well, and I found myself pushing through the sections dealing with my less favorites, so that I could get to the characters I really liked. Also, the scope of the novel makes it difficult for Piercy to tie all the stories into a coherent whole. There is too little connection between the story of Louise, Daniel, Abra, and Oscar and that of the Siegal family; this can be aesthetically unsatisfying to the reader. Another problem is that because of Piercy's scrupulous inclusion of all types of characters (no group except blacks is left out), one becomes aware of her plotting plan. The outline shows through, so to speak.[41]

Nevertheless, though perhaps failing to achieve an "epic stature," *Gone to Soldiers* is an impressive achievement, one of the few attempts so far at adapting a feminist sensibility to historical materials.[42] For the most part, Piercy resists the temptation to give her characters thoughts that people in the 1940s would not have. Thus, the novel retains a historicity that such an approach would have destroyed. At the same time, Piercy shows us the difficulties of women during these years and how sexist attitudes affect the relationships of the characters. She also deserves praise for her treatment of the adolescent girls in the story, showing their insecurities and the growth through which each must struggle in a difficult environment. It will be interesting to see if Piercy tries this sort of novel again with a different historical period, perhaps one even farther removed in time from the contemporary world.

Gone to Soldiers was followed by *Summer People* (1989), set on Piercy's own Cape Cod, and some reviewers saw it as a definite retreat from her prior radicalism and feminism.[43] Probably Piercy's weakest novel, *Summer People* concerns an "alternative lifestyle" triangle involving three unconventional 1960s types: Dinah, a composer; Susan, a fabric designer; and Susan's husband, Willy, a sculptor whose politicized works are no longer in vogue. Piercy focuses on the breakup of this strange relationship, which apparently has existed in health for ten years. Susan has become bored with the quiet life on Cape Cod and longs to work in New York for Tyrone, a powerful and cold business tycoon who owns a nearby summer home.

In *Summer People* Piercy's politics are still obvious, though here she seems less interested in strictly feminist issues; the theme of the novel is the contrast between the "frozen-souled glamour" of the urban life represented by Tyrone, who finally rejects Susan, and the quiet, simple, genuine, close-to-nature life of the year-round residents of the Cape Cod community. In an interview Piercy stated that she wanted to show how people [like Susan] who choose false images dictated by the society "suffer heavy penalties."[44] However, reviewers felt the novel lifeless and boring, without the feminist fervor of her earlier works. As *The New York Times* scathingly put it:

[Piercy's] the sort of feminist sage whose fiction and poetry flourished in the 1960's and 1970's, when her *epater le bourgeois* posture, and the ramshackle social architectures she proposed fit the *zeitgeist* more snugly....[her] timeworn polemic can't enter the 1990's blowing the same old steam, so she's not waving banners and fomenting revolt here; she's not even pitting male values against female.[45]

Though Tyrone's cold, masculine attitudes do pit "male" values against female, other men in the novel at least to some degree represent the humane values of a feminist outlook.

In the final analysis, what makes *Summer People* weak is not a missing "timeworn polemic" but uninteresting characters whose internal monologues bore the reader. As Patricia Craig said, "We learn much more than we want to know about these self-absorbed people," all of whom are desperate to "achieve some banal doctrine of self-fulfillment."[46] The language is often clichéd; the story lacks the passion of earlier Piercy and the interesting characters and scope of *Gone to Soldiers*. Does the failure of this "least feminist" of Piercy's novels suggest that the feminist fiction she represents is a phenomenon of the 1970s and 1980s, no longer relevant to a new generation of readers? This is a question to be considered in the conclusion of this study.

The above question was written before the publication of Piercy's latest novel *He, She and It* (1991), for with this science fiction novel she returns to her radical feminist critique of American society. Perhaps she was affected by the tepidness of *Summer People*'s reception, but in any case, *He, She and It* definitely shows us much of the old Piercy, although admittedly somewhat muted, not quite as fierce and dogged. In my estimation, this makes the novel not as powerful as *Woman on the Edge of Time*, which it resembles in many ways.

He, She and It is set in the middle of the twenty-first century. As in the dystopian part of *Woman on the Edge of Time*, the world is divided into a number of huge corporate multis, where people exist to serve the state, social classes are rigidly stratified, and matters of sexual identity such as appearance are dictated. The ravaged earth shows what our present environmental abuse has led to. Humans must live in shelters such as domes because of the destruction of the ozone layer, and global warming has radically altered plant and animal life. Most people eat "vat food" grown from algae, and owning a pet is a rare privilege. Not all people are allowed to be in the multis; in fact, the majority live in the "Glop" (from megalopolis), steamy slums terrorized by gangs, where people make do by theft and hustling. The "Glop" is obviously just a tiny step from our present urban nightmare but, true to Piercy's radical roots, it also contains hope for the future. A few of the gangs are beginning to plan to change life for themselves in concert with the "free cities," enclaves of democratic freedom where people live in harmony with nature as much as possible (the cities must be covered with "wraps" during the day). The free cities resemble to a large degree Mattapoisett in *Woman*. Technology in the free cities serves people, not dominates them; for example, household work is done by cleaning robots, and women cook or clean only for pleasure. The implication is that our present world *could* be saved by political unity between the lower classes and those few educated people who have not allowed themselves to be formed by corporate society.

As in *Woman*, Piercy's radical politics are reflected in this future world, but there are major differences between the two novels, results of the nearly twenty-year gap. There is more stress in *He, She and It* on the effects of environmental abuse and our neglect of the cities. Piercy seems to have rejected technology that would radically change the reproductive process, certainly a move toward cultural feminist thinking. In *He, She and It*, the power to give birth is treasured. It stresses the negative and positive effects of technology more. People can "plug" into a worldwide Network of information and travel mentally (and apparently physically) from their locations, which vastly enhances their experience and knowledge. This, of course, is only a small step from present-day technology's creation of simulated environments with computer graphics. However, information pirates and multis can enter the "Net" and steal information or destroy people's brains. People can also have their bodies surgically "enhanced," to make themselves stronger (one of the important minor characters is an "amazon" named Nili) or more sexually attractive. In fact, in the multis both men and women are encouraged to have operations to achieve a certain "look."

He, She and It concerns Shira, a Jewish worker for Yakamura-Stichen (the Axis powers of World War II have come together), one of the most powerful multis; her former lover, Gadi, a creator of "stimmies," media experiences that allow the audience to feel the actor's feelings (very like the "feelies" in Huxley's *Brave New World*); and Yod, a sensitive, handsome cyborg (a combination of hardware and biological elements) who has been created by Avram, Gadi's scientist father. Shira has recently left the male-dominated multi after having her son taken from her in a divorce; she returns to her roots in the free Jewish city of Tikva, decides that her love for Gadi is finally over, falls in love with Yod, and retrieves her child. The emphasis on Jews and Judaism reflects Piercy's own interest in her Jewish roots.

Through this plot Piercy explores a number of themes common to science fiction, but with a feminist twist. To the question "What is a human being?" she asks if through careful programming a machine (Yod) could be created that would be more sensitive, multidimensional, and loving than a "real" man, who is programmed to have sexist thoughts and reactions to women, and finds it difficult to experience happiness and pain. The answer is obviously yes, which may confirm antifeminists' beliefs that feminists are man-haters. Piercy also pursues this question in her alternate story, told to Yod by Shira's grandmother, Malkah, of the sixteenth-century Prague ghetto where a rabbi Judah Loew creates a golem to save the Jews from pogroms. The golem, Joseph, turns out to be a rather slow but kindly man. The fate of both these human-created "persons" shows Piercy's conviction that intelligent beings should not be controlled. As Malkah says, "Yod was a mistake.... It's better to make people into partial machines than to create machines that feel and yet are still controlled like cleaning robots. The creation of a conscious being as any kind of tool—supposed to exist only to fill our needs—is a disaster."[47]

Piercy also deals with a number of more traditional questions common to recent feminist fiction: through Shira's relationships with Ari, her son, and her mother, Riva, and her grandmother, Malkah, who raised her, Piercy examines issues related to motherhood and daughterhood. Shira has a passionate bond with Ari, and feels closer to Malkah than to her own mother, an adventuress who roams the earth as an information pirate. Apparently mothers are important, though biology is less important than physical proximity. Through the creative, brilliant Malkah, who programs Yod's emotions and "tries him out" sexually, Piercy explores questions relating to older women in our society.

Science fiction is not my favorite genre, and I found some of this amusing (when humor apparently was not intended), and perhaps too obvious. The social/political criticism and the technological innovations seemed rather similar to other science fiction I have read. I found middle-class Shira to be a less interesting character than Connie Ramos, and some of her musings about her love for Yod (since he is in every way a person, their love is made acceptable to the reader) to be immature and clichéd. Nonetheless, some of the technology was fascinating, Piercy's descriptions of the "Glop" were sinister, and her male characters were well rounded and not morally inferior to the women. As in much of Piercy, though one finds fault, one is drawn on, absorbed by plot and characters. What *He, She and It* does show is that Piercy is not done with her criticisms of contemporary society, though it has been some time since she has written an effective novel set in the present. Her politics do appear to be less radical than in the 1970s in the sense that men are not portrayed as evil, and traditional female concerns are valued and given prominence.

A CRITICAL ASSESSMENT

After eleven novels written over some twenty years, how can one assess Piercy's contribution to contemporary literature? I have indicated some of her strengths and weaknesses in my discussions of the novels. Perhaps the most important question is that raised by nearly all critics of feminist writing, particularly radical feminist writing. Is this art or is it political propaganda? Do the politics weaken the literary qualities or, as Anne Mickelson asked of *Small Changes*, does "personal experience undergo the transmutation into art?" (176). A fair number of critics over the years have said no: Piercy's novels fail as art because they are excessively political.

Piercy dismisses these charges as bias. Such critics disagree with her feminist politics, so they devalue her work. She maintains that any literary work "embodies ideas of right and wrong, male and female, who's smart and who's stupid...."[48] Thus works by male writers not believed to be "political" do embody political ideas. Piercy believes it is very difficult for a feminist writer to become acclaimed by the literary establishment because the majority of critics are not feminists. Further, she argues that her works *are* art, in that her fiction is about the choices people make based on their characters and circumstances; her work does not attempt to say things that could be said as well in a political pamphlet (*PCB* 148).

However, in the same interview she also says that she is "driven," that she hopes to change people's thinking, that she speaks for those unspoken for. Though few authors would deny that they hope to affect people, Piercy hopes to change the world, and it is the sweeping nature of the changes she hopes for and her urgent desire for that change that lead to the problems critics find in her work. For example, characters are "excessively heightened," there is too much reliance on coincidence (one example is the meeting of Jacqueline and Gloria, Oscar's sister, in *Gone for Soldiers*), melodramatic scenes seem created to move the reader, and political speeches seem placed into the mouths or minds of the characters. These charges are made not just by male critics but also by those who agree with her feminist agenda. Mickelson sums it up by saying, "...the political and social perspective dominate the story rather than tell the story" (*RO* 177).

Although I have already cited examples of these problems, a few more might be helpful. Donna in *Braided Lives* has such a horrendous life that we have difficulty believing so many terrible things could happen to one person; Leib's seduction of Naomi seems gratuitously added to *Gone to Soldiers*, to remind us of the sufferings of young girls at the hands of unscrupulous men in earlier times ("See, sexual abuse has always been a problem; it's not just an invention of feminists"). Though Piercy says she rarely places her own ideas in the mouths of her characters (*PCB* 148), it is quite easy to spot speeches and mental monologues that sound like her own beliefs, for example, in *Small Changes* and even in *He, She and It*. Finally, as I have said, the absence of decent men weakens the verisimilitude of some of the works.

Nevertheless, despite such flaws, why do I obviously believe Piercy deserves attention not only for her feminism but also as a contemporary writer? First, she *is* a fine writer. Although uneven, her novels are rich in detail, the kind of detail that personalizes characters and creates memorable scenes. Along with this eye for detail Piercy reveals an ear for dialogue when she resists the desire to have her characters speak or think in whole paragraphs. She has done this less in the more recent novels. Although sometimes one can find examples of clumsy or clichéd prose, her technical skill with words has improved, and she can turn some mighty pretty and/or odd metaphors that are arresting. For example, in *Gone to Soldiers* she describes Bernice in her plane: "... she put on the little plane like a flimsy extended body, insectlike around her, beautiful as a dragonfly although jeweled only to her and burst into flight" (97). In sum, her characters and situations, for the most part, are real and involving.

Further, the charges of "polemical" do seem to have an element of bias, that is, such charges would not be made if the politics were not feminist. As Anne Mickelson says, the same criticisms (stereotyped characters, improbable coincidences, etc.) have been made in the past of writers like Dickens and Theodore Dreiser. These charges were justified, yet we still revere those men as great writers and study their works. Why? Because, like Piercy, they spoke movingly of the oppressed; they told harsh truths about the evils of their societies, truths that needed telling; and they told damn good stories (*RO* 177). No doubt their works have effected changes, and we can only hope that Piercy's have done likewise. If the novels have not always provided convincing solutions to the problems they disclose, we should remember that most protest literature in the past has not. To provide detailed plans for social change is the job of others besides the novelist.

Piercy, despite her complaints of being rejected by the literary establishment, has been a very popular author and has sold thousands of books. This brings to mind a final charge, one that has been made of popular feminist writing in general, to which I briefly alluded in speaking of *Fly Away Home* and *Gone to Soldiers*. Is this writing merely popular melodrama—the "domestic" novel, the historical novel, the romance—done up in feminist trappings? This charge carries all kinds of elitist underpinnings, assuming, for example, that novels containing strong doses of adventure and romance are "popular" and therefore inferior to "serious fiction." It also ignores how many "serious" writers deliberately adapt popular genres for their purposes.

Such a charge is difficult to refute if one just scans plot summaries of Piercy's novels. She has indeed adapted some popular forms, especially in the case of *Gone to Soldiers* and her science fiction novels. However, as I have shown, her treatment of the material reveals a depth of theme and character not found in popular romance/adventure/historical sagas such as those by James Michener and Herman Wouk. Though she is not "arty" or subtle, operating almost exclusively in a realistic mode, her novelistic skills take her writing beyond the scope of much popular fiction. As I have suggested, this realism and didacticism of Piercy puts her at a disadvantage in the contemporary literary world.[49]

At the same time we recognize that Piercy's novels go beyond the scope of much popular fiction, there are nagging doubts that she can be ranked with some other women writers who reveal feminist concerns in their themes, such as Toni Morrison, Mary Gordon, and the Canadian Margaret Atwood. Andrea Freud Loewenstein, in her review of *Gone to Soldiers*, explains this doubt best. There is a side to her, Loewenstein says, that devours Piercy novels with the same injudicious fervor with which she read *Marjorie Morningstar* as a girl: "... this [*Gone to Soldiers* is] a book that forces itself on you, making you carry it around, sneaking a read on the bus or risking it in the bath." And, then, there is an "English major" side to her that "insists that whatever Piercy's virtues in terms of readability and politics, there is a dimension she does not reach.... There is a flat completeness about even the most interesting figures here."[50]

Despite what I have said about well-drawn characters and absorbing plots, I would have to grudgingly agree. Nonetheless, says Loewenstein, we should not too easily dismiss the growing pile of Piercy novels, the work of a radical feminist who has found a wide audience for her ideas. Then, too, some feminist critics would say this tendency to "rank" writers (I once overheard a colleague telling a crestfallen student that his favorite writer, Steinbeck, is only a 6, while Dostoevsky is a 10) smacks of male hierarchical thinking. Therefore, despite our doubts, perhaps produced by years of literary training that taught us to devalue what is "accessible," and "polemical," we should grant Piercy her due. Her novels remain powerful fictional treatments of ideas, as well as absorbing stories of contemporary women and men.

NOTES

    1. Anne Mickelson, *Reaching Out: Sensitivity and Order in Recent American Fiction by Women* (Metuchen, NJ: Scarecrow, 1979), 182. Hereafter abbreviated *RO*.

    2. Deborah Silverton Rosenfelt, "Getting into the Game: American Women Writers and the Radical Tradition," *Women's Studies International Forum* 9 (1986), 363.

    3. Besides Marge Piercy, Rosenfelt includes in the left feminist tradition the work of Grace Paley, Alice Walker, and Mary Lee Settle, and "implicitly" the writing of Tillie Olsen. If one includes the latter (writing that "implicitly" seems to advocate changes in society), then one could include most of the writers I have already discussed.

    4. Marge Piercy, *Parti-Colored Blocks for a Quilt* (Ann Arbor: University of Michigan Press, 1982), 164-165. Hereafter abbreviated as *PCB*.

    5. Marge Piercy, "In the Fifties: Through the Cracks," *Partisan Review* 41 (1974), 202-216.

    6. Piercy explains her disillusionment with the New Left in "The Grand Coolee Dam," reprinted in Robin Morgan, ed., *Sisterhood Is Powerful* (New York: Random House, 1970), 421-438.

    7. Marge Piercy, "Mirror Images," in *Women's Culture: The Women's Renaissance of the Seventies*, ed. Gayle Kimball (Metuchen, NJ: Scarecrow, 1981), 192.

    8. Elizabeth Hardwick, "Militant Notes," *New York Review of Books* 15 (7 January 1971), 3.

9. Marge Piercy, *Dance the Eagle to Sleep* (Garden City, NY: Doubleday, 1970), 145-146.

10. Piercy, "Mirror Images," 192.

11. Margaret Ferrari, "Exploring the Self, Ordering the State," review of *Small Changes* by Marge Piercy, *America* 129 (1 December 1973), 507.

12. Marge Piercy, *Small Changes* (New York: Fawcett Crest, 1972), 19.

13. Carol Burr Megibow, "The Use of Story in Women's Novels of the Seventies," in *Women's Culture*, ed. Gayle Kimball, 201.

14. See, for example, Carol Farley Kessler, "*Woman on the Edge of Time*: A Novel 'To Be of Use,' " *Extrapolation* 28 (1987), 310-318; Carmen Cramer, "Anti-Automaton: Marge Piercy's Fight in *Woman on the Edge of Time*," *Critique* 27 (Summer 1986), 229-233; Frances Bartkowski, *Feminist Utopias* (Lincoln: University of Nebraska Press, 1989), 61-78.

15. Marge Piercy, *Woman on the Edge of Time* (New York: Fawcett Crest, 1976), 26.

16. Bartkowski, *Feminist Utopias*, 65.

17. Rosenfelt, "Getting into the Game," 370.

18. Quoted in Meg McGavran Murray, ed., *Face to Face: Fathers, Mothers, Masters, Monsters—Essays for a Nonsexist Future* (Westport, CT: Greenwood, 1983), 298-301.

19. Judith Kegan Gardiner, "Evil, Apocalypse, and Feminist Fiction," *Frontiers* 7 (1983), 75.

20. Piercy, "Mirror Images," 193.

21. Critical views on *High Cost* were decidedly mixed. For example, Christopher Lehmann-Haupt, "Books of the Times," *New York Times* (19 January 1978), sec. 3, 18, found the characters absorbing and not pushed around by ideology, while the reviewer for *The New Yorker* felt the novel abounded with stereotypes (53 [13 February 1978], 124).

22. Bonnie Zimmerman, "What Has Never Been: An Overview of Lesbian Feminist Criticism," in *Making a Difference: Feminist Literary Criticism*, ed. Gayle Greene and Coppelia Kahn (New York: Routledge, 1985), 177-210. Zimmerman provides an excellent summary of the development of a lesbian feminist criticism, and outlines some of the major issues tackled by lesbian critics. Like most lesbian scholars, she is critical of the "heterosexism" of most feminist scholars (179).

23. Linda Abbandonato disagrees about the relative importance of lesbianism to *The Color Purple*, saying that Celie's flouting of the requirement of "compulsory heterosexuality" is the *key* to her break from her oppressive situation. "A View from 'Elsewhere' ": Subversive Sexuality and the Rewriting of the Heroine's Story in *The Color Purple*," *PMLA* 106 (October 1991), 1110. White heterosexual feminists, she says, do not want to look too closely at this theme.

24. Paulina Palmer, *Contemporary Women's Fiction: Narrative Practice and Feminist Theory* (Jackson: University Press of Mississippi, 1989), 144-148.

25. See Ginette Castro's *American Feminism: A Contemporary History*, trans. Elizabeth Loverde-Bagell (New York: New York University Press, 1990), pt. II, ch. 4, for a discussion of various viewpoints on lesbianism in the movement. Castro suggests that the proselytizing done by radical lesbians led to their rejection by the movement, rather than the movement's rejecting them out of hand. Zimmerman states that separatism is an important ingredient in the thinking of many lesbian

fiction writers and critics, certainly not an attitude we see in this mainstream fiction, not even Piercy's (182).

26. Celia Betsky, "Talk with Marge Piercy," *New York Times Book Review* (24 February 1980), 36.

27. See, for example, Elinor Langer, "After the Movement," review of *Vida*, *New York Times Book Review* (24 February 1980), 1, 36. Marge Hershman, "Books in Short," *Ms.* 8 (January 1980), 90; Lore Dickstein, review of *Vida*, *Saturday Review* 7 (1 March 1980), 44. All these critics found *Vida*'s sense of the times to be compelling.

28. Marge Piercy, *Vida* (New York: Fawcett Crest, 1979), 124.

29. Elaine Hoffman Baruch, *Women, Love, and Power: Literary and Psychoanalytic Perspectives* (New York: New York University Press, 1991), 140.

30. Jennifer Uglow, "Weighing up the Seventies," *Times Literary Supplement* (7 March 1980), 258.

31. Katha Pollit, "A Complete Catalogue of Female Suffering," review of *Braided Lives* by Marge Piercy, *New York Times Book Review* (7 February 1982), 30.

32. Both Mickelson and Palmer argue that "political" fiction or "fiction of ideas" does not purport to imitate reality and should not have to conform to standards of probability (*RO* 177; *Contemporary Women's Fiction*, 45, 56). However, I find such arguments less than persuasive when a writer adopts a realistic mode. Departures from such fictional requirements are easier to accept in more experimental types of fiction.

33. Marge Piercy, *Braided Lives* (New York: Fawcett Crest, 1982), 2.

34. John Leonard, "Book of the Times," review of *Vida* by Marge Piercy, *New York Times* (15 January 1980), sec. 3, 10.

35. Ellen Sweet, "Books in Short," *Ms.* 12 (March 1984), 32.

36. Marge Piercy, *Fly Away Home* (New York: Fawcett Crest, 1984), 423.

37. Jeanne McManus, *Washington Post Book World* (19 February 1984), agrees, feeling that Piercy lets her politics get in the way of her characters.

38. See, for example, the already discussed "Flying from Work" by Arlyn Diamond, *Frontiers* 2 (1977), 18-23; Elaine Reuben, review of *Fear of Flying* by Erica Jong, *New Republic* 170 (2 February 1974), 27; and Patricia S. Joyne, "Women's Lit," *National Review* 26 (24 May 1974), 604.

39. Marge Piercy, *Gone to Soldiers* (New York: Fawcett Crest, 1987), 105.

40. Mary Biggs, review of *Gone to Soldiers* by Marge Piercy, *The Women's Review of Books* 4 (July-August 1987), 24.

41. Ibid., 23.

42. Ibid.

43. Carol Iannone, in "A Turning of the Critical Tide," *Commentary* 88 (November 1989), 59, lambastes the novel for its clumsiness and declares that it shows that radical writers are finally coming home to more middle-class themes and attitudes.

44. Mickey Pearlman and Katherine Usher Henderson, ed., *Inter/View: Talks with America's Writing Women* (Lexington: University Press of Kentucky, 1988), 66.

45. Stephen Schift, review of *Summer People* by Marge Piercy, *New York Times Book Review*, (11 June 1989), 4.

46. Patricia Craig, review of *Summer People* by Marge Piercy, *Times Literary Supplement* (15 September 1989), 997.

47. Marge Piercy, *He, She and It* (New York: Knopf, 1991), 426.

48. Piercy, *Parti-Colored Blocks*, 143.

49. In 1973, in reviewing *Small Changes*, Richard Todd said that the tone of Piercy's writing recalled the "moralistic insistence" of the nineteenth century, in this age of relativism certainly a negative observation on any writer. *Atlantic* 232 (September 1973), 105.

50. Andrea Freud Lowenstein, "Iron Fist Fiction," review of *Gone to Soldiers* by Marge Piercy, *Nation* 245 (4/11 July 1987), 26.

5

Mary Gordon: Christianity and Feminism

During the first twenty years of contemporary feminism, scholars devoted a great deal of attention to exposing the patriarchal underpinnings of the Judeo-Christian tradition. To some secular feminists the idea of a Christian feminist seems nearly a contradiction in terms. Nearly every aspect of theology and church structure has come under attack, from concepts of the deity as male, to sexist language, to the almost exclusively male power structures in most churches.[1] Certainly no Christian faith is seen as more patriarchal than Roman Catholicism, the denomination whose leadership is most implacably opposed to women clergy. Because of this male bias in Christianity, a good many feminists in the 1970s and 1980s abandoned their traditional faiths to search for less male-oriented methods of spiritual development, some turning back to ancient concepts of the Mother Goddess.[2]

Nevertheless, many feminists have chosen to remain in their traditional churches and to work for change from within. In 1976 the American Episcopal Church ordained its first women priests, and efforts continue within the church to reform liturgy and to be sensitive to the needs and concerns of women. Other mainstream Protestant faiths ordain women and have active feminist movements. Within Roman Catholicism laywomen and nuns work unceasingly for fuller participation of women within the church, including the ordination of women, although with the present pope, this prospect seems very dim. Feminist theologians have worked with traditional materials, attempting to create a more "female friendly" theology.

This involvement of feminists with religious change was not reflected to any great degree in the literature of the 1970s and 1980s. As I explained in Chapter 2, most of the searches of contemporary women documented in the novels of this period were social searches, with protagonists struggling to find themselves in relation to others in society, particularly to the pa-

triarchal structures of society. Most protagonists did not search for a tran-
scendent Being, either within or without traditional religion.[3] This lack of
a religious context for the search of these protagonists no doubt reflects the
secular milieu of the writers; however, it also reflects a gap in the docu-
mentation of contemporary women's experience, since many feminists are
trying to incorporate their ideas into new concepts of the deity and their
own roles within traditional religion. They resist giving up the spiritual
richness of their traditions, but at the same time see those traditions in
conflict with their new ideas.

One feminist novelist who has not entirely rejected her religious roots,
and in fact has celebrated their gifts, is the Irish Catholic Mary Gordon.
Unlike most of the writers discussed so far, who either maintain a secular
viewpoint or see patriarchal religion as woman's enemy, Gordon has portrayed characters who reject that which is life-denying in their faiths but
embrace that which is life-enhancing. Further, their searches engage them
in profoundly moral questions involving not only their social relations but
also questions of love, sacrifice, and an examination of the holy in the world.
Though Gordon's answers would not always please the Church, either the
pre- or post-Vatican II version, her protagonists are never able to completely
discard their religious roots, which provide them a basis from which to
examine those fundamental questions.[4]

Mary Gordon is unusual as a feminist fiction writer concerned with spiritual questions, but in another way she seems representative of novelists of
the 1980s who reflected cultural feminist concerns such as motherhood and
female friendship. One of her four novels is centered on the meaning of
motherhood in the lives of contemporary women, and two others feature
motherhood as a central theme. Through her revision of Christian views of
body and spirit, she has been able to develop a view of immanence rather
than transcendence that brings together the physicality of the female and
Christian views that seem to deny the body.[5]

Like Marge Piercy, Mary Gordon was the child of Jewish-Christian parents raised in an urban ethnic environment, the Irish ghetto of Queens. Her
father, David, a Jewish scholar, was a "ne'er do well" who cared for Mary
while her self-sacrificing Irish mother worked to support them. He converted
to Catholicism and like many converts became more devout, even fanatical,
than those born to the faith, being a right-winger who felt that history
stopped with the Reformation. According to Gordon, he kept starting
"doomed little right-wing magazines with articles like 'Roosevelt: The
Anti Christ.' " Though an immensely literate man, he ripped pages out of
books he did not like and was a very "unphysical" man. Gordon says she
is not sure how she was conceived.[6]

Though David died when Mary was eight, he had a great influence on
her spiritual and intellectual development. Today, although she rejects his
conservative beliefs, she confesses her "absolute love" for him and has

difficulty in explaining to others the complexity of the relationship: "I think I always chose my father over my mother, and that's it. My father is always the star for me and the hero—which is odd for a feminist."[7] Two important male characters in Gordon's novels strongly resemble David Gordon: Joseph Moore in *Final Payments* and Father Cyprian in *The Company of Women*. Gordon now says that David's Jewishness, as well as his Catholicism, might have had an effect on her as a writer by empowering her to speak despite the strong coercive nature of her environment: "... being the kind of Irish Catholic I was brought up among, I could never have written. It was such an interdicting environment, such a silencing environment.... And, I think my father's Jewishness gave me a kind of license to speak" ("RD" 81).

Like many bright Catholic girls in such a restrictive environment, at first Gordon was a docile achiever, pinning religious medals to her undershirts, writing religious treatises and poetry, reading about the saints and virgin martyrs, and fantasizing about the pure life of the cloister. However, "puberty drove out God," who was replaced by boys ("MG" 5). Gordon rebelled against the tyranny of the nuns in school and eventually won a scholarship to Barnard, which lifted her forever away from her ethnic milieu. She now says that going to Barnard was the most important thing she ever did ("RD" 82).

At Barnard, Gordon's intellect was awakened and her social consciousness developed with various 1960s political issues. She participated in Columbia's uprising of 1968, shouting "Up against the wall" like the others ("MG" 5). At this point, one assumes, she rejected most of the political ideas of her conservative father. In the classroom her mentor was Elizabeth Hardwick, who taught her a respect for finely crafted language and urged her to switch from poetry, her original literary medium, to prose. In the future critics were to point again and again to the poetic qualities of her prose. Since graduate school at Syracuse, Gordon has taught English at several colleges, has been married twice, and is the mother of two children. From 1978 to the present she has produced four novels and one book of short stories. In 1981 Gordon discussed Virginia Woolf's "A Room of One's Own" and agreed with Woolf that women have achieved less because they have had children. At the same time she believes that women's experiences have enriched them in ways that can feed their artistic efforts.[8]

FINAL PAYMENTS: A CATHOLIC BILDUNGSROMAN

Gordon's first novel, *Final Payments* (1978), was given high acclaim by critics. Typical were comments such as "The best American feminist novel yet.... an eloquent comment on the nature of woman's fate" and "This is a well-made, realistic novel of refined sensibility and moral scruple, informed by the values of orthodox Christianity."[9] Even a critic who disliked Gordon's rejection of some aspects of Christian belief admitted her challenging themes: "We could picture this as a feminist Rent-a-Joyce saga of guilt and liberation, but it is more than this. . . . The Church is portrayed in exasperating complexity."[10] Over the years Gordon has achieved a good amount of positive critical attention. This is partly due to her unusual, "electric" prose, but it is also due to her religious themes, which provide critical content not often found in contemporary fiction.[11] As Ann-Janine Morey puts it, "Gordon's novels are ideal territories for people interested in the relations between religion and literature."[12] Then, too, though she obviously reveals feminist themes, she is not overtly "political" in the way Marge Piercy is. Thus she cannot be attacked as a polemicist.

Final Payments is the *bildungsroman* of Isabel Moore, an attractive, clever, but naive thirty-year-old Irish Catholic from Queens who, at novel's beginning, has recently been released from an eleven-year servitude to her patriarchal, arch-conservative and godlike professor father, Joseph. Thus, Gordon introduces us to a peculiarly feminist theme: sacrifice through caregiving. As Wilfrid Sheed says, service to God knows no sex, but taking care of a cranky old man does.[13] Another theme is Catholic guilt, in that Joseph was an invalid due to a heart attack suffered after catching the nineteen-year-old Isabel in bed with her boyfriend, David. Barbara Rigney sees the theme of Mariolatry here. Through her "sin" with David, Isabel took on the corruption of Eve; to compensate, she submits herself to the will of the Lord (her father) and lives the pure life of the Ever-Virgin Mary. Unfortunately, by giving up her freedom to her father (who also represents the Church), Isabel also gives up her humanity.[14]

Isabel and Joseph even fantasize about a son she will have from this brief encounter, a Christlike child that will be passed off as the result of a rape or virgin birth. When no pregnancy occurs, Joe has a heart attack, thus becoming in effect Isabel's child as well as a domineering yet loving father. Rigney points out the obvious Freudian implications of this father-daughter relationship (throughout the novel Gordon uses a psychoanalytic approach), as well as the "lethal" effect of the Freudian idea of no "pure acts." Isabel believes—in fact, her experiences teach her—that there are no real acts of personal sacrifice; if a person sacrifices, it must involve some payoff for her/ him, and all selfish acts must be paid for. Thus her life becomes a kind of lifelong penance to absolve herself from guilt (40).

The years of servitude were routine but not unhappy, since Isabel loved her father and joyfully martyred herself for him, the experience giving a sense of uplift described by those who sacrifice from religious conviction. At Joe's funeral Isabel reflects that the day her father became helpless "was of my whole life the day I felt most purely alive."[15] Isabel believes she sacrificed herself out of the love of God, but later we discover it was done for personal love, the love of child for parent. Now she is acutely aware that her identity is gone, and her frightening and yet immensely exciting future looms before her: "I felt light, as from the removal of a burden, light as a spaceman in a gravityless universe" (7). Throughout the story Gordon emphasizes the existential nature of Isabel's crisis; without the dictates of her father and her culture, she faces the abyss: "I no longer knew whom or what I represented.... What if you represented nothing but yourself only?" (165).

At this point, it appears that *Final Payments* will be similar to other feminist *bildungsromans* of the 1970s, and in some ways it fulfills those expectations, detailing Isabel's struggles with the world of romance and work. However, Gordon deals with larger spiritual questions as well, and these make the novel unique. As John Neary says, Isabel's crisis at her father's death is metaphysical as well as social. Spiritual certainty, in which words and things have absolute significance beyond the metaphorical, has disappeared from her life. Though Isabel has long left the Church and thinks she has lost her faith, she has not faced up to what that means. In effect, her father became God for her; now, God is dead and the universe has become random and chaotic (100).

Though *Final Payments* centers on the brief period immediately after Joseph's death, flashbacks are important to give us a full understanding of Isabel's character and the background she tries to escape. Isabel's mother died when she was young, and her father hired a spinster, Margaret Casey, whom Isabel hated and eventually sent away. Margaret also martyrs herself for others, but always whiningly and grudgingly—the sort of woman who appears to be a "saint" (she loves novenas and holy pictures) but in fact is a nasty, unloving person. She represents a horrifying possibility for Isabel, what she might become if she cannot break away:

You cannot imagine how unbearable the brown patches on her skin—they were not moles but large, irregular in shape, like the beginning of a cancer—were to a child, or even worse to an adolescent.... Her feet were flat as a fish, except where the bunions developed like small crops of winter onions. The sound of her slopping around the house in her slippers is the sound of my nightmares. (27)

Though she escapes Margaret at this point, Margaret later reappears as the agent by which Isabel will endure a new martyrdom. Even more than the lepers of medieval times, Margaret is "crippled in both body and spirit."[16]

Through Isabel's struggles to escape her milieu, Gordon shows the power of the Church even for those who reject its teachings. Although Isabel has not left Queens, she has kept in touch with the world's changes through friends and reading. Pretending to attend church to please her father, she rejects the Church's indifference to women, recalling how when the priests used to visit her father to discuss theology, they expected to be served by her but never remembered her name. The one priest she maintains contact with, the alcoholic Father Mulcahy, is a friend rather than a spiritual adviser. Thus, when Isabel begins her secular search for self, she wrongly believes she can proceed free of the encumbrances of tradition and faith.

Mary Gordon generally devotes a good deal of attention to women's friendships in her fiction, and *Final Payments* is no exception. As in many novels of the 1970s, Isabel's friends, Eleanor and Liz, who stand on her right and her left during the funeral, seem to suggest alternative possibilities for the protagonist. Throughout her years with her father, Isabel has derived comfort and support from both women. Eleanor is dreamy, male dependent, and timid, her unhappy life revolving around her lovers, whom she eventually gives up because they cause her too much pain. Together, Isabel and Eleanor talk "about ourselves, about our natures, checking on one another against our childhoods to see what we had become, as though external events had no consequence" (6).

In contrast with Eleanor is Liz, who "was slapped by the principal for passing notes during the Consecration" (7). With Liz, Isabel discusses radical politics in the same way that other women discuss their love affairs. This they must do secretly, to conceal their ideas from Joseph. Though on the "liberal" side on most social questions of the times, Isabel and Liz laugh at the changes in the Church, perceiving them as insincere trendiness:

nuns in Ship'n Shore blouses who made her [Liz] want to join the Green Berets just to be on the opposite side; priests with no sense of irony losing their virginity in their forties; ... And, of course, Eugene McCarthy was the man every Catholic girl had dreamed of marrying, as Dan Berrigan was the priest we yearned to seduce. (13-14)

The mocking Liz is Isabel's touchstone with reality during these isolated years, a strong, practical, independent woman who "ought to have led men across the Antarctic" (9), and instead married a boorish cad, John Ryan. As a result she has found love with other women. Though both women help Isabel in her quest, neither provides an answer in her self-seeking. In Gordon's treatment of these friendships, Elizabeth Abel's and Judith Kegan Gardiner's theories of complementarity/commonality do not seem to fit.

A central issue in most of Gordon's fiction is "ordinariness," the lives most women lead, giving up pursuits of the spirit and mind to immerse themselves in the flesh—husbands and babies. Isabel has long speculated why she allowed herself to be caught with David, an ordinary young man. Perhaps it was oedipal feelings, a desire to show her father that their relationship was in danger: "Was I trying to punish my father for something; for his lack of attention to my obvious adulthood, for his lack of jealousy at the intrusion of so clear a rival ... ? Perhaps I was outraged at his lack of outrage at what could so obviously have separated us" (21). Isabel now realizes that this crazy act was caused by her desire to resist "ordinariness," a life of "cooking Sunday dinner for my father and David and our children" (22), in effect choosing the peculiar and intense life with her father, studying together and debating theological issues. Because, of course, her father's heart attack prevented her from having another man in her life in an intimate sense. Most of Gordon's protagonists struggle against an "ordinary" existence; usually they eventually embrace such a life, but always with nostalgia for the idealized purity of the spiritual life.

Isabel's grief is short-lived, and ignoring who she is, she recklessly seizes her new "ordinary" life, seeking female pleasures in new clothes and makeup, perceiving a beauty and sensuality in her body she did not expect: "I opened the bag and took out a pair of nylon bikini underpants: dark green with ivory lace.... Quickly, I pulled off my heavy underpants and slipped on the silky new ones. The effect was immediate and delicious. I laughed, in embarrassment, in pleasure" (50-51). Unlike traditional Catholic thinkers, who would argue that Isabel's "sin" is her enjoyment of the flesh, or like some feminist thinkers, who would say that Isabel is too concerned with enhancing her beauty for the world, Gordon says Isabel's mistake is her lack of self-awareness, of not understanding who she is.

Throughout Gordon's writing the demands and pleasures of the spirit and flesh are in constant conflict. Discussing the importance of her religious past, Gordon attacks two "sins" of the Church: abstraction and dualism. Abstraction is "the error that results from refusing to admit that one has a body and is an inhabitant of the physical world," and dualism "admits that there is a physical world but calls it evil and commands that it be shunned." These ideas have been "the cause of . . . much human misery."[17] Furthermore, the male Church has held that women are in thrall to their flesh, being forced to obey the imperatives of nature to conceive and bear children. Because of their relentlessly physical natures, women have more difficulty approaching the divine, of being spiritual.

This physicality of women also has a negative effect on men, in that in women's lust to satisfy themselves, they tempt men from spiritual callings. Thus women must be excluded from the personal and official lives of male clergy. Gordon finds this hatred and fear of the flesh not only antifemale but also anti-Christian, for the meaning of the Incarnation must be found in the divine taking on physical form. The human body is not an evil vessel.[18] For Isabel this means that she must seek a synthesis of body and spirit by rejecting the body hatred she has been taught, without giving in to complete self-indulgence.

In the next sections of the novel, Gordon shows Isabel's quest in the worlds of sexuality and work. Though not a virgin, Isabel is sexually unawakened. Like other feminist heroines, she encounters sex first with a woman-abuser, John Ryan, the caddish husband of Liz. Like Marge Piercy, Gordon acknowledges the attractiveness of the "rat," the woman-hater who embodies the masculine qualities our society values. Isabel feels somewhat degraded by this drunken encounter, but true to her frank, shrewd nature, admits she enjoyed the act. In the episodes with John, Isabel discovers something discovered by other feminist heroines: sex without caring may be exciting, but it can lead to a denigrated sense of self and will. When John makes love to her a second time, Isabel feels diminished, yet also feels that since he has had her once, he therefore has a right to her body: "I kept my eyes on the damp stain on the ceiling, imagining it a snail.... Since I had wanted him once, he deserved me now.... By wanting him once I had forfeited the right ever to deny him" (173).

Perhaps these adventures, which, as Maureen Howard says, "could be found in any contemporary fiction about the working girl and her problems," are less interesting than the insights Isabel gains through her new job (32). Isabel visits foster homes for the elderly in an experiment to determine whether such care provides more emotional warmth than institutions. Gordon describes these visits in a series of masterful vignettes that critics called the best parts of the novel.[19] Here she introduces a theme central to all her work: the limitations of divine or Christian love versus human love. During her visits Isabel discovers that foster care provides little more than nursing homes. Without the kind of love she gave to her father, the elderly may as well die: "If that was what you wanted—someone to love you for yourself more than anyone else—there was nothing worth living for once you had lost it" (230). When an elderly woman begs for help in committing suicide, Isabel hesitates little before providing it. She now realizes she cared for her father out of love rather than some kind of female masochism.[20]

This theme of the particularity of love—the impossibility of human love without particular love for the love object—seems to reject the Christian idea of agape, selfless love of the Other who may not be known. Christian critics have harshly criticized this aspect of Gordon's moral theology, saying that she perverts doctrine or at least does not understand it. John W. Mahon, for example, says that in human love one finds the promise of divine love; this promise of God's love should keep the individual, who has once experienced human love but has lost it, from the despair that would lead to suicide.[21] Gordon would probably argue that the promise of divine love is not enough for most mortals.

Isabel's reckless love affair with a married man, Hugh Slade, leads to the novel's crisis. Hugh's wife, Cynthia, is a miserable "harridan" who hates his affairs but stays with him for security. In characters like Margaret Casey and Cynthia, Gordon supports another of her often-repeated themes disliked by Christian critics. Some people in life are losers, randomly set aside in the doling out of good looks, attractive personalities, talents, money, or loving families. Though it seems unjust in a universe supposedly ruled by a benevolent deity, these people exist and suffer for their lack of life's gifts. And, Christian charity aside, it is impossible for most of us to love them.

In her affair with Hugh, Isabel embraces the body and rejects the Church's admonitions: "It was possible that today I was doing something that would cause pain to strangers, but I did not care. I felt I had finally joined the company of other ordinary humans. It was the first time I had wanted anything in adulthood: I wanted him" (168). She decides that people are religious only because their bodies have not given them enough pleasure, thinking, "Pleasure. I held the word in my mouth like a plum" (171). It seems here as if Gordon is totally rejecting the anti-body outlook of the Church for a hedonistic embrace of the fleshly. However, subsequent events show that Isabel goes too far in her self-indulgence and will need to temper her love of the body with some restraint.

When Hugh's affair with Isabel is revealed in a melodramatic but believable confrontation with his wife, Isabel wallows in her guilt and shame. She starkly realizes she is still her father's daughter, yet without his support. Isabel, exposed to the scorn of society for the adulteress, finds that the wife's words bring up her guilt: "I had murdered my father." For the first time, she truly realizes that her father *is* dead; she will never see him again, and she grieves. "I was entirely alone. I wept like an animal. My mouth was open. I rock and rocked" (232-234). Without the security of her good reputation, her father's love, and her culture, she realizes how comforting those supports were:

As the daughter of my father I lived always in sanctuary. Think of the appeal of sanctuary, the pure shelter.... I had won sanctuary by giving up my portion, by accepting... far less than my share... by giving up youth and freedom, sex, and life.... It was as though I had been in a fire; I was exposed to faces that would close when they saw me. (238-239)

This idea of "shelter," like questions of body versus spirit and the limitations of love, is central to all of Gordon's fiction. Gordon believes that much human action, such as marriage, is motivated by a need for shelter or sanctuary. This need for refuge from the depredations and terrifying freedom of life needs to be attended to, but it also can be restrictive, especially for women, who often give up so much freedom to achieve it. In Isabel's case, she temporarily gives up her quest for the sanctuary of martyrdom, a mistake that nearly destroys her.

The next events are Isabel's attempt to reconstitute certainty in the randomness into which she has been thrown (Neary 103). She will return to the absolutism of the Church and do penance for her pleasure, just as all the martyrs have done. This penance includes (1) abasement of her body (often used by women martyrs) through an orgy of eating and (2) sacrificing herself to care for that which is most unlovable, the odious Margaret Casey. "It would be a pure act, like the choice of a martyr's death which, we had been told in school, is the only inviolable guarantee of salvation" (249). Isabel's decision is misguided, not only because she is seeking martyrdom but also because she does not love Margaret.

While staying with Margaret, Isabel returns to the long rejected Church;

however, without belief, the forms have no meaning. And, as so often happens in Gordon's work, the institutional church fails her.[22] At confession, the priest's mechanical absolution gives no relief, and as he counsels her against "sins of the flesh," her menstrual blood reminds her of her filthy femaleness (275-277). Earlier, she had sought help from Father Mulcahy, but he, who has spent his life following the example of Christ, loving the unlovable in the abstract, cannot manage to hear his troubled friend's confession; he blubbers and passes out in a puddle of whiskey on the rectory floor. Scornfully turning from his human misery and fear, Isabel thinks, with the righteousness of the martyrs, "Coward." Though Isabel calls him a coward, she fails to apply the lessons of his life by cowardly hiding with the unappreciative Margaret and trying to love, not as a friend but in the abstract.

Gordon masterfully explains Isabel's "resurrection" as a coming together of body and spirit. "Selfish pleasure" is reawakened by a letter from Hugh. Father Mulcahy comes to visit her as a friend and aids in the healing process of regeneration. His inability to hear her confession has been a blessing, for he now warns her of the disaster and even sinfulness of her self-abasement: "Watch your weight, honey. God gave you beauty. If you waste it, that's a sin against the first commandment" (297). The body does have value.

When Margaret accuses Isabel of being with the priest too long, Isabel shouts, "You are a wicked, wicked, woman," in a scene that makes the reader want to cheer, and sweeps Margaret's dishes to the floor. To Margaret's "I am a poor woman," Isabel retorts, "the poor you always have with you" (298). Later she reflects on the story of Judas, Mary Magdalene, and the anointing of Jesus' feet. When Jesus said "The poor you always have with you, but me you have not always" he meant that

the pleasure of the hair, that ointment must be taken.... We must not deprive ourselves, our loved ones, of the luxury of our extravagant affections. We must not try to second-guess death by refusing to love the ones we loved in favor of the anonymous poor. And it came to me...that I had been a thief. Like Judas, I had wanted to hide gold, to count it in the dead of night, to parlay it into some safe and murderous investment. It was Margaret's poverty I wanted to steal, the safety of her inability to inspire love. So that never again would I be found weeping, like Mary, at the tombstone at the break of dawn. (298-299)

I quote at length here because this passage exemplifies the essence of Gordon's central theme: that the pleasures of particular love, sexual or otherwise, are to be preferred to the "spiritual," abstract love of traditional Christianity; that, in fact, such a love is "Holy," being a mirror of the Incarnation. Furthermore, Isabel has tried to evade her freedom and herself by hiding from life with Margaret; this craven seeking of sanctuary has been a sin against herself. According to Sarah Gilead, in this revised interpretation of the biblical passage Gordon has feminized Christian doctrine by integrating the best from her two heritages, "the feminist and the patriarchal, the unauthorized and the authorized."[23]

Unlike many feminist writers, Gordon does not rail at the male tendency to love women for their beautiful bodies: Isabel realizes she will have to lose weight:

I tried to imagine a love that would make no distinctions, that would not be tried by flesh that lost its smooth surface, that would not be tested by ingratitude, or sadness, or betrayal or a simple coldness of the heart. . . . I had at that moment a flash of revelation about the body that had the simplicity . . . of great art. The body changed. . . . What I had done to myself was not final. . . . I would make things happen to my body that would allow him to love it again. (300-301)

Isabel allows her spirit to heal by attending church on Good Friday. Acknowledging her father's death and realizing that she is not guilty, she takes comfort in the ritual that confirms our own mortality: "We were here to say that we knew about death, we knew about loss, that it would not surprise us" (302). And, of course, with the acceptance of death lies the hope of all the pleasures of new life because, if death is important, so is the physical world, including the body.[24] Life may be transitory, random, and without absolute truth, but it offers its own form of holiness.

Isabel's regeneration is complete when she reunites with Liz and Eleanor, who all along have tried to sway her from her disastrous course: "How I loved them for their solidity, for their real and possible existences, nonetheless a miracle. For they had come the moment I called them, and they were here beside me in the fragile and exhilarating chill of the first dawn" (307). Thus, the novel ends as so many of the 1970s *bildungsromans*, with the protagonist as a "new Eve," coming to terms with her past and moving into a future that is full of promise. Though we are not sure what her future holds, we know that Isabel will live an "ordinary" life, loving the lovables and not trying to be a saint or virgin martyr. Some feminist theologians have suggested that women need to reject the traditional myths of Mary and women martyrs, that they are antifemale and counterproductive to women's quests; Gordon seems to be suggesting that, with revisions, the myths can offer women guidance in their spiritual quests.[25]

As Isabel prepares to leave Margaret, she acknowledges the dangers of a life of freedom, that she is now making herself vulnerable to life's pain: "Margaret's unlovableness rendered her incapable of inflicting permanent pain. She could decay the soul, but she could not destroy. Only love could do that, and the accidents of love" (304). As a "final payment" Isabel leaves all of her inheritance from her father, twenty thousand dollars, on the kitchen table. Barbara Rigney sees this final payment as puzzling: If Isabel is not guilty, why the need for further payment? However, Gordon could simply be having Isabel "purge herself" completely from her old life (46).

Although Sarah Gilead feels that Isabel has exorcised her patriarchal past and has opted for a future of humanistic, feminist values (226), some critics find this feminist "deconstruction" of traditional Christian values a perversion. John W. Mahon states that Isabel should try harder to love Margaret and follow Matthew 18: "If thy brother shall trespass against thee, go and tell him his fault between thee and him alone: if he shall hear thee, thou hast gained a brother" (52). Carol Iannone quotes Paul's words in 1 Corinthians: "Though I bestow all my goods to feed the poor . . . and have not charity, it profiteth me nothing." The twenty thousand dollars on the table is an insult to Christ's teaching.[26] Gordon would likely reply that Paul's exacting ideal is impossible for most of us, or, as Wilfrid Sheed says, "Loving the unlovable is largely a charade one plays for one's own benefit" (14).

THE COMPANY OF WOMEN: FEMALE BONDS AND PRIESTLY MENTORS

With *The Company of Women* (1980) we move into territory more typical of the feminist novel of the 1980s. Less important is the sexual relation of the protagonist to males. In fact, a central theme in *Company* is the relation of the protagonist, Felicitas Taylor, to women in her life, as well as the relations of all these women to each other. The story concerns a small community of women who live in a state of intimate friendship that one equates with the early Christians. However, such a description would be incomplete, because equally important to the relations among the women is their connection to a strong male figure, the fascinating Father Cyprian.

In an interview while working on *Company*, Gordon stated: "I want to be talking about women and their spiritual mentors, and the female habit of abdicating responsibility for their inner lives to the men—priests, lovers—who in one way or another compel them."[27] Gordon has admitted to an "almost erotic" preoccupation with priests, an interest noticed by a number of critics.[28] For her, priests seem to have a "hidden magical potency that is powerful, because it is both sexually inaccessible and directly connected to spiritual ritual and the mystical."[29] It is a quality withheld from women, who are made to feel they can never have such a direct connection to God. As one from a Catholic girlhood, I can attest to the attractiveness of the handsome priest whose access to God makes him enviable and desirable.

The plot of *Company* concerns a group of Irish Catholic women "left to take care of their parents because they had not been chosen by a man," and therefore pitied by society.[30] Two of them, Charlotte Taylor and Elizabeth, are widows; one, Mary Rose, has a mentally ill husband whom she cannot divorce because of her religion; Muriel is a bitter spinster like Margaret Casey, whom the others tolerate out of Christian charity; and Clare, another spinster, at one time wanted to be a nun but now manages her family's business. All of these women have focused their maternal instincts on Felicitas, Charlotte's bright, shrewd, and rebellious daughter, named after the one Christian martyr "whose name contained some hope for ordinary human happiness" (3). These mother figures, along with Father Cyprian, hope for great things for her, far beyond ordinary human happiness. Although she cannot be a priest, perhaps she will become a great religious scholar.

Father Cyprian, the towering presence in this novel, as Joseph Moore is the dominant force in *Final Payments*, comes from a humble Polish farm background. Always believing himself different from his environment and wishing to "prove he was not flesh" (47), Cyprian is forced to withdraw from his order because he cannot accept the changes in the Church—folk masses, young priests wearing chinos, soft-drink vending machines in the monastery. Like Joe Moore, he is convinced such changes at best are misguided and at worst are the work of the Devil. As Joe is for Isabel, Cyprian is the patriarchal force against which Felicitas must struggle in her quest.

In *Company* Gordon depicts how powerful priests enjoy their ministry to women who let them dominate their lives. Cyprian has established a retreat in upstate New York for single, working women. This "company" abdicates responsibility to Cyprian in most areas of their lives; for example, he gets Mary Rose's husband committed to Bellevue Hospital, but then will not give her permission to divorce and remarry, keeping her in bondage to his community. In the earlier sections of the novel Cyprian does not see that his attitudes toward others (he calls human tenderness "womanish") actually are prideful and contrary to the spirit of the Incarnation, in which God took on fleshly form to bring himself closer to us.

The adolescent Felicitas enjoys her centrality in this odd little community, where she spends her summer vacations being fussed over by the women and taught the classics and theology by Cyprian, who also counsels her against the evils of modernism. As the young Mary Gordon and Isabel were to their fathers, Felicitas is at first a docile pupil to Cyprian, who admits he loves her as much as—no, more than—God. Though she is sometimes a bit embarrassed at her strange life, Felicitas prides herself on her difference from other girls. She loves the praise Cyprian gives, the attention that celebrates her singularity: "She valued more than anything in life that look in his eyes, the look that said, " 'You are the chosen one' " (45). Cyprian tells her that she will not "throw her life away on some man," but at the same time, because of his contempt for the womanish, always lets her know "all that she was not and would not be" (36).

Through the relationship between Cyprian and Felicitas, Gordon again stresses the feminist theory that women are associated with nature and body, seen as inferior to culture and spirit. Cyprian especially counsels Felicitas against pantheism, the "Protestant" view that God can be found in nature: "Natural beauty is only a reflection of divine beauty. It has no meaning in itself" (36). When Felicitas, her senses swimming with the wondrous odors of fresh grass, remarks, "I think heaven will smell like this," the angry Cyprian forces her to smell manure until she vomits, telling her: "I will not have you poisoned by the sentimental claptrap that passes for religion in this age. Christ and the Virgin movie stars. The Passion just another cowpoke episode. Heaven a garden.... It is the spirit... that is life eternal." As Cyprian says, "It was womanish to say, 'how sweet the grasses are' " (44-45).

The intelligent Felicitas burns with the injustice of the farmer and Cyprian laughing at her: "In that laugh she was *the other*. She would know always in that laugh what it was to be the outsider, the woman among men, the black among whites, the child among adults, the foreigner among natives" (42). Gordon presents the scene as symbolic of masculine contempt for feminine sensibility, as well as the beginning of Felicitas's rebellion against her background.

Now that Felicitas sees the faults of Cyprian's thinking, like Isabel she must confront secular society and the flesh, moving outside her milieu in order eventually to see its value. In her decision to attend Columbia, against the advice of the group, Felicitas completely rejects her roots:

The lives of the women she loved were bankrupt. She was tired of their efforts to live the lives of bankrupts making do with God and each other, purchasing the icon of a man, a tyrant... who stood out on the landscape not for his distinction but because it was a desert. (98)

As Gordon will show, Felicitas, who at eighteen thinks she is infallible, is only partly right about Cyprian and his company.

As with *Final Payments*, some reviewers did not care for the protagonist's adventures in the world outside her milieu, stating that the characters, mostly 1960s counterculture types, are poorly drawn.[31] Felicitas's seduction by the caddish Robert, a political science professor, seems fairly typical of other feminist novels. As Helen McNeil says, Robert worships at the altar of St. Herbert [Marcuse] and espouses sexual freedom by having a harem of women whom he abuses with their willing participation. His commune "demonically parodies" Cyprian's group.[32] In these sequences Gordon exposes some of the results of the move for sexual liberation for women of the late 1960s. Robert's woebegone harem and the horrifying group of used women visiting illegal abortionists show what happens to women when the protections of traditional morality are ripped away without options for women's lives or greater self-esteem.

Like other feminist writers, Gordon shows how women give up self-esteem in their quest for romantic love; though Felicitas has scorned the "ordinary lives" of most girls, with Robert she behaves like any other love-struck teenager. She gives up her virginity easily, considering it an honor to be wanted by such a brilliant man. As readers, we see Robert as a mediocre thinker who mouths inanities such as "Now I wish that I had been born a woman. A black woman" (148). Robert, however, is handsome and, as Ann-Janine Morey says, Felicitas finds the claims of "pure spiritual intellect clashing with the insistence of flesh. She has a woman's body to answer to, but few resources from the intellectually wrathful pedagogy of the priest with which to do so" (1060). Felicitas has always wanted to read Plato in Greek, but now "the beautiful face of Robert Cavendish eclipsed it, muddying the cold transparent water that was her mind... making it turbulent and brackish" (*Company* 104).

Although Felicitas has plenty of confidence in her intellectual ability, she has no self-esteem when it comes to her attractiveness to males:

Why should any man love her, having the face she had? She had no beauty, and she knew what beauty bought, had always known, although abstractly, for never in her life had anyone suggested that beauty would be her portion. Even as a child she had been valued for her sense. (132)

Because of her perceived lack of beauty, Felicitas takes less than her portion and is humbly gratefully for the crumbs of attention Robert throws her, telling herself that she "had always known, from the moment she considered being Robert's love, that she would want him more than he wanted her" (135). Felicitas pursues Robert and painfully shares him with others, since he tells her in the jargon of the 1960s that her approach to their relationship is "incredibly bourgeois." Following Robert's instructions, she sleeps with Richard, another man in the commune, to demonstrate the insignificance of sex. This section of the book could be faulted for being included as part of a feminist agenda, but the episode rings true to many readers—the spectacle of an intelligent woman, low on self-esteem, allowing herself to be debased because of romantic love.

Here Gordon also seems to be contrasting traditional male and female attitudes toward sex. The unsure Felicitas begins to wonder if her attitude is too sentimental. Could it be that it really did not matter with whom one had sex? She knows she simply does not feel for others what she feels for the particular—Robert. She feels sorry for hurting Richard, since he obviously loves her. Felicitas absolves Robert of his cruelties to herself and others because men are clearly masters: "Part of his majesty was that he was a man, with a man's bodily strength, never having had to question the propriety of his inheritance" (136). Though the relationships are different, Felicitas defers to Robert in all things, in the same way she deferred to Father Cyprian, believing them both superior to her by virtue of their sex.

In the reaction of Charlotte and the other women to Felicitas's disastrous course (in a sense they have contributed to it by isolating her), Gordon emphasizes the powerlessness of mothers and the mother-guilt that she stresses in her next work, *Men and Angels*. Charlotte is distraught and angry when Felicitas fails to come home at night, and turns to her friends for solace. Helpless against her child's attempts at independence, she struggles very little when Felicitas decides to move into the commune:

Charlotte saw herself as a wall in front of which her child, her tree had flourished. With Charlotte near, Felicitas did not have to bend in the wind.... But she knew her child had to grow, had to grow unprotected, needed exposure, needed loss of shelter. She had to leave her alone. (199)

Felicitas rejects not only her mother but other members of the company, too, including Cyprian, who counsels her against her new radical political ideas. She coldly but truthfully tells Clare, who pleads with Felicitas to have more respect for Cyprian, "It was an ego trip for him" (172). An auxiliary member of the company, Joe, the perennial suitor of Mary Rose, cautions her she may be in trouble in her relationship with Robert: "I'm a man. I know what men are like. They don't want what they can get easily" (194). Felicitas responds to this concern as an attack on her attempts to achieve selfhood.

However, she turns to the company at the novel's crisis—an unplanned pregnancy. Because of her involvement with Richard, Felicitas does not know who is the father of her child. After obtaining information about abortions, Felicitas witnesses a common event in feminist novels—the horror of illegal abortion complete with a "small, depressed Hispanic" doctor and a woman who hemorrhages on the floor, causing Felicitas to flee. On her way back to the commune, she notices a group of marchers protesting the invasion of Cambodia, but she cannot join them because she is "going to have a child" (237). This event emphasizes her turning away from the world and toward maternity—the life of ordinary women.

The concluding section of the novel, set in 1977, shows the working out of Felicitas's "ordinary" destiny. In this section, each member of the company is given time to tell her/his story in first person (the preceding sections are narrated in the third person, suggesting that the Felicitas of the final section has become herself). We discover that the company, including Cyprian, has welcomed and supported the pregnant Felicitas with true Christian warmth. No longer the intolerant adolescent, Felicitas does not choose to examine their motives: "Kindness is a rare thing, and having been saved by it, I no longer choose to mar its luster by too close examination" (252). She has made her peace with the elderly Cyprian and, in fact, holds him in reverence, despite the paucity of his ideas: "I revere him for his labor, for his passionate excluding love, for the dignity of his priestly calling he wears with him everywhere: the habit of his grand impossible life" (266).

Gordon's treatment of Felicitas's motherhood illustrates cultural feminist ideas: the restrictive nature of the institution of motherhood but its profound pleasure. By opting for the life of an ordinary woman, Felicitas gives up the exalted spiritual calling planned for her. Like many new mothers, at first she finds it difficult to love her daughter, Linda; rebelling at the restrictions of her own freedom that the child represents, she understands the impulse of mothers to kill their children: "It is life they must punish, for cheating them, for trapping them in the oldest trick in the world, the female body; for telling them, often children themselves, 'you are tied to this life now; your life is over' " (246). However, after about a year, Felicitas, who has numbed her feelings, begins to recover from her ordeal and discovers new beauty in the world. With this rediscovery comes a passionate love for Linda that amazes her with its force. She finds now that she must work not to spoil the child, who, as she once was, is the center of attention for the childless company, being seen as "superior to all others of her age in beauty, grace, and wisdom" (289). Although maternity threatens and restricts women, it yet has the potential to humanize through its rich physical love, which in some sense illuminates the mystery of the Incarnation.

The most important effort in Felicitas's drive to be ordinary is her impending marriage to a local businessman, Leo, a silent "ox." Felicitas hopes that marriage will humanize her. Marriage scares her in some ways: its potential for "diminishment," to make her "one more woman who lives in the country, is good around the property, occasionally reads books." She wonders if she is marrying for "shelter," like so many women. But she thinks not, because she is *choosing* to marry, relatively late in life—it is "not an act of nature visited upon me" (262). And she feels that a sexual life will humanize her with intimacy; too many single women she sees have a certain "cruelty of judgment."

This conclusion disappointed some reviewers, who felt that marriage to Leo indeed suggests a "diminishment" for the brilliant Felicitas, a kind of retreat into a serenity "ominously like quietism." Felicitas's one disastrous experience in the world of men causes her to back away from "sexual struggle," into a disappointing passivity in a world of sexless women and "oafish" men.[33] Gordon, however, defends her conclusion by saying that the novel is not about a woman who goes through rough times, "pulls herself up by her boot straps and goes and works for *Ms.* And most people do have severely limited lives. I mean, life does not always get out of the way so that we express ourselves to the fullest." She also states that Felicitas is "damaged." "She is not going to marry Alan Alda" ("RD" 74-75).

Here again we have the controversy I discussed in Chapter 2. Should fiction about women provide role models, portraying them as active doers, as makers of their destiny, or should it portray the reality of women's lives? Perhaps it is necessary to point out here that, in fact, Felicitas *has* consciously created her destiny, and what she has chosen is the life of most women, a life that *does* have value and meaning. It is only when we judge her life by the standards of male achievement that we find it wanting. As Felicitas herself tells us, men can make the desires, emotions, and thoughts of women seem foolish: "the sage as fire in whose flame must burn the fat female mind" (266-267). She believes that, in fact, she has a better mind than Cyprian.

Though *Company* is Felicitas's *bildungsroman*, it is also Cyprian's, and we find that he undergoes a radical transformation. He now realizes that he was wrong to oppose the changes in the Church with such unchristian wrath, that he joined the priesthood not to love God and humans but to exalt himself. Surprisingly, these insights have come from the example of women. He once saw the affection of these women as second best, as contemptible; and though he let them near him, he always patronized them. Now in his old age he feels "the great richness of the ardent, the extraordinary love I live among" (283-284). Sometimes he feels he betrays his priestly vows by loving these women so much; by loving as a brother and father he lacks the abstract love of the spirit: "They have won me, they have dragged me down to the middling terrain of their conception of the world, half blood instinct, half the impulse of the womb." These, however, are the residual thoughts of the patriarchal Church. Occasionally, Cyprian gets flashes that perhaps human love is enough, that it helps him understand the Incarnation for the first time: "Christ took on flesh for love, because the flesh is lovable" (285). And when he reflects on little Linda's beauty and cleverness, and considers the many mediocre men who have become priests, he prays every day for the ordination of women.

Needless to say, this transformation of the once patriarchal, austere Cyprian was not to the liking of some reviewers. Carol Iannone believes that the "doomed, savagely devout" priest represents the old Church itself, which, Gordon says, "needs to be cut loose from its male spiritual chauvinism . . . humanized, feminized, and brought down to earth by (the company of) women. . . . It is the female principle that will save Catholicism," but how the substitution of one orthodoxy for another will improve the Church is a mystery (65). This view sees the change in Cyprian as a kind of emasculation, similar to what Charlotte Brontë does to Rochester in order to make him worthy of Jane Eyre.

In my discussion of *Company*, I have neglected the relationships among the company—the intertwined lives of Charlotte, Elizabeth, Mary Rose, Clare, and the embittered Muriel, who, as one of life's losers, is psychically outside the company, being permitted there only out of abstract Christian charity. Gordon devotes considerable time to each of the women, who are types that illustrate various ideas about women but are also carefully drawn individuals. To me, the most interesting is Clare—the almost-nun businesswoman who describes herself as one of a dying breed: "the wise virgin, the well-dressed, clever spinster, interested in style but not in sex" (276). Clare has always been embarrassed that she does not desire sex and marriage like other women, but "she had never for one second wished another human to have access to her body" (25). Clare finds acceptance with her friends even though most of them have been married.

As we have seen with *Final Payments* and *Company*, like other feminist novelists Gordon has been very interested in friendships between women and skillful at describing them. As critics have pointed out, Gordon has a sharpness of observation on how women "are with each other."[34] In 1979 she discussed her ideas about female friendship, the essence of which is that though relations between men and women come and go, friendships with women endure. Just as the older women in *Company* find themselves nearing the end of their lives in the company of women they have been close to since childhood, most women can name such relationships in their own lives. Thankfully, the Women's Movement and novels like Mary Gordon's and others discussed in this study have made us realize the importance of these friendships to our lives; we are beginning to develop cultural traditions and romance about women's friendships similar to those of men's.

Gordon suggests that women have been notorious for deserting their women friends for men. Since women have been told by their society they are incomplete without men, they have been quick to break dates with women for men. And perhaps, says Gordon, these small betrayals have enriched our friendships, in that we have understood and forgiven them: "We did not expect salvation from women." It is true that men can give women something their women friends can't—sex (Gordon speaks of heterosexual women), and since sex is so highly charged, it "creates an instant and instinctive bond that nonsexual friendships cannot create." It also, however, encourages dishonesty, a kind of theatricality; sex is so powerful a force that it is very easy to be wrong about a person to whom you are attracted. Though the "most compelling of passions," sex is also the shortest-lived.[35] For a little while, we are totally absorbed, and then the storm subsides, to be replaced by indifference or, over time, love, in the same way love develops between women. It is to the benefit of women's friendships that they are less hectic than relations with men; they begin more slowly, and perhaps that explains why they often last longer.

Before considering Gordon's last two novels, I need to discuss a point made by several critics about both *Final Payments* and *The Company of Women*: their similarity to nineteenth-century novels, especially those by Charlotte Brontë and Jane Austen.[36] (Gordon has admitted she read *Jane Eyre* many times as a child.) In *Final Payments* Isabel says, on her father's death, "If it were the nineteenth century, I'd have become a governess" (63). Sarah Gilead notes the numerous parallels between *Final Payments* and nineteenth-century *bildungsromans*. The heroine begins as an orphan and quests for her self in a patriarchal world, thereby illuminating the "Woman Question"; friends are used as possible alter egos for the protagonist as well as enemies (Margaret Casey is cited by Isabel as one horrid possibility for her future in the same way that Bertha Rochester represents Jane's darker nature);[37] solutions are offered by Liz (jokingly) that resemble a Jane Austen novel—Isabel could be an aunt to Liz's kids, a sister to Liz

and a confidante to John, her husband; an important theme of the novel is
self-abnegation, often seen as a female virtue in the nineteenth century.
Gilead asserts that these similarities represent Gordon's conscious efforts
to tap into that rich female tradition, to assert many of its structures and
moral themes, at the same time adapting these themes to an era far more
"questioning of patriarchal traditions" (226). Her skillful use of these can-
onical works should not diminish our respect for Gordon's literary invention: she has made her "final payments" to the great literature of earlier
women writers (213).

MEN AND ANGELS: MOTHERHOOD AND SPIRITUAL EMPTINESS

With her third novel, *Men and Angels* (1985), Gordon moves away from
her Irish Catholic milieu to treat life in a family of "yuppies." According
to Gordon, this automatically makes the book less interesting to critics:
"Nobody wants to write about yuppies. It's much more interesting to write
about a closed, slightly secret, marginal group."[38] She says that *Final Payments* partly was successful because she was writing about a place that "the
sophisticated had not visited" ("RD" 81). However, though the physical
setting may be different, we find that the themes of *Men and Angels* are
similar to those of the first two novels, for the central concern is the contrast
between maternal love, love in the particular, and the abstract Christian
love of 1 Corinthians: "Though I speak with the tongues of men and angels,
and have not charity, I am become as a sounding gong or a tinkling cymbal."
A new theme, but related to earlier ones, is the conflict between a woman's
career and her role as mother.

Gordon's protagonist, Anne Foster, is mother of a son and a daughter
and "faculty wife" of Michael, a professor at a small college in upstate New
York. A thoroughly secular person, Anne represents a twentieth-century
rational woman, someone who has been reared outside any religious tradition, who has no consciousness of the holy and does not understand the
religious impulse in others.[39] Religious people embarrass her; she thinks
they "shouldn't talk about such things in public; it was like a libertine
bragging in front of virgins."[40] The main conflict in the novel stems from
the coming together of Anne and her children's nanny, a needy, disturbed
girl named Laura, a religious fanatic, who also represents the disastrous
effects of lack of mothering.

Margaret Drabble calls *Men and Angels* "deliberately domestic," almost
claustrophobic in its emphasis on the details of the life of the small-town
faculty wife: social life with friends and neighbors, all the gossip and infi-
delities resulting from this, housekeeping, and so on (1). Anne has a lovely
home, a shelter that she enjoys making comfortable for her family. Though
she loves domesticity, she escapes its "diminishment" through her work as

an art historian. At the beginning of the novel, Anne has received a challenging opportunity to write a catalogue describing the paintings of Caroline Watson, an artist who, like Mary Cassatt, concentrated on mothers and children, and whose work has therefore been neglected. (One sees a resemblance to the "undiscovered" women writers who have not been given their due because of their domestic subject matter.) At the same time, Michael will be taking a sabbatical abroad. Thus Gordon presents a problem typical in these families who have it all: what to do when husband's and wife's careers conflict. Though Anne's career has always been second to Michael's, she longs to accept this exciting commission, and Michael, like a good yuppie husband, is supportive (no domineering chauvinists here). The problem of the children is solved by hiring the doomed Laura, thus alleviating Anne's mother-guilt. In Chapter 3 I discussed how other authors have portrayed this guilt. In "Mary Gordon's Mothers" Ruth Perry describes it as

the freefloating mother-guilt felt by nearly all mothers in Anglo-American culture, independent of their individual circumstances—a guilt ready to attach itself to any phenomenon, a nagging feeling that we never do enough for our children or do it quite right, never properly protect them from danger and disappointment in the world, and are never quite sure that we have acted in their best interest.[41]

Gordon explores motherhood through the conflicts between Anne's family life and her job, and insights she gains on the project itself. Although Anne loves her job, she admits that her "ruling passion" is maternity, and as Drabble says, Gordon "tellingly evokes" that passion. Anne ruminates on the mystery of this powerful emotion: "No one had told her what it would be like, the way she loved her children. What a thing of the body it was, as physically rooted as sexual desire, but without its edge of danger" (22). She is painfully conscious that this love prevents women from achieving in the outside world, but it is impossible to not value that love above all, given its pleasure: "A mother was encumbered and held down ... [but Anne] felt that she was fortunate in that she loved the weighing down, the vivid body life the children lived and gave her" (74). These are the same sorts of feelings that Felicitas has for Linda—the ambiguity or double-edged sword of maternity—its restricting nature and compensations that give gifts not received by men. Unlike a writer like Marge Piercy, however, Gordon never suggests alternatives to the physicality of motherhood, for it is this "bodiliness" that humanizes women.

As Ruth Perry says, Gordon skillfully draws parallels between Anne's situation and Caroline Watson's (216). When Anne studies Caroline's work, she is astounded by its beauty and power, and angered at its neglect. She also finds herself angry at Caroline when she learns that she was a bad mother to her illegitimate son, Stephen, whom she never loved, feeling him to be a detriment to her work. When Stephen married a young woman named Jane, Caroline found she loved Jane and preferred her to Stephen, who died at twenty-eight, a miserable alcoholic. As Anne studies the family letters, she is struck by her own interest in the domestic life of Caroline. Surely we would not be concerned with what kind of father a male artist was. Why, then, do we want to know the "grossest facts" about successful women? We are curious because

for a woman to have accomplished something, she had to get out of the way of her own body. This was the trick people wanted to know about. Did she pull it off? . . . One wanted to believe that the price was not impossible for these accomplished women, that there were fathers, husbands, babies flourishing beside the beautiful work. For there so rarely were (82).

Society's expectations for mothers often prevent their artistic achievements, and, unlike fathers, we are not so willing to forgive the woman who is a poor parent.

Perry provides an interesting interpretation of Gordon's treatment of the conflict between maternal love and artistic creativity. Feminist scholars have shown that cultural attitudes draw an either/or dichotomy between a woman's impulses toward maternity and creativity. If a woman creates with her body, she cannot create with her mind. In *Men and Angels*, in her description of Anne's working process as she does her research on Caroline, Gordon brings together these seemingly disparate poles, showing many parallels between them. In fact, she provides in the novel a picture of Sara Ruddick's "maternal thinking" in action, "a blending of looking, holding (as opposed to acquiring), self restraint, humility, and empathy that comprises the maternal discipline" (215). Far from limiting a woman, motherhood can provide skills and insights useful in creative work. For example, in the case of a writer, characters in novels often take on a life of their own, just as children are intransigent, stubbornly refusing to be molded. Perry believes that Gordon is one of the first feminist novelists to integrate motherhood and intellectual life, showing their interconnections and "equally privileging" them (221).

Gordon also treats the theme of female friendship in *Men and Angels*. Jane, Caroline's powerful daughter-in-law, becomes a mentor to Anne, just as Caroline mentored Jane. Jane, unlike Anne, has a religious life, which surprises and discomforts Anne. Jane tells Anne that she turned to religion to alleviate the terrible guilt she felt at neglecting her husband in favor of his mother, and perhaps hastening his death. Religion, says Jane, "showed the possibility of forgiveness for the unforgivable" (280). This female mentorship of Anne by the older Jane is similar to those found in several other novels of the 1980s.[42] Anne finds she desperately wants Jane's approval: she courts her and hopes their friendship will be a deep one, not beginning in "intimacy and playing out in small talk, like some women's friendships"

(154). She fears that Jane will disrespect her love of marriage and maternity (Jane has lovers but has never remarried). In this analysis of Anne's and Jane's relationship, Gordon perceptively shows how maternity can divide women. Anne also has close relationships with women her own age—Barbara, a housewife who seems threatened by Anne's achievements, and Ianthe, a coworker whose flamboyant love affairs fascinate Anne.

Though he appears several times, Michael plays a secondary role in the story, which is unusual for a domestic novel, even one written from a feminist viewpoint. A loving, sensitive man and an active father, Michael supports his wife's career and is everything a contemporary woman could want. This deemphasis of a male as central in the life of the protagonist can "ghettoize" a writer, says Gordon. If a man is out of the central focus of a novel, critics "think you're writing for the Ladies Home Journal." Gordon also suggests that someone like Sue Miller has been successful because although she is writing about motherhood, a man is really at the center ("RD" 71). According to Ruth Perry, male/female sexuality need not play a central role in this novel because of the eroticism of both motherhood and the creative process, and the centrality of that process to Anne's life (219). She tries briefly to seduce Ed, an electrician who becomes a friend while Michael is gone, but is not especially upset when he refuses her.

Gordon ties her theme of motherhood to the religious conflict of the novel: Anne's inability to love the frightening, "radically damaged" Laura, who has been an unloved, unwanted child. Believing she is possessed by the Spirit, Laura feels that one should forget the love of the flesh: "Can a woman forget her sucking child, that she should have no compassion on the child of her womb? Even these may forget, yet I will not forget you" (Isaiah). She hopes she may "save" Anne and her family from the unholy life of the body. The warped Laura represents all that is distorted in the Christian tradition, the hatred of the flesh to extreme.

Through Laura, Anne, Caroline, and Jane, Gordon shows the mystery of love and what the lack of love can do. Ellen Macleod Mahon states that Laura attempts to find mother-love with Anne, who is unable to return it, being rooted in the physicality of love for her own children.[43] Susan Suleiman suggests a kind of doubling: the characters make possible our fantasies that mothers are either all good or all bad, and omnipotent in the lives of their children. Anne is a good mother to her own children and bad to Laura; Caroline Watson is a bad mother to her own son and a good mother to Jane, who is not her daughter. In this interpretation Anne and Laura are "two sides of a coin." Anne can use the crazy Laura, who endangers the children, to confirm her own goodness.[44] As Perry says, Gordon stresses the "inexplicability of maternal failure." Why did Caroline love Jane and reject Stephen, and Anne's and Laura's mothers reject Anne and Laura, to favor other children? (212-213). The answer to this puzzle is unknowable, part of the randomness of life that is so important in Gordon's worldview.

If the causes of maternal love or rejection are unknowable, however, a child's need for love is not. Luckily, most people get love somewhere. Both Anne and Michael have been somewhat neglected by their mothers, but Anne had a devoted father, and Michael's mother, though she failed to make an economically secure home for her fatherless son, gave him plenty of love, "a steamy rich affection, redolent of the cave" (30). Ed acts as surrogate mother (his wife is ill) for his son, who has obviously thrived under his love.

As in her other novels, in *Men and Angels* Gordon again examines the impossibility of spiritual love unconnected with the particular, this time connecting it with her theme of maternal love. As in *Final Payments*, the protagonist tries "spiritual" love, but it fails. In Anne's case, her impulse lies in secular, liberal good intentions, but the effect is the same. Although she dislikes Laura instantly and suspects there may be something wrong with her, Anne hopes to extend charity by hiring Laura and paying her small courtesies like gifts and a birthday party. Nevertheless, Anne's antipathy grows, and eventually her inability to love drives her to paroxysms of guilt—"I am an unjust person...I am a person who hates" (310). Like Margaret Casey and Muriel in "the company," Laura, one of life's losers, cannot inspire love.

The denouement of the novel has an ironic twist. Anne always sought to protect her family from danger, but has exposed them to it, for it is her son, Peter, who discovers Laura's blood-drained body in the bathtub. Deceived by Anne's kindnesses at first, the now-rejected Laura (fired because she endangered the children's lives) has decided that the only way she can get Anne's attention is through a blood sacrifice. The bloody water running down the living room walls symbolically shows the damage caused to Anne's family, which, unlike the water, cannot be cleaned up.

These horrible events are not easily resolved, certainly not by a turn to orthodoxy. As Anne asks, how can she "love a God who let a young girl bleed...? The only sane thing to say was that God was not within the Universe" (376). Jane provides the "revised" orthodox answers to the puzzles of Laura's life, saying that her death shows the dark, fearful side of God. But it should be remembered that Laura did not understand the Gospels—that she *was* greatly beloved. Even if she had, however, it would not have been enough, because "the love of God is always insufficient for the human heart. It can't keep us from despair as well as the most ordinary kindness from a stranger" (387). Anne weeps, not for love of Laura but for life, which

would raise its whip and bring it down again and again on the bare tender flesh of the most vulnerable. Love was what they needed and most often it was not there. It was abundant, love, but it could not be called. It was won by chance. (388)

Strangely, Anne feels, Laura has been a sacrifice for her work on Caroline Watson; if she had not been hired by Anne, the girl would still be alive. Here Gordon reiterates her theme in *Final Payments*: the "monstrousness" of life, which in doling out the good fortune of love, is seemingly so random and unjust (294). At the funeral the priest's words from Psalm 121—"I will lift up mine eyes unto the hills/from whence cometh my help?... The Lord shall preserve thee from all evil"—do not comfort. Obviously, Laura's God has not preserved her from life's dangers. At novel's end, Anne, still in her secular universe, rocks Peter and speculates on the impossibility of completely protecting children from life. She will try, she thinks, and will continue to turn from that impossible task to the refreshment of her work on Caroline Watson.

As with Gordon's two earlier novels, reaction to *Men and Angels* varies according to the reviewer's own position vis-à vis traditional Christianity. Though the feminist critics I have already cited found the story innovative, even brilliant, in its depictions of maternity, John Mahon points out the limitations of Gordon's view of love. Laura is correct in recognizing the "emptiness of the lives around her" (58). Mahon and Ellen Mahon note the eerie physical resemblance between Anne and Laura, John Mahon suggesting their spirits may be equally distorted. He hopes that Anne may come to acknowledge "the love that transcends human love, that consoles even in cases like Laura's." Secular families like the Fosters, outside the absolute love of the Christian community, can be at best only a "foster" family.[45] No doubt Gordon would point out that this universal community does not exist for ordinary people. She admires these traditions, which have been realized by a very few saints, but is concerned with finding a more truthful description of the way life is for most people.

THE OTHER SIDE: THE IRISH IMMIGRANT EXPERIENCE

Eleanor Wymward has pointed out that in *Men and Angels* and her collection of short stories, *Temporary Shelter*, Gordon seems to be moving away from "a readily identifiable Catholic tradition, thus muting her theme of religious affirmation" (158). However, close examination of Gordon's most recent novel, *The Other Side* (1989), shows many of the same themes: the clash between spirit and body so prevalent in Catholic tradition, and the related concept of the limitations of human love. The setting, too, is similar: an Irish Catholic neighborhood in Queens. One important difference is Gordon's choice of protagonist. In her earlier works she concentrated "on one woman's relationship to the world," but in this novel she focuses on an entire Irish immigrant family of four generations.[46] Though the novel says a great deal about the immigrant experience, the true focus is family life, the "domino effect" of how characters' actions affect not only their own children but also those farther down the family tree.

A "richly patterned domestic," *The Other Side* (the title refers to the term the immigrants gave to the New World) concerns the MacNamara family, a close-knit clan containing sixteen people (not including husbands, wives, and lovers, each of whom is also given attention).[47] The action takes place during one day in August 1985, with the past being told in a series of flashbacks going back to turn-of-the-century Ireland. Unlike Gordon's other novels, there is considerable attention to male characters—in fact, action centers on the eighty-eight-year-old patriarch, Vincent MacNamara. His life provides the "single line that stretches through the generations, through one house, through a life lived beside one woman, through children going out and coming back to do him honor."[48] Though Vincent, described by his granddaughter Camille as a gentleman and a prince, provides a focus, Gordon's attention moves from character to character as each contemplates past and present, the mysterious connections of love and hate between them all.

Vincent, his wife, Ellen, and their descendants have had the classic immigrant experience: laborers, union organizers, and now middle-class professionals. Though they have "made their journey to the outside . . . they came home to live" (21). These are people to whom family is everything. Incapable of sharing themselves with outsiders, they live in a steamy society of their own, full of anger, beauty, shame, fear, and sometimes joy. Gordon's chief concern is how their characters were formed and how they relate to each other; the purpose is not to illuminate their pasts so they may change, since few of these people seem capable of change.

Through Ellen's story, Gordon shows the obstacles faced by women in traditional Irish society. Though Ellen made a happy marriage to Vincent, a deformed childhood had warped her personality and she has not loved all her children equally, thus deforming them. Ninety years old and dying, Ellen is still furious at the past. Her mother was a beautiful, happy woman, the center of life and warmth for her daughter. However, a series of miscarriages, some witnessed by Ellen, change her whole life. Ellen's father, a wealthy publican and grocer, "sickened by the women's mess of it" (88), took a mistress and effectively left his family, causing his wife to go insane and his daughter to become bitter.

In the story of the degeneration of Ellen's beautiful mother, who becomes "fat and gibbering," Gordon shows sympathy for the "barren" women, a failure in the Irish society of 1911, but she also sympathizes with the confused husband and the helpless child:

Her mother took to resting in the afternoons. She was nearly always pregnant, or getting over the loss of a child. But she was never whole with child. The children broke her, or they broke her heart. He [the father] went on doing it, the thing he did to her that made it happen. (91)

Ellen now hates her father, whom she had always loved and felt was like herself. When the guilt-ridden man comes to her for forgiveness, he is given "stone." He accepts this punishment, believing he deserves it, and admires Ellen for her hatred, bragging to the villagers that Ellen has a "great head for business, better than any man in the district" (94-96). The culprit here is not the individual man, but a society that bases a woman's entire worth on her reproductive ability.

This experience causes Ellen to develops a chip on her shoulder for the entire world but especially for her own sex. She sees most women as weaker than she, who worked so capably in her father's business and took care of her demented mother. Ellen internalizes the lesson that her own sex is somehow contemptible. Later, when she has three children—Teresa, Magdalene, and John—she obviously prefers the boy. The girls, not suffering in childhood as she did, seem weak and unremarkable to her; like most American girls they are concerned with trivialities like boys and clothes.

In the story of the young immigrant Ellen, Gordon dignifies these young women who suffered, worked, and made lives for themselves. Haughty Ellen realizes the degradation of her first job as a lady's maid; she will not give up her day off as a special favor to her employer, telling a friend after she quits: "I'm out of service and I thank God for it. You're a fool if you don't get out" (120). During her next job, as a needlewoman, Ellen meets one of her few female friends, Bella, a fierce young Communist who introduces Ellen to radical ideas. Together they talk not about silly girl things, or relationships with men, but ideas: "the fierce, shy friendship of two girls, made up of adoration, mutual humility, a sense of honor, and momentarily the lifting of the curse that is their life: poverty, hard labor, the female sex" (121). As she does elsewhere, Gordon shows that women's friendships go much beyond boyfriends, husbands, and babies, and are based partly in the knowledge of their difference, the fact that they are not men and not valued. Later Ellen and Bella become involved in the Women's Trade Union League and try to organize the other girls in the shop. Bella is also a spiritual mentor, and through her, Ellen learns to despise the conservative, antiunion Church that says women should have babies and keep out of public life.

Ellen's relationship with Bella supplies her with intellectual stimulation, but her relationship with Vincent satisfies her passionate nature, which she attributes to her licentious father. Within Ellen there is a consciousness, instilled by the Church and her society, that her woman's body is a curse and a weakness. With the change to a woman's body—"breasts, hair, blood, monthly pain," and the birth of children—she feels a loss of self (121). However, the passionate love of her young husband, Vincent, for that body makes her happy, and later she never doubts the rightness of her union to Vincent, whose body she loves as he does hers:

They had been beautiful, young. High-colored. They had talked, though not as well as she could talk with Bella. Vincent hadn't the quickness of Bella's mind, hadn't read as much. But talk with them had come from and gone back to the body. Garlands their words were, that twined around them, joining them, limb to interlocking limb. It was more truthful, what they said because of that knowing. (137)

It is that physical side to her nature that keeps Ellen from living a public life, unlike Bella, who never has children. Once again Gordon reiterates how until very recently the life of the body kept women from achieving in the outside world. Though Ellen reads avidly about politics and argues about issues with her family, she fears speaking up at union meetings, and after retiring she seldom leaves her home or invites people into it. Unlike Bella, she is unable to shake the restrictions of her background. Though some feminist critics might fault Gordon for not making her main female character a "role model" like Bella, having known older immigrant women, I found Gordon's rendering of Ellen sympathetic and realistic. As feminist theorists explain, a woman like Ellen is afflicted by lack of self-esteem; though she cannot articulate it, she senses how her sex and her background have restricted her, and she directs her anger toward other women.

The complexity of Ellen's character is rivaled by that of her granddaughter Camille, a divorce lawyer who, like her great-grandmother in Ireland, suffers from her female body. However, in this convoluted family one cannot understand a character without looking at parental, especially maternal, relationships. Camille is the daughter of Magdalene, one of Ellen's two rejected daughters (the other, Teresa, is a cold, austere religious fanatic who cannot love her own children). As a child Magdalene cannot get attention from Ellen, who resists the softness of her maternal feelings. In contrast with Ellen, Vincent prefers his daughters to the son, but the negative effects of Ellen's lack of love seem to outweigh the positive effects of the father's love.

Because she struggles as a child to achieve love, Magdalene develops "no notion of herself apart from the responses she could engender" (165). All is surface to Magdalene, who seeks images of female glamour in movies and attention by leaving home to marry young. To do this, she has to have sex, which shocks the naive Magdalene. Since she gains no attention from having sex, she sees no profit to it and is frigid. Eventually, after her young husband's death, Magdalene develops into a successful entrepreneur—the owner of a beauty parlor. Though she gives her daughter, Camille, some love and attention, she leaves her during the day with Ellen. Ellen perceives Magdalene is bringing up the child to be insubstantial, like herself, and takes charge of her education, sending her to public schools and encouraging her reading. Thus, Cam's achievements as a lawyer are in large part due to Ellen, one of the few examples in the novel of positive female influence on younger women. For her part, Magdalene's resentment toward Ellen grows stronger as she grows older, her lack of self-confidence and her softness leading her to alcoholism and agoraphobia.

Besides documenting the effects of lack of mothering, Gordon examines the role of daughter. Camille has become Magdalene's mother, feeling that somehow she has caused her mother's problems. People often remark how different she is from her mother, and in the "matrophobia" of Adrienne Rich, Camille denies her ties to Magdalene:

Not for her the fashionable romance dragged up, patched together, by her friends and fellow feminists.... *Mother. Darling. We are the same. Only the wicked system made us push away*.... When her friends speak like this she doesn't even pretend interest. When they talk about their mothers she feels like a Bolshevik listening to White Russians talk about the old life. (318-319)

Camille believes that she does not love her mother, who represents "everything I never want to be..." and also reminds her of her own mortality: "You show me what I will become" (317-318). Though Camille does love her mother and is brokenhearted by her decay, her feelings are decidedly ambivalent, similar to the feelings of most women in feminist novels toward their mothers (as we saw in Chapter 3). Just as the theorists on mother-daughter relations discuss, we can see here the tensions produced by identification with the mother as victim. In other Gordon novels this ambivalence predominates: Isabel Moore has no mother, Anne Foster is unloved by her mother, Felicitas bitterly rejects her mother, and most of the mothers and daughters in *The Other Side* are estranged in some way.

Camille's story also brings to light other feminist themes, including the pressure on women to marry and the indifference of the health care establishment to women's problems. In the 1960s Camille married a Catholic boy she did not love mostly because she was so grateful to be desired by a man at the age of twenty-four. Their marriage immediately goes bad because of painful intercourse due to undiagnosed endometriosis, a disease few doctors then understood. Some tell Camille it is in her head, and she finally has a hysterectomy in her thirties, becoming the barren woman so pitied in Catholic society. At the same time, ironically, her lack of children makes her more impressive to her prospective boss. For these Irish Catholics, motherhood disqualifies women for success in the workplace. After her operation Camille's weak, ineffectual husband, Bob, who has blamed himself, never attempts to have sex with her again, although they continue to live together in a sexless marriage.

Throughout *The Other Side* Gordon shows a great deal of sympathy for her male characters caught in the traditional roles of marriage. Besides poor Bob, we see that the courtly Vincent regrets the changes that motherhood has brought about in his feisty, curious Ellen. Cam's lover, Ira, is a sensuous Jewish man who is sometimes relieved that Cam does not want to live with him:

He is terrified of the imperialistic life of women in a house. She [Cam] doesn't live like that.... He remembers his anguished attempts to satisfy those domestic hungers in his wives: the time he bought a child's paintbrush and spent a week painting antique molding. . . . He recalls agonized trips to paintshops, wallpaper books that blurred before his eyes. (328)

More than most other feminist novelists I have studied, Gordon shows how traditional roles tyrannize and limit both sexes. These are characters who live the roles dictated to them, whether Irish immigrants, or lower-middle-class, or yuppies. In keeping with the broad themes found in all of Gordon, most are not able to surmount the dictates of culture.

I have left a great deal out of the warp and woof of this complex family tapestry, but I have shown how Gordon uses these relationships to bring out her perennial themes. Characters suffer because they are not loved enough, and sometimes this deforms them to the extent that they harm others; they suffer because of guilt induced by the traditional Church or society, guilt that makes them hate or fear their own bodies. Yet despite this suffering, they experience closeness and joy in their relationships, and this closeness somehow mirrors, though perhaps less obviously than in Gordon's earlier novels, the human relationship to the divine.

As Madison Smartt Bell points out, the world in *The Other Side* is a fallen world, perhaps even a world without a traditional God. For Vincent, God is "some person whom your tears will interest," but he also wonders if he has made God up. Ultimately, the novel celebrates what Dan, another of the grandchildren, calls "the wholeness" of life, "the intricate connecting tissue . . . this terrible endeavor, this impossible endeavor" (349). All of us in some way impinge, sometimes awfully, "monstrously," on each other, but we also connect in a mysterious whole that with love provides a sense of unity. This is mighty close to the universal Christian community of the early Church.

A CRITICAL ASSESSMENT

What kind of feminist writer is Mary Gordon? Certainly she cannot be labeled "radical," as Marge Piercy can be. Although she certainly condemns society's treatment of women, we do not see the sweeping condemnation of "patriarchy" that we find in the radical feminist writers. Despite what some critics have said, her novels do not seem to be written with her eye directly on feminist theories, although she certainly shows an awareness of such ideas, and much of what she deals with has little to do with radical feminist issues; her work lacks the monolithic concern for women's oppression as *the* primary issue that people must face. Then, too, her novels celebrate (as well as criticize) the traditional roles of women, such as motherhood, in a way that radical feminist writing does not. In this sense she could be called a cultural feminist. Studying a writer like Mary Gordon shows it is unwise to label women writers or to tie them too closely to particular feminist ideologies.

As I stated in my introduction to this chapter, Mary Gordon has generally achieved critical acclaim for all her novels, especially *Final Payments*. Reviewers have praised her passionate, poetic style, her sensitive rendering of women's quests, her sympathy for her characters, and above all, her ability to weave profoundly religious themes into all her works. However, as I have mentioned, there have been detractors, and a reply to some of these may further illuminate Gordon's achievements.

Like other novels about women's lives, Gordon's works have been scornfully referred to as "women's novels," just a step above the fiction in the better women's magazines: "Without the defining element of religion, the resemblance of her novels to the genre known as 'women's fiction' (in which omnicompetent heroines battle through impossible odds toward inevitable triumph) would no doubt have been more readily discerned."[49] As we have seen, Maureen Howard feels that there are elements in *Final Payments* which resemble "working girl" fiction, but the religious and social themes push the novel farther than this. Even the term "domestic novel," used to describe Gordon's novels, reveals a subtle bias toward Gordon's concentration on the lives of married women and children, a kind of "ghettoization." On the other hand, critics like Margaret Drabble, Francine du Plessix Gray, and Ann-Janine Morey have praised Gordon's insights into women's lives: "Gordon genuinely likes women. She is interested in them as a group and as individuals, and her writing is somehow different because of this interest." Unlike the works of the revered male writers such as John Updike, where women are the "cosmic generic," woman are participants and individuals in Gordon's universe. Through women protagonists, Gordon examines themes of universal human significance, and "most of us cannot afford or endure such self-satisfied parochialisms" as dismissing a writer as a "woman's writer."[50]

Then there is that group of critics who, rather than calling Gordon a superficial, lightweight writer, object to her treatment of religious themes and philosophical questions. Paul Ableman says that because Gordon tries so earnestly to invite judgment by "moral rather than literary criteria," the characters are not real. This is theology posing as fiction. Though Gordon is a "natural writer" who has the ability to write a splendid novel, she needs to drop the moralizing.[51] Even du Plessix Gray feels that Gordon's concern for moral questions makes her perhaps more germane to the philosophical tradition than to the novel.[52] This criticism seems influenced by the postmodernist view that fiction should take a disinterested view of the universe, certainly a view at odds with the nineteenth century with which Gordon identifies. The truth is that literary fashion changes; one hundred years ago most critics would have condemned writing that did not adopt moral positions. Many of Gordon's readers, including myself, find her treatment of moral issues in a fictional framework fascinating and refreshingly unique.

Finally, there are those critics, some of whom I have already cited, who dislike Gordon's moral conclusions, whether because she revises traditional Christian teaching or because she reflects feminist ideas. Brenda Becker, for example, says that Gordon's work reflects the "feminist dirge" that "men, self, God and Happiness don't work in any combination." When the Christian framework is "emptied of conviction, it is not a kind, ethical retreat for battered women, but a monstrous, lying fraud." Because the figure of a personal Christ is missing, Gordon is "cheating" (28). To Carol Iannone, Gordon reconciles the self-serving tenets of materialism and the "agitated emptiness" of feminism with the demand for self-renunciation of Catholicism. Her heroines can have some of the gifts of faith without believing in God; they can "have it all"—husband, children, friends, rewarding career, and warm spiritual ideas—without giving up anything (66). However, even these critics seem to be provoked by Gordon's ideas and grant her powers of observation about her social milieu, as well as her extraordinary skill with language.

One perceived weakness of Gordon's writing is male characters, especially in the first two novels. She did "unsexed" males such as priests or the priestlike father in *Final Payments* brilliantly, but her "sexed males," those who have sexual contact with the protagonist, are unconvincing. James Wolcott says that Gordon admits she does not know what goes on in men's heads. Thus her men are "figures hewn from trees and imbued with the spirit of brooding gods." Susan Lardner agrees, saying that men in Gordon are gods or oafs.[53] Surely, however, one's reaction to Gordon's men depends in part on one's own view of the sex. Gordon points out that male critics said Robert in *The Company of Women* was "totally unrealistic," but many women said, "I knew him" ("RD" 73). Certainly in her last two novels Gordon has portrayed males much more sympathetically and skillfully. As I have pointed out, some other feminist novelists, after portraying men in rather one-dimensional ways in earlier works, have achieved more complex portrayals.

One might also object to Gordon's insistence on the "monstrousness" of life and the women characters' seeming inability to surmount the dictates of their cultures. However, Gordon also insists on the beauty and mystery of life and the gifts of love. Though she indeed revises orthodox Christian ideas, her characters always demand of themselves the elusive ideal of Christian love of the Other, although they do not achieve it (as most of us do not). And many of her characters do make happy lives, in the process achieving a good amount of self-understanding, sometimes even rejecting limiting parts of their culture. Though she does not always provide the role models demanded by some feminist critics, Gordon's stories about women's lives explore important moral truths and real problems faced by many women in our society.

As Ann Janine Morey says, one should not emphasize the universality of Gordon at the expense of the particular. Her novels explore the particular problems of women as well as universal human questions. Though her protagonists do not find belief, they are able to find happiness in a synthesis of traditional Christian ideas with the ideas of contemporary feminism. That Gordon has been able to do this is a "nigh impossible task."[54] Is Gordon still a Roman Catholic? In 1987 she said, "It shifts back and forth, and I feel that I should be allowed to shift. I can change back in the next month" ("RD" 81). Whether or not Mary Gordon remains a practicing Catholic is beside the point, for it is doubtful that her writing will cease to reflect the rich insights her heritage has given her.

NOTES

1. Several studies discussing patriarchy in traditional religion are Mary Daly, *The Church and the Second Sex* (Boston: Harper, 1968) and *Beyond God the Father: Toward a Philosophy of Women's Liberation* (Boston: Beacon, 1973); and Naomi Goldenberg, *Changing of the Gods: Feminism and the End of Traditional Religions* (Boston: Beacon, 1979).

2. See Monica Sjoo and Barbara Mor, *The Great Cosmic Mother: Rediscovering the Religion of the Earth* (San Francisco: Harper & Row, 1986); Anne E. Carr, *Transforming Grace: Christian and Women's Experience* (San Francisco: Harper & Row, 1988); Carol P. Christ and Judith Plaskow, eds., *Womanspirit Rising: A Feminist Reader in Religion* (San Francisco: Harper & Row, 1979); Rosemary Radford Reuther, *Sexism and God-Talk: Toward a Feminist Theology* (Boston: Beacon, 1983); and Mary Jo Weaver, *The Contemporary Challenge to Traditional Religious Authority* (San Francisco: Harper & Row, 1988) for some examples of woman-centered theologies.

3. See Bonnie Hoover Braendlin, "Alther, Atwood, Ballantyne, and Gray: Secular Salvation in the Contemporary Feminist *Bildungsroman*," *Frontiers* 4 (1979), 18-22.

4. Joseph J. Feeney, "The American Religious Imagination and Three Contemporary Imaginers: A Look at Mary Gordon, Tom McHale and Andre Dubus," in *The Incarnate Imagination: Essays in Theology, the Arts, and Social Sciences*, ed. Ingrid H. Shafer (Bowling Green, OH: Bowling Green State University Popular Press, 1988), 163.

5. John Neary, "Mary Gordon's *Final Payments*: A Romance of the One True Language," *Essays in Literature* 17 (Spring 1990), 108.

6. Nan Robertson, "Mary Gordon, Mary Gordon," *Critic* 37 (September 1978), 4, 5. Hereafter abbreviated "MG."

7. M. Deiter Keyishian, "Radical Damage: An Interview with Mary Gordon," *The Literary Review* 32 (Fall 1988), 76. Hereafter abbreviated "RD."

8. Mary Gordon, "The Fate of Women of Genius," *New York Times Book Review* (13 September 1981), 7.

9. Bruce Allen, "First Novels," review of *Final Payments* by Mary Gordon, *Sewanee Review* 86 (Fall 1978), 616; David Lodge, "The Arms of the Church," *Times Literary Supplement* (1 September 1978), 965.

10. Brenda Becker, "Virgin Martyrs," review of *The Company of Women* by Mary Gordon, *The American Spectator* 14 (August 1981), 28.

11. John Leonard, "The Saint as Kill Joy," review of *Final Payments* by Mary Gordon, *The New York Times* (4 April 1978), sec. 3, 31.

12. Ann-Janine Morey, "Beyond Updike: Incarnated Love in the Novels of Mary Gordon," *The Christian Century* (20 November 1985), 1060.

13. Wilfrid Sheed, "The Defector's Secrets," review of *Final Payments* by Mary Gordon, *New York Review of Books* 25 (1 June 1978), 14.

14. Barbara Hill Rigney, *Lilith's Daughters: Women and Religion in Contemporary Fiction* (Madison: University of Wisconsin Press, 1982), 39.

15. Mary Gordon, *Final Payments* (New York: Ballantine, 1978), 6.

16. Maureen Howard, "Salvation in Queens," review of *Final Payments* by Mary Gordon, *New York Times Book Review* (16 April 1978), 33.

17. Mary Gordon, "Getting Here from There: A Writer's Reflections on a Religious Past," in *Spiritual Quests: The Art and Craft of Religious Writing*, ed. William Zinsser (Boston: Houghton Mifflin, 1988), 26-29.

18. In "Coming to Terms with Mary," *Commonweal* (15 January 1982), 11-14, Gordon discusses antifemale attitudes in the Church and suggests that Mary, the sensuously sweet Mother of God, can provide a bridge between body and spirit.

19. See Howard, "Salvation in Queens," and Sheed, "The Defector's Secrets."

20. Peter Prescott, "Living Sacrifice," review of *Final Payments* by Mary Gordon, *Newsweek* (10 April 1978), 92.

21. John W. Mahon, "Mary Gordon: The Struggle with Love," in *American Women Writing Fiction: Memory, Identity, Family, Space*, ed. Mickey Pearlman (Lexington: University Press of Kentucky, 1988), 52.

22. Eleanor B. Wymward, "Mary Gordon: Her Religious Sensibility," *Cross Currents* 37 (Summer/Fall, 1987), 157.

23. Sarah Gilead, "Mary Gordon's *Final Payments* and the Nineteenth-Century English Novel," *Critique* 27 (Summer 1986), 226.

24. Neary, "Mary Gordon's *Final Payments*," 108.

25. See Rosemary Radford Reuther, *New Woman, New Earth: Sexist Ideologies and Human Liberation* (New York: Seabury Press, 1975); and Marina Warner, *Alone of All Her Sex: The Myth and Cult of the Virgin Mary* (New York: Pocket Books, 1976). Mary Daly says that the cult of Mary harks back to the Great Goddess, but lost the reverence for the female. Mary contains no significance without the fact that she is the Mother of God.

26. Carol Iannone, "The Secret of Mary Gordon's Success," *Commentary* 79 (June 1985), 64.

27. Mary Gordon, "Works in Progress," *New York Times Book Review* (15 July 1979), 14.

28. See Francine du Plessix Gray, "A Religious Romance," *New York Times Book Review* (15 February 1981), 1.

29. *Contemporary Authors*, ed. Frances C. Locher, vol. 102 (Detroit: Gale Research, 1981), 225.

30. Mary Gordon, *The Company of Women* (New York: Ballantine, 1980), 24.

31. For example, see James Wolcott, "More Catholic Than the Pope," *Esquire* 95 (3 March 1981), 23; Becker, "Virgin Martyrs," 29.

32. Helen McNeil, "Miraculous Births," *Times Literary Supplement* (3 July 1981), 747.

33. See ibid.; Wolcott, "More Catholic Than the Pope," 21; and Susan Lardner, "No Medium," *New Yorker* 57 (6 April 1981), 177-178.

34. Becker, "Virgin Martyrs," 30.

35. Mary Gordon, "Women's Friendships," *Redbook* 153 (July 1976), 31ff.

36. Besides Wymward, Sheed and Leonard cite similarities with Jane Austen, Leonard saying that Gordon is as good with female friendship as Austen.

37. Sandra M. Gilbert and Susan Gubar, *The Madwoman in the Attic: The Woman Writer and the Nineteenth Century Literary Imagination* (New Haven: Yale University Press, 1979). In this study Gilbert and Gubar discuss the use of doubles in nineteenth-century women's fiction, often of a sinister nature, in order to illuminate a heroine's darker side.

38. Joseph Berger, "Being Catholic in America," *New York Times Magazine* (23 August 1987), 65.

39. Margaret Drabble, "The Limits of Mother Love," *New York Times Book Review* (31 March 1985), 1.

40. Mary Gordon, *Men and Angels* (New York: Ballantine, 1985), 270.

41. Ruth Perry, "Mary Gordon's Mothers," in *Narrating Mothers: Theorizing Maternal Subjectivities*, ed. Brenda O. Daly and Maureen T. Reddy (Knoxville: University of Tennessee Press, 1991), 210.

42. See, for example, Celie's relationship to Shug in *The Color Purple*, ch. 3, and Justin's relationship to Ursula in Gail Godwin's *The Finishing School* (New York: Viking, 1985).

43. Ellen Macleod Mahon, "The Displaced Balance: Mary Gordon's *Men and Angels*," in *Mother Puzzles: Mothers and Daughters in Contemporary American Literature*, ed. Mickey Pearlman (Westport, CT: Greenwood, 1989), 91-99.

44. Susan Rubin Suleiman, "On Maternal Splitting: A Propos of Mary Gordon's *Men and Angels*," *Signs* 14 (1988), 25-41.

45. Ellen Mahon, "The Displaced Balance" 93; John Mahon, "Mary Gordon," 58-60.

46. Michiko Kakatani, "Past Traced to the Present in a Family's Intricate Story," *New York Times* (10 October 1989), sec. 3, 21.

47. Madison Smartt Bell, *New York Times Book Review* (15 October 1989), 9.

48. Mary Gordon, *The Other Side* (New York: Viking, 1989), 9.

49. Iannone, "The Secret of Mary Gordon's Success," 63.

50. Morey, "Beyond Updike," 1060, 1062.

51. Paul Ableman, "Last Things," *The Spectator* (13 January 1979), 23.

52. *Contemporary Authors*, ed. Frances C. Locher, vol. 102, 224.

53. Prescott, "Living Sacrifice," 92; Wolcott, "More Catholic Than the Pope," 21; Lardner, "No Medium," 177.

54. McNeil, "Miraculous Births," 747.

6

Toni Morrison: African-American Women and Men, an Uneasy Alliance

In her review of Toni Morrison's critical study *Playing in the Dark: Whiteness and the Literary Imagination* (1991), Wendy Steiner asserts that at present Morrison is the closest we have to a national writer. While building her deserved reputation Morrison has had an advantage in being a woman and black because it seems that now the "path to a common voice runs through the partisan."[1] Through her portrayals of black women and men, Morrison has forced white Americans to confront their own dark side and has celebrated the joy and pain of being human, thus achieving a truly universal worldview.

When I began this study four years ago, a growing body of Morrison scholarship already existed, but little dealing directly with feminist themes in her writing or using feminist critical theories to discuss her work. Such is no longer the case; several excellent studies have been published, to my mind the best being Barbara Rigney's *The Voices of Toni Morrison*, which connects Morrison to the theories of the French feminists.[2] The French feminists such as Julia Kristeva, Hélène Cixous, and Luce Irigaray have called on women writers to write from the body, to penetrate the unconscious zones outside the language of the patriarchy, and allow their language to become "unruly" and loose. Then, in Morrison's own words, "it can bring things to the surface that men—trained to be men in a certain way—have difficulty getting access to."[3]

Though Rigney carefully qualifies her approach, saying that one can never separate the work of black writers from their race, Morrison delineates what the French feminists call a feminist practice of writing, "a zone that is 'outside' of literary convention, that disrupts traditional Western ideological confines and modifies patriarchal inscriptions" (*VTM* 1). Such writing can be more radical than that more closely adhering to traditional conventions of form and language. Being black has been especially useful, because in Western culture blackness has always represented a "wild zone," the contemplation of which can allow whites to deal with what they deny in themselves. As Rigney points out, the French feminists themselves use blackness as a metaphor for marginality and "radical dissidence."[4] Rigney makes a persuasive argument that Morrison's fiction includes the linguistic disorder and anarchy that is feminist and politically radical.

It may be wondered why I chose to examine Toni Morrison rather than an Afro-American woman writer more easily identified as a feminist, such as Alice Walker, Gloria Naylor, or Paule Marshall. To my mind, Toni Morrison more obviously represents the difficulty of applying white feminist ways of thinking about women's problems and women's literature to black writers. Her work, though always celebrating the strengths and deploring the sufferings of black women, shows far more sympathy to men than does the work of white feminist writers, and even some other black women writers. She often explains the abuse of black women by their men as a result of the crippling institutions of society that deny black men their manhood. In addition, in her celebration of the nurturant power of black women, she calls into question the goals of some factions of the white feminist movement. Like many black women, she is not always sympathetic to the seeming obsessions and results of "women's liberation." To her mind, women free themselves from their traditional roles as lovers of men and nurturers of children at their own peril as women and human beings.

From the beginning of the Women's Movement, many black women hesitated to speak out about sexism, recognizing that although black males often held sexist attitudes, it seemed disloyal and distracting to focus on the problems of women when the oppression of blacks was such a pressing concern. Further, the experience of black women made it difficult for them to identify with the concerns of white middle-class housewives or young women struggling to enter the professions. Black women had long worked outside the home to help support their families, often at low-pay, low-status jobs. Although some black women, especially those in academe, have come to identify themselves as feminists, it is always as black feminists, and their relationship with white feminists has been wary. Alice Walker has coined the term "womanist" to describe her own brand of black feminism. A womanist writer "will recognize that, along with her consciousness of sexual issues, she must incorporate racial, cultural, national, economic, and political considerations into her philosophy."[5] The womanist writer, says Walker, is "committed to survival and wholeness of entire people, male *and* female."[6]

The term "womanist" has been applied to Morrison's view as well.[7] Her *primary* project is, as a black writer, to expose, through writing that is always political in theme and purpose, the injustices of black life in America.[8] Her vehicle for this project is the experience of black women, who "are the touchstone by which all that is human can be measured." Because they have been marginalized, abused by white men, excluded from the pedestal of white women, and served as the buttress of their men and children, black women have understandings that are deep and an angle of vision on American life that is unique.[9] Morrison is especially annoyed when critics praise her for moving beyond the viewpoint of a "black woman writer," to some kind of abstract universal view. Surely, says Morrison, her focus on black women should not deny her universality. It is important to qualify her concern with black women, however, by stressing that at no point does Morrison identify with the political feminism associated with white feminism. Morrison surely shows the "differences" within American feminism—that ways of viewing women's experience are varied and sometimes contradictory.

Near the beginning of her writing career in 1971, Morrison discussed the black woman's attitude toward the Women's Liberation Movement. This interview illuminates the tension in her writing between feminist issues and black liberation. First of all, she says, white feminism is white, and therefore automatically suspect. Second, black women, who see themselves as tough and capable, often lack respect for white women, soft and helpless "ladies." The black woman feels little in common with the privileged white housewife, who may have a black maid. To some extent, Morrison agrees with Ida Lewis, editor in chief of *Essence* magazine, who said, "The Women's Liberation Movement is basically a family quarrel between white women and white men."

As Morrison sees it, the job of the black woman writer and scholar is to document the different experiences of black women, a group that so seldom has been spoken for. Black women writers should examine the female archetypes—the sexy, sassy Geraldine; and Sapphire, the nagging wife of Kingfish—which, even if concocted by men, contain the "sweet smell of truth." These types can be offensive because they portray the strengths of black women as weaknesses, but they are true because they show the triumph of the black woman over terrible odds. The black woman has raised her family, worked outside the home, and "had nothing to fall back on: not maleness, not whiteness, not ladyhood, not anything. And out of the profound desolation of her reality she may very well have invented herself." Like Sapphire, sometimes she fought and nagged her husband, who found it difficult to deal with a "competent and complete personality," and was driven by his shame to leave her and their children. Thus black women have had the freedom white women crave, but it is not sweet because it has been forced on them.[10] It is this invention of herself, the use of the black woman's bitter freedom, that Morrison has documented so well.

The details of Morrison's life have often been told, but perhaps there are a few points that need to be stressed. One is her roots in Lorain, Ohio, in some sense a peculiar place for an American black to grow up—not rural South, not urban North. This was a working-class community of many ethnic groups, and Morrison learned not the inferiority imposed on southern blacks but the value of ethnic differences. From her parents, who were educated and encouraged her reading, she gained strong role models of women and an intense dislike for white people. She describes her home as "racist." Her mother and father shared roles in the family, and there was a sense of "comradeship" between them and her grandparents, who lived with them.[11] In her family and the black community of Lorain, Morrison learned through stories and myth that there are "ways of knowing that encompassed more than concrete reality."[12]

Morrison is one of the most celebrated authors in the United States. Her works have all the complexity and ambiguity demanded by the literary establishment; her first five novels were all greeted with extravagant praise; the verdict on the most recent, *Jazz* (1991), is still pending. Because her work offers such a fertile field for criticism, it has been exhaustively examined: for example, her narrative strategies, her marvelous imagery, replete with symbolism, her adaptation of Afro-American fable and folklore, her depictions of black communities, and her incorporation of Western myths such as the quest. Her style is varied, sometimes spare and direct, elsewhere lush, almost florid. Perhaps the best description of her prose is Barbara Christian's "fantastic earthy realism."[13] In her stories people fly, nature is anthropomorphized, and ghosts exist; yet unlike some white writers' use of the fantastic, the reader accepts, perhaps because she understands the author does, too. When asked by an interviewer whether she believed in ghosts, Morrison returned the question with "Do you believe in germs?"[14] In Afro-American culture, the dimension of the spirit has a reality not acknowledged in white culture. As Barbara Rigney says, with Morrison "magic realism" is not an oxymoron (*VTM* 27).

THE BLUEST EYE: A SAD BLACK GIRLHOOD

Morrison's first novel, *The Bluest Eye* (1970), is a dark work, holding little hope of triumph over the terrible conditions it depicts. Pecola Breedlove's story shows her complete victimization by both white and black culture.[15] Unlike the protagonists of the hopeful white feminist *bildungsromans* of the early 1970s, Pecola has no way to invent herself because she and her family totally accept white standards of beauty, and according to them, Pecola is ugly.[16] Pecola hopes for blue eyes because then she would be pretty and loved. This is a theme especially relevant to women because in the black culture, as in white, a woman's self-esteem is derived more from her beauty than a man's is from handsomeness. Thus, black women labor under a twofold yoke: the impossible standards of beauty of white culture and the importance their own culture places on female beauty.

In all her novels Morrison is concerned with motherhood, but even more than some white feminist writers, she exposes the dangerous side of mothering. In the relationship between Pecola and her mother, Pauline, Morrison successfully deconstructs the myth of the Afro-American matriarch, the sort of woman depicted in Lorraine Hansberry's *A Raisin in the Sun*. This image of the strong, nurturing, self-effacing, wise mother who supports her children, often with her man gone or broken by white oppression, has been powerful in black culture and, indeed, in the culture as a whole.[17] Though Morrison shows great sympathy for Pauline, she also shows the devastating effects of her lack of nurturing, for Pauline gives Pecola virtually no love nor self-esteem.

According to feminist theory, the nurture of daughters calls for *self-nurture* on the part of mothers.[18] A woman with little faith in herself (and in patriarchy she may develop little) will pass her self-hatred and passivity to her daughter. As she identifies with the values of her oppressors, her daughter is proof of what she despises in herself. As the daughter grows, she learns to efface herself, suppress her rage, and demand little from people around her; thus, we get a continuity of female self-hatred and helplessness through the generations.[19] Paula Bennett argues that this situation describes Pauline and Pecola, but it is complicated by race; Pauline has no faith in her sex or her blackness.[20]

Barbara Christian states that another aspect of Pauline's problem is her uprootedness, the "loss of center" suffered by many migrants from the South.[21] Pulled out of her rural southern environment by her marriage, Pauline can find no coherence in her life, unlike the rural southern women, with whom Morrison contrasts her. Both types of women suffer from white oppression, but Pauline lacks the "functional traditions, as embodied in the land" (49). She also suffers because she accepts the myths of romantic love and physical beauty of white culture.

These myths come into play when she meets Cholly Breedlove. Her limp has always made her feel "separate" and unworthy.[22] But when her family moves to Kentucky, Pauline enjoys keeping house, especially establishing order, arranging shelves, mending fences, and the like. At puberty, though, as so often happens in female *bildungsromans*, discontent appears, and Pauline spends much time dreaming about a someone, "a Presence, an all-embracing tenderness with strength and a promise of rest.... She had only to lay her head on his chest and he would lead her away to the sea, to the city, to the woods ... forever" (88). When Cholly arrives with his attentions to her, "all of the colors" of her childhood come together, and she is in love. In the hymns Pauline sings in church, Jesus had been the romantic Presence; now she has a real man to substitute for Jesus. When the family moves north, she expands her dreams of romance with images of the beautiful people she sees in the picture shows; from them she also discovers what constitutes female beauty and decides she is ugly, a self-hatred she passes to Pecola.

In Lorain, Ohio, life in the Breedlove household degenerates into almost a sociological paradigm of some poor black families. White society continues to take its toll by preventing Cholly from supporting his family and forcing Pauline into the role of breadwinner. The children watch their parents fight with terrified fascination, but Pauline actually enjoys her martyrdom, the fights giving her "tiny, undistinguished days some grandeur and relief" (31). Neglecting her own duties to her family more and more, Pauline allows her job as maid to satisfy her natural impulse for making order. Like Sula, Pauline may be a frustrated artist who lacks an outlet for her talents. Since she cannot make her own family into the storybook white family depicted in the primer that tells of Dick and Jane, which Morrison uses to frame her narrative, Pauline lives a false vision with the white family.

Failing to see how she has damaged her children (the boy, Sammy, like many black males in Morrison, is able to run away), Pauline ignores and abuses the "ugly" Pecola, slapping her for accidentally spilling a hot cobbler and comforting the little daughter of her white employer. As Trudier Harris says, Pauline belongs to the Fishers in the same way that a southern mammy belonged to the master.[23] Again, I should stress Morrison's sympathy for Pauline; though the reader is horrified at her lack of motherly concern, one can also see how she has been affected by her degraded circumstances.

Morrison juxtaposes this horrifying image of motherhood with the healthy image of Mrs. MacTeer, the narrator Claudia's mother. Not the all-perfect mother of myth, Mrs. MacTeer can be impatient with her daughters, and she does buy Claudia the hated white baby doll. Yet, though she is poor and does have some of the damaging white values, she creates a secure, warm home that the mature Claudia recalls as happy. Claudia recounts a time when she is sick with a cold and her harassed mother scolds her for vomiting, leaving her to snuffle in self-pity. Now, however, she reflects that it was not really as painful as she remembers: "Only mildly. Or rather, it was a productive and fructifying pain. Love, thick and dark as Alaga syrup, eased up into that cracked window. I could smell it—taste it—sweet, musty, with an edge of wintergreen in its base—everywhere in that house" (7). Later, Morrison contrasts these scenes of the richness of mother love with the indifference of Pauline.

Like the theorists on motherhood, Morrison shows that the self-esteem generated by the security of love will help keep a child from adopting distorted values. Pecola loves to drink from the MacTeers' Shirley Temple cup and eventually wants Shirley's blue eyes, but Claudia instinctively hates her white baby doll: "I could not love it. But I could examine it to see what it was that all the world said was lovable. Break off the tiny fingers, bend the flat feet, loosen the hair, twist the head around" (14). Claudia later transfers her hatred of the white doll to little white girls. When she learns that such "disinterested violence" is considered repulsive, she for a time succumbs to a "fraudulent love" for Shirley Temple (16). Thankfully, when the mature Claudia tells the story, she has moved beyond this fraudulent love and has achieved the full understanding denied to the doomed Pecola. Claudia's achievement provides the hope in this otherwise tragic story; as Joanne Frye points out, Claudia's *bildung* is subversive because she manages to resist her society's images of female beauty.[24]

Morrison creates some other significant portraits of black women in *The Bluest Eye*, types that recur in all her novels. In contrast with the culturally uprooted and degraded Pauline are the old women of the southern culture, Cholly's Aunt Jimmy and her friends. Morrison describes these culture-bearing women in lyrical passages: they suffered, worked, supported husbands and children, and had a sense of pride, control, and understanding of their worth. Not as close to the mass-media culture, as young women they were not obsessed with their lack of beauty by white standards, but pleased with their sexuality. As old women they had a place of value in the culture as repositories of lore. And always, despite the suffering, there was the friendship of other women, with whom they could exchange stories of their troubles.

According to Elliott Butler-Evans, another group of black women, the three black prostitutes, are ambivalent figures who show Morrison's conflicted feelings about what black women can and should be. Cynical and competent, they control their lives in a way the respectable women of the community cannot do. Hating all men from all races and disrespecting most women, they do not regret their loss of innocence and, in fact, regret they had not been wiser sooner. In short, by inventing themselves they become feared by the community, but can be seen as a positive portrait of how black women have responded to the forces in their lives, in contrast with Pauline and Geraldine Peel.[25]

Also unlike Pauline and Geraldine Peel, they are the only women, with the exception of Mrs. MacTeer, who treat Pecola decently. Pecola seeks out their "maternal space," the warm preoedipal bonding she never got with Pauline (*VTM* 11). They sing to her, and their laughter is music in her drab world. Their man-hating, however, is a danger, says Barbara Rigney, because they are outside the community, which for Morrison is a sad fate for any black person. According to Rigney, in later novels Morrison suggests even more directly to "women readers and feminist critics" that if women castrate men, out of love or spite, they will end up alone (*VTM* 89). Like other "liberated" women in Morrison, the prostitutes are ambiguous figures—to be admired and feared simultaneously.

Though Morrison sympathizes with the distorted, poverty-stricken Pauline, she scorns the middle-class black women, who wholeheartedly adopt white values. Hardly in the "wild zone" of the French feminists, these "thin brown girls" keep perfect homes, go to land grant colleges "to learn how to do the white man's work with refinement," read uplifting literature, sing in the church choir, and always worry about the "edges of their hair." These women make excellent wives, though they may not let their husbands smoke in the house, and view each sexual encounter with distaste. When a man marries such a woman, "he will sleep on sheets boiled white, hung out to dry on juniper bushes, and pressed with a heavy iron. There will be pretty paper flowers decorating the picture of his mother, a large Bible in the front room.... they smell the coffee and the fried ham" (65). These women are afraid of "funk," that "unruly," dreadful eruption of erotic passion and naturalness. In *The Bluest Eye* they are epitomized by the light-skinned Geraldine Peel, who calls Pecola a "little black bitch," and throws her and the MacTeer girls out of her house. Though Morrison usually accords her characters a great deal of sympathy and takes pains to explain their cruel or negative behavior, such is not the case with Geraldine and her kind.

Butler-Evans says that Morrison's view of these women is more sympathetic than it appears, that this is not simply the black nationalist's rejection of white bourgeois values. Women like Geraldine have been taught to suppress sexual and self-assertive desires in order to achieve security. Through control of their passions, they have attained what is valued in both white and black society. Therefore, when Geraldine sees the disheveled Pecola in her kitchen, she sees everything she has been working to get away from:

the dirty, torn dress, the plaits sticking out on her head, hair matted where the plaits had come undone, the muddy shoes.... She had seen this little girl all of her life. Hanging out of windows over saloons in Mobile, crawling over the porches of shotgun houses on the edge of town, sitting in bus stations holding paper bags and crying to mothers who kept saying "Shet up!" (71-72)

Geraldine is protecting the stability of her home not from authentic blackness but from disorder (*RGD* 72). It seems clear to me, however, that in Geraldine and the "thin brown girls" Morrison creates characters we are meant to dislike. By describing them through their husbands' eyes, their human desires for self-assertion have been obliterated. Further, in her careful detailing of Pauline's and Cholly's pasts, Morrison takes pains to explain the reasons for their cruelty to Pecola; with Geraldine there are no mitigating circumstances.

In *The Bluest Eye* the tension between Morrison's sympathy for the pain of black women and her need to support black men in their struggle toward racial justice can best be seen in Cholly's rape of Pecola, the pivotal event of the novel. Prior to the rape, Morrison takes us carefully through Cholly's youth, creating sympathy for him. In this sense, Morrison's treatment of the rape contrasts with the way rape and incest have been handled in white feminist novels, or in Alice Walker's *The Color Purple*, where little attention is given to why Celie's father might sexually abuse her.

Abandoned by his mother and raised by Aunt Jimmy without a father figure in his life (his father later rejects him), Cholly is humiliated by his first sexual experience. Caught with his girlfriend, Darlene, by a group of white men, he is forced to continue the act, and later deflects his hatred for the men onto Darlene. This episode suggests that much abuse of black women by black men could be deflected hatred of whites. Later, without family and adrift, Cholly leaves home and lives a free life, working when he can and loving a number of women. When he must settle down to marriage, this earlier socially imposed freedom leads Cholly to discover that marriage is confining: "The constantness, varietylessness, the sheer weight of sameness drove him to despair and froze his imagination." Because white society will not allow him to support his family, he finds that "only in drink was there some break, some floodlight" (126).

Morrison describes the rape mostly from the drunken Cholly's point of view. He is guilty and angry because Pecola looks so unhappy, and even though he loves her, he cannot make her happy. "What could he do for her—ever? What give her? What say to her? What could a burned-out black man say to the hunched back of his eleven-year-old daughter?" His frustration momentarily wells up in hatred, but fatefully Pecola scratches the back of her calf in a gesture exactly like Pauline's. Cholly's confused emotions dissolve into a "tender" lust. He wants to "fuck her—tenderly. But the tenderness does not hold," and he thrusts fiercely into her. Lest the reader forget Pecola, we hear her only sound, "a hollow suck of air in the back of her throat," see her "sad and limp" panties around her ankles (127-129). The French feminists have called on women to break their silences, but Pecola's silence speaks far more than words ever can (*VTM* 21-23). As Paula Bennett says, Pauline has failed to give her daughter a voice (136).

This rape scene has been analyzed: by Madonne Miner as a paradigm of Greek myths of incest and rape, and by Michael Awkward as a revisitation of the Trueblood episode in *The Invisible Man*.[26] Both critics stress the importance of Morrison's speaking for the violated female. However, such interpretations overlook Morrison's effort to create sympathy for Cholly and the attention she gives to his reaction. As a reinforcer, Morrison reminds us at the end of the novel, after Pecola descends into madness, that Cholly was one of the few people who loved her. In a later interview Morrison explained how she wanted to show Cholly's powerlessness to help Pecola's pain, and that for him, "the embrace, the rape, is all the gift he has left."[27] As Butler-Evans says, "[Morrison's] description of Cholly's life leads the reader to view his brutal treatment of Polly, as well as his rape of Pecola, as acts ultimately generated by a brutal system of dehumanization" (*RGD* 78). This portrayal of both rapist and victim as victims produces a "dissonance" in the reader, resulting from Morrison's dual allegiance to feminism and the black liberation movement, in this case two "contradictory" positions (*RGD* 40).

This dissonance between racial and "womanist" loyalty is also clear in Morrison's depiction of an episode between Pauline and her white employer. Because Cholly has been abusing Pauline, Mrs. Fisher says she will withhold her wages until she leaves Cholly. Pauline rightly resents this controlling white woman who cannot even clean her own house. When Mrs. Fisher tells her to have self-respect and asks her what good Cholly is, Pauline thinks, "How you going to answer a woman like that, who don't know what good a man is, and say out of one side of her mouth she's thinking of your future but won't give you your own money so you can buy baloney to eat?" (94). Pauline remembers the early happy days and the moments of pleasure Cholly and she still have together. At these times, Pauline feels "a power. I be strong, I be pretty, I be young" (101). Although a woman may be abused by a man, she feels empowerment in her sexual relation with him, in the case of a poor black woman an empowerment found nowhere else in her life.

Butler-Evans points out that in rejecting Mrs. Fisher, Pauline places "race above any romanticized concept of sisterhood, yet her involvement with Cholly is essentially destructive" (RGD 75-76). On the other hand, one can argue that although her employer's criticisms of Cholly do contain truth (in a way Pauline is enslaved to Cholly), they are negated by Mrs. Fisher's exploitation of Pauline. In any case, we again see a tension between Morrison's view of black women's relations to black men and the role played by white society in racial oppression. Morrison does not provide a clear resolution to these conflicting issues because the solution, in fact, is not clear; however, questions of black women's oppression must always be couched in the context of black oppression. Finally, white feminists who ask black women to reject their men lack understanding of the black woman's experience.

One final point should be made about *The Bluest Eye*, and Morrison's other novels as well, and that is her ambiguous portrayal of the Afro-American community. She places great value on the sense of continuity and belonging given by community membership. Those who voluntarily exclude themselves or are rejected by the group suffer—they are "outdoors," beyond the pale, so to speak; those who are part of the community experience a warmth that is positively maternal. There is, however, a dark side to community that uses the ugliness of pariahs like Pecola and Cholly to hone its own image of goodness. The community is a necessary force for conformity and rationality, Rigney argues (*VTM* 52-53); people like Cholly *are* dangerous. Too much conformity, however, can be a danger to people, especially women, who are less able to flee their communities and seem less psychically able to resist social pressures. We will see this theme clearly in later novels, especially *Sula* and *Tar Baby*.

SULA: BLACK GIRLFRIENDS

Sula (1974) presents some obvious differences from *The Bluest Eye*, though again it raises feminist issues. Here Morrison deals with a pariah who chooses her fate (*BWWW* 129). Another difference is that *Sula* switches focus from white oppression of blacks to female friendship, a subject not dealt with extensively by white novelists until the 1980s. Morrison deliberately set out to write about women's friendship:

> Friendship between women is special, different, and has never been depicted as the major focus of a novel before *Sula*. Nobody ever talked about friendship between women unless it was homosexual, and there is no homosexuality in *Sula*. Relationships between women were always written about as though they were subordinate to some other roles they're playing. (*BWWW* 118)

Another central idea in *Sula* is the nature of evil, not often explored in the context of female behavior. As Anne Mickelson points out, feminist readers may find it difficult to accept evil in a woman character, but Morrison does not shy away from this unsettling theme.[28] A less discussed theme in *Sula* is motherhood. The bonding of mother and child is a mystery that gives warmth and belonging but can be a serious danger to self, both for the mother and for the child. According to Marianne Hirsch, though black women writers have celebrated the influence of their mothers in their public statements and nonfiction writing, their portrayals of the maternal presence in their fiction are disturbing and contradictory.[29]

The two protagonists of *Sula*, Sula Peace and Nel Wright, represent two opposite aspects of the same person: a kind of Dostoevskian double.[30] Sula is the Jungian shadow: individualistic, fearless, amoral, and self-aggrandizing; Nel is the conventional, orderly, kindly, and self-effacing side. Yet they are also similar, with "distant" mothers and "absent" fathers. When they first meet in childhood in the Bottom, the black neighborhood in the small town of Medallion, Ohio, a community similar to Lorain, "they felt the ease and comfort of old friends. Because each had discovered years before that they were neither white nor male, and that all freedom and triumph was forbidden them, they had set about creating something else to be."[31] Thus, as Meredith Cory states, "Morrison uses male destructiveness as a background which helps to define what it means to be girlfriends."[32]

Their surface differences are attractive; each seems to fulfill certain needs of the other: Sula for order and stability, and Nel for excitement and even chaos. At first Elizabeth Abel's theory (see Chapter 3) of complementarity seems to apply to these friends.[33] Sula has been raised in the "throbbing disorder" of the Peace household by her matriarchal grandmother, Eva, and her mother, Hannah, an easygoing, man-loving women who wanted "some touching every day" (46). Somewhat like the three prostitutes in *The Bluest Eye*, the Peace women operate outside the community; not quite pariahs, they exist in the "wild zone" where human needs for conformity are ignored.

I have called Eva a matriarch, but she is hardly the stereotyped, all-giving, perfect mother. After being deserted by her ne'er-do-well husband BoyBoy

(males in Morrison often have diminutive names), she painfully struggles
to support her children on nothing at all. Willing to maim herself by possibly
losing a leg in order to support her family, she offers love and concern to
her drug addict son, Plum; but his illness threatens her integrity, and she
imagines he is trying to crawl back into her womb. His insatiable need and
immaturity overpower Eva, and one night she kills him by burning him,
but not before embracing him one last time. Eva could be seen as the dreaded
all-powerful Phallic Mother whom we all need to embrace and then break
away from, or as a tormented, loving mother who cannot stand to see her
beloved son suffer, and who feels her very being consumed by him.[34] Marianne Hirsch believes that Eva's burning of Plum can illustrate the powerlessness of mothers. In despair over his drug-induced impotence (forced to
fight in the white man's World War I, he has become an addict), Eva kills
him out of her own impotence to alleviate his suffering (179). In Morrison
child and mother sometimes threaten each other.

In contrast to the wildness of Sula's upbringing, Nel lives in an orderly,
middle-class home. Helene Wright, another Geraldine Peel, is so fearful of
funk that she has rubbed any sparkle Nel originally had to a dull glow; she
makes her wear a clothespin on her nose at night to make it longer. Morrison
explains Helene's conventionality by telling us that she is rejecting her own
mother, a New Orleans whore; raised by a proper grandmother, Helene
hates her own blackness. With each other, Sula and Nel are able to shake
off these influences of their families and be themselves: "In the safe harbor
of each other's company they could afford to abandon the ways of other
people and concentrate on their own perceptions of things" (55). Together
they seem to provide each other a healthy balance between rationality and
feeling.

Sula and Nel share many common experiences, but the most important
is the "accidental" drowning of the boy Chicken Little. Morrison depicts
this as partly the result of Sula overhearing Hannah tell a friend that she
loves Sula but does not like her. Though Hannah only tells the truth, children
do not allow their mothers to have ambivalent feelings toward them, and
Sula is deeply hurt by Hannah's comment. Shortly after, the girls run to the
river and play in the grass, digging holes with sticks, an act that Margaret
Homans sees as aggressively asserting their femaleness against their subconscious oppression.[35] They then silently "defile" the holes they have dug
by tossing in debris. When Chicken Little flies into the river, he becomes
the "ritual sacrifice to female power" (*VTM* 50) or, as Hirsch suggests, a
rejection of femaleness or maternity, at least on Sula's part.[36]

Significantly, the next major scene in the novel describes the death of
Hannah, who catches fire while incinerating trash, as Sula watches with
"disinterested" fascination (78); Sula's behavior contrasts with that of Eva,
who leaps out the window to try and save her daughter. Cynthia A. Davis
finds Morrison's tendency toward women rejecting their mothers and grand-

mothers (matrophobia) to be disturbing; as we have seen, this is a tendency found in some recent white women's fiction as well.[37] However, from another point of view, some rejection is necessary since all people, men and women, must break away from the power of the mother. Sula's rejection is extreme and later involves rejecting maternity for herself.

The subsequent events of the novel—Nel's marriage to Jude, Sula's life of experimentation, and her seduction of Jude—are fraught with questions and contradictions. Though Morrison sympathizes with Nel's pain, clearly she is most at fault because she ruptured friendship by choosing another to be more important in her life. In addition, raised in a home where sexual fidelity was unknown, Sula truly did not realize that taking Jude to bed would so deeply hurt Nel:

> They had always shared the affection of other people: compared how a boy kissed. ... Marriage, apparently, had changed all that, but having had no intimate knowledge of marriage, having lived in a house with women who thought all men available ... she was ill prepared for the possessiveness of the one person she felt close to. (119)

Sula had always felt that she and Nel knew why other women became jealous; they were afraid of losing their jobs as wives. Now Nel had joined the rest of the town and was part of the boredom and conformity that Sula had found in her travels.

Morrison further enlists our sympathy for Sula by having her expose the shallowness and immaturity of Jude. Jude marries for security and to be mothered:

> Whatever his fortune, whatever the cut of his garment, there would always be the hem—the tuck and fold that hid his raveling edges; a someone sweet, industrious and loyal to shore him up. ... Without that someone he was a waiter hanging around a kitchen like a woman ... the two of them would make one Jude. (83)

As she did in *The Bluest Eye* and as many white women writers have also done, Morrison debunks this ideal of romantic love, showing how marriage does not make one whole person of two already diminished people. Sula is able to attract Jude's attention by acting the opposite of the traditional female supportive role. Like many black men, Jude continually complains about his "hard row to hoe," and Nel plays the role of supportive wife (and mother?), exuding customary "milkwarm commiseration." One day Sula speaks up:

> "I don't know what the fuss is about. I mean, everything in the world loves you. White men love you. They spend so much time worrying about your penis they forget their own. ... And white women? They chase you all to every corner of earth,

feel for you under every bed. . . . Colored women worry themselves into bad health just trying to hang on to your cuffs." (103-104)

Despite its humorous tone, Morrison is chiding the black man for at least some of his lamenting about his miserable position. And, if black men allow themselves to be mothered too much, they should not be surprised if they are emasculated.

In an interview Morrison said that in *Sula* she wanted to show the lack of choices for black women in these times;[38] she further explained Sula's behavior by showing us that for Sula, sexual love is her only creative outlet. All along Sula has been looking for an outlet for her creative mind:

In a way, her strangeness, her naiveté, her craving for the other half of her equation was the consequence of an idle imagination. Had she paints, or clay, or knew the discipline of the dance, or strings . . . she might have exchanged the restlessness and preoccupation with whim for an activity that provided her with all she yearned for. And like any artist with no art form, she became dangerous. (121)

As Marianne Hirsch says, the artist Sula rejects the traditional plot for women and tries to rewrite the book, but at that time there were few other outlets for women (183). With Nel, Sula for a while has the alternative to the "heterosexual romance" that Nel finally opts to live. Once Nel goes that conventional route, the frustrated artist Sula turns to sex and becomes a dangerous force in the community.

Still, despite Morrison's effort to explain Sula, the reader is deeply disturbed by her betrayal of friendship. In the traditional view, because one recognizes that possession of a man is so important for a woman, one does not "steal" a friend's husband. Further, for a feminist reader, Sula's behavior seems to fly in the face of sisterhood's telling us to cherish our relationships with women friends. Such behavior makes women rivals for the attentions of men and suggests that the betrayer values the sex (or "romance") more than the friendship. Because we have earlier been asked to identify with Sula's questing, free life, this betrayal shocks and disappoints us. Hortense Spillers puts it this way: " . . . we confront . . . the entanglement of our own contradictory motivations concerning issues of individual woman-freedom. Sula is both loved and hated by the reader, embraced and rejected simultaneously."[39]

More than her seduction of Jude, Sula's "putting Eva out" illustrates for the reader her evil in conventional terms. In the traditional black community, putting the elderly "outdoors" is a grave sin against the loved one and the community. After her period of self-invention by embracing an "experimental life" of travel, college, and affairs with many men, Sula returns to Medallion in 1937. Eva, not completely outside the traditional value system, scolds her for not having babies and "floatin' around without no man."

Sula retorts with the feminist argument that she "don't want to make somebody else. I want to make myself" (92). In retaliation, and to gain possession of the family home, Sula puts Eva in an old people's home.

With Sula, Morrison has created the woman who loves the "free fall": "... she lived out her days exploring her own thoughts and emotions, giving them full reign, feeling no obligation to please anybody unless their pleasure pleased her" (118). Taking Sula entirely outside conventional moral absolutes, a place women in literature have seldom been allowed to be, Morrison asks, "What would happen if a woman were *entirely* free?" Spillers says that in much black fiction, if a woman cannot be powerful, she can be good, and the same can be said about some heroines of white feminist novels. In their powerlessness as victims of patriarchy, they present alternatives of full humanity, the goodness that our society pays lip service to but cannot really encourage because it does not lead to profit and domination. Sula embodies no such absolute moral goodness. However, since she is outside moral absolutes, in the wild zone, one could argue she is not really evil, lacking a conscience or "center" (105); she is the part of ourselves that most of us submerge in our superego.

Lest the reader views Sula as an inhuman symbol of evil, Morrison humanizes her by describing her affair with Ajax. Here Sula acts like any other women; she tries to possess a man and thus loses him. Sula's male counterpart, Ajax is an unabashed hedonist.[40] Like Cholly and like Son in *Tar Baby*, Ajax is the free black male, a man who is denied the work he craves (a pilot) and refuses menial jobs. Not needing nurturing like most men and having a mother he respects as a person, Ajax is fascinated with Sula's brilliance and independence, and in him Sula finds a temporary outlet for the artist inside. Their sex is described as the creation of a beautiful sculpture, with Sula chiseling down through Ajax's black skin to the "gold leaf" and "black loam" underneath (130). Sula's love for Ajax, however, leads her to the desire for possession she despises in other women, and when Ajax detects the "scent of the nest," he leaves (133). Though suffering, Sula realizes she would have tried to know him too deeply; total union with another is not possible. Knowing she has felt all the pain there is—"I have sung all the songs there are"—Sula, unlike Nel, lets go of the experience of loss (137).

The deathbed confrontation between Sula and Nel sets forth the issues in the novel. In her defense, Sula reiterates some common feminist arguments for women's freedom. When Nel tells Sula she cannot live like a man, Sula asks, "Why?" Anyway, being a black woman is like being a man, presumably meaning that a black woman's circumstances free her from some of the constraints placed on white women. Nel calls attention, as Eva did, to the "unnaturalness" of a childless woman, pointing out that Sula would not have been free with children. Sula replies, shocking us further, that if she had children, she would have left them; after all, most black men leave their

children, and there seems to be little condemnation of that.[41] Morrison
seems to say here that children present an insurmountable obstacle to freedom for women; black men are free partly because they do not take care
of their children. For Sula, the price one pays for a free life, loneliness, is
worth it. Most colored women are dying slowly, "like a stump," while she
is "going down like one of them redwoods," having lived a full life. Her
loneliness is *hers*, while Nel's loneliness was handed to her by someone
else—Jude.

Before Nel leaves, Sula asks how she knows if she was really the good
one. "Maybe it was me" (144-146). After all, Nel deserted the friendship;
all Sula did was sleep with Jude. And, even if this is so important—and
Sula obviously feels it isn't—why couldn't Nel get over it? In this debate
between rebel and conformist, Morrison poses tough philosophical questions. Is being one's own person, living free from the boring confines of
society, worth loneliness and death at thirty? Is it finally only life that
matters, wresting from life as much pleasure and experience as one can? Is
Nel's lack of forgiveness a greater evil than Sula's affair with Jude? How
the reader answers these questions will depend on the degree to which he
or she accepts moral absolutes.

After she steals Jude, Sula is a pariah and, as a scapegoat, gives the black
people of Medallion a way to gauge their own goodness in the same way
that Pecola's ugliness makes the people of Lorain feel beautiful. This is
Morrison's dark side of community, the side that breaks the nonconformist
and uses her/his difference to deny its own evil.[42] Sula's evil benefits Medallion because it causes people "to protect and love one another.... and in
general band together against the devil in their midst" (117). After Sula's
death, the people slip back into their evil ways, hurting each other on a
daily basis. Wives pay less attention to husbands; ironically, daughters put
their elderly relatives in nursing homes. Society needs scapegoats, however,
and Morrison uses this aspect of the story to comment on her views of good
and evil. She believes black people view evil differently than do whites; evil,
though hated and feared, is an integral part of life, part of the pattern of
the universe: "...they did not wish to eradicate it [evil]. They wished to
protect themselves from it, maybe even to manipulate it, but they never
wanted to kill it.... Evil is not an alien force; it's just a different force.
That's the evil I was describing in *Sula*" (*BWWW* 129). In this view, Sula
is *not* really outside the community; she is that fourth person in the Holy
Trinity that completes the mandala of life (*VTM* 55).

Elsewhere Morrison has argued that, contrary to some people's views,
the people of Medallion were "nourishing" to Sula, that the little town was
the only place a woman like her could have lived (*BWW* 343). Morrison
has also stated that black women have less a need to change things (to
eradicate evil?) than do white women. There is more acceptance among
them of the natural order of things, to "allow things to go on the way

they're going" (*BWWW* 123). Though this attitude could be due to women's powerlessness, she thinks not. Such an attitude may have something to do with black women's reluctance to become involved with radical feminist plans for changing women's roles.

The loneliness of the rest of Nel's life clearly shows that her ready acceptance of community norms has not brought happiness. Because she is a "respectable" woman, she cannot take a lover, and lives celibate, eventually being left by her children. Nel does not end her quest without understanding, however; during a powerful scene between the supposedly senile Eva and Nel, Morrison makes Nel confront issues of good and evil. With eyes that "look sane," like the conjure-woman that she is, Eva tells Nel that she knows about Chicken Little, that Nel watched and therefore is an accomplice. Eva tells the prideful Nel that she was never different from Sula. For the first time Nel admits it was exciting and satisfying to see Chicken Little die. Who has been evil and who good? The person who actively participates, or the person who watches and does nothing to alleviate evil? Nel realizes that she never felt guilty for Chicken Little's death because she had given the responsibility to Sula, her alter ego (B-H 30).

In Nel's final, moving epiphany, she recognizes not only her complicity in evil but also that the best experience of her life was Sula's friendship. In all her lonely years it was Sula she missed, not Jude. " 'We was girls together,' she said as though explaining something. 'Lord, Sula,' she cried, 'girl, girl, girlgirlgirl.' It was a fine cry," says Morrison, but Sula is gone and so it has no ending, "just circles and circles of sorrow" (174). As Margaret Homans says, in this primal scream Nel has finally found her voice ("her very own howl") as a black woman, but it is terribly sad to have it come so late (194). Although girlfriends may go on forever, in this case beyond death, Sula will never know how she was loved. We could see this as a resurrection for Sula;[43] nevertheless, it is a resurrection that brings little joy to Nel, who reenters the "wild zone" of her childhood with Sula only after her friend is dead. Marianne Hirsch believes that Nel's epiphany recognizes that the plot of "sisterhood" and female friendship can provide an alternative to the heterosexual love plot and maternity (184). However, the fact that the realization comes too late suggests to me that in the world of which Morrison writes, it may be a fantasy rather than an actual possibility for women's lives.

The sad endings of both women can be viewed as an argument for balance. A life of excessive social conformity or a life of total rebellion will produce unhappy, alienated people; Sula dies "outdoors," and Nel, though she has her brief moment of self-awareness, lives most of her life self-alienated (B-H 31). In such an interpretation, both women have failed in their quests. According to Dorothy Lee, Nel's spirit has been rubbed down by her family, and Sula's "preoccupation with experience for its own sake and with gratification of whim regardless of the feelings of others is destructive. Through such pursuit of gratification, she loses Nel . . . 'the other half of her equation.' "[44] The circumstances of Sula's death show she cannot be a model for women's quests. Some critics believe, however—and I would side with them—that Morrison is valorizing the free life in Sula, choosing it over the staidness of Nel. As Barbara Rigney says, the rose tattoo epigraph shows Sula's heroic status: "Nobody knew my rose of the world but me. . . . I had too much glory. They don't want glory like that in nobody's heart" (Lilith's Daughters, 18).

In this view, Sula is not a Cain (her tattoo can also be seen as the mark of her outcast status), she is a Christ figure who sacrifices herself so that the community will be free of sin and guilt.[45] The purging is completed shortly after Sula's death when the crazed war veteran Shadrack, one of the few people who always cared for Sula (he keeps her belt after the Chicken Little episode), like the Pied Piper leads the people into the new railroad tunnel, where a large number drown. Thus the community's guilt for Sula's death is expiated.

Like all great characters in literature, it is these multiple ways to view her that make Sula so memorable. The different ways of viewing her rose mark emphasize the ambivalence even of Morrison, for despite her boldness in creating Sula, Morrison is obviously uncomfortable with her. She tries to provide justifications for Sula's behavior—her home life, Hannah's careless remark, her lack of an artistic outlet, her willingness to suffer for her freedom (RO 132). The unease that Morrison and readers feel about Sula shows only that we are all, unless we are sociopaths, bound in some way to the moral absolutes of our society.

In Sula one finds the same sort of ambivalence toward women's issues that we saw in The Bluest Eye. Some black men do desert their families, but they do so because white society denies them manhood. Some men, like Ajax, "love and leave" women, but women should not deny them their right to "fly." Finally, in Medallion women like Hannah and Sula are not allowed to live. Sula's brave words about "making herself" and going down "like a redwood," set against her sad death "outdoors," cut off from Nel and the community, may show that women cannot reject marriage and maternity and be totally free. Though feminist concerns are present in Sula, as Elliott Butler-Evans says, they are "fragmented and elliptical." Because Morrison's primary concern is to explain the workings of good and evil in a black community, issues of women's freedom inevitably take second place. In Sula we have "contending discourses" (RGD 89), a condition not found in white feminist novels, whose primary purpose is to explore issues relating to the freedom or lack of freedom of women. If evil is meant to exist, including not only Sula but also the evil of men deserting their children, then the sufferings of women become part of "the way things are" rather than something we should struggle to change. Finally, if we choose to believe that Sula's selfish behavior is not a model for female quests, then we may be thrown back toward traditional attitudes about women.

SONG OF SOLOMON: FEMALE STRENGTH/MALE FLIGHT

In *Sula*, Ajax would like to fly, and in Morrison's highly acclaimed *Song of Solomon* (1977) the metaphor of flight takes center stage. Most critics judged the novel, which won the National Book Critics Circle Award, to be her most ambitious work, longer and more complex than the two earlier novels. One important difference is her switch to a male protagonist. In addition, *Song* has a number of settings, ranging from Michigan to the South and the roots of the characters. Morrison has said that in books about males, one must have a more expansive setting, since women have lived out their lives in houses, whereas men have had a greater freedom to roam. This expansive setting has given *Song* a more sprawling character.[46]

As many critics have stated, despite its male protagonist, women are really the focus of *Song*; and again Morrison says much about their strengths and weaknesses, their sufferings and triumphs, and their relations with black men. As in her earlier novels, in *Song* Morrison shows the deep conflict between the pain of black men and what that pain causes them to do to their women. She also shows how too much mothering can "emasculate" both men and women, how women are the carriers of the culture in the black community, and how women's insights can lead men to a deeper understanding of themselves, for it is through his Aunt Pilate that Milkman achieves the goals of his quest.

Song is the *bildungsroman* of Macon (Milkman) Dead, Jr., a young, middle-class black raised in a northern city in a cold and sterile home. Milkman has no consciousness of his roots in black culture, his father, a successful businessman, being ashamed of his own humble past. Macon, Sr., is a bitter man who hates his only sister, despises the poor blacks he exploits, and struggles to accumulate as many bourgeois trappings as he can, one being his light-skinned wife, Ruth, the daughter of the only black doctor in town. Macon represents patriarchal values to an extreme. He treats his wife and daughters with contempt (they are women) and is especially contemptuous of Ruth because he suspects that she had incestuous relations with her father. Raising Milkman to take over the family business one day, Macon has given him very little sense of self; Milkman wants nice things and enjoys being an important man in the black community, but he hates the power his father has over him. Thus the story has strong oedipal resonances.

The plot of *Song* concerns Milkman's figurative and literal journey to the land of his ancestors in order to discover who he is. The journey involves all the aspects of the typical Western quest: physical danger and pain; rebirth (journeys into and out of caves and forests); encounters with strange, wise people, male and female, who help him on his way; beautiful women who offer love and advice; and fights with men who then become comrades. Milkman's quest ostensibly begins in a desire to locate the family fortune, some bags of gold that his father and aunt had discovered in a cave as children; the "gold" he eventually finds is his real family name (Solomon or Shalimar) and the knowledge that his great-grandfather was an African chief who flew away from slavery, back to Africa. In the process of the search he learns that he, too, can "fly": "If you surrendered to the air, you could *ride* it."[47] Through knowledge of self and one's roots, through acknowledgment of one's bonds with others, and through pain and self-examination, one can achieve spiritual transcendence and rise to new heights of involvement in the great business of life.[48] According to Barbara Rigney, one must enter the "wild zone," beyond the constraints of the dominant culture and consciousness, the zone that women find easier to inhabit than do men.

Milkman's (his name derives from his prolonged nursing by Ruth) most important guide and the most important character in *Song* is his Aunt Pilate. Morrison has said that black novels should have an ancestor, "timeless people whose relationships to the characters are benevolent, instructive, and protective" (*BWW* 344). As the ancestor in *Song*, Pilate shows Milkman how to love and forgive, the value of a natural life, the unimportance of material possessions, and the importance of learning one's identity. Even though she has no navel, implying her isolation from others, and thus has been rejected throughout her life, Pilate has a firm sense of self, carrying it symbolically on a piece of paper in a little metal box made into an earring. She has never let her hardships, which include losing several lovers, being ostracized many times by various black communities, and being hated by her own brother, defeat her (*RO* 136). She dies by a bullet meant for Milkman on the spot where Solomon flew away (ironically, a woman named for the Christ killer gives her life for another), and as she dies, she tells him, "I wish I'd a knowed more people. I would of loved 'em all. If I'd a knowed more, I would a loved more" (336).

This lesson of universal love is not lost on Milkman, who realizes that "without leaving the ground" Pilate could always fly. It is through love that we give life meaning, love that comes through self-knowledge and acknowledgment of our duties to others. It could be argued that this is an advance on the moral vision we saw in *Sula*. Sula's flight destroys, while Pilate's enriches. In *Song* there is no ambiguity about the value of living in harmony and consideration for others.

Song of Solomon is equally Pilate's *bildungsroman*.[49] Morrison shows us Pilate as a woman in harmony with her natural environment; she scorns material possessions and cares little about her personal appearance, refusing to wear shoes, and makes wine for a living. Though what she does is illegal, she refuses to allow the usual activities of a wine house (prostitution) to take place on her property. As a typical Morrison pariah, Pilate cannot be part of the community, and so she invents a lifestyle for herself, creating a home for her daughter, Reba, and granddaughter, Hagar, that is a refuge, a place of warmth and comfort that contrasts with the sterile environment of Milkman's house. In an early scene of the novel we see Macon Dead standing outside his sister's home, irresistibly drawn to its enveloping warmth:

They were singing some melody that Pilate was leading. A phrase that the other two were taking up and building on. Her powerful contralto, Reba's piercing soprano in counterpoint, and the soft voice of the girl Hagar ... pulled him like a carpet tack under the influence of a magnet. Treading as lightly as he could, he crept up to the side window where the candlelight flickered lowest and peeped in. Reba was cutting her toenails with a kitchen knife or a switchblade, her long neck bent almost to her knees. The girl Hagar was braiding her hair, while Pilate, whose face he could not see because her back was to the window, was stirring something in a pot. (29)

Ironically, Macon has forbidden Milkman to enter Pilate's house, but he himself cannot keep away. As Rigney says, this is the nurturant, warm "preoedipal maternal space" that all Morrison characters, male and female, would love to enter; it contrasts with the masculine world of Macon's business, in which he easily evicts a poor family.

Song could be seen as incorporating cultural feminist values. Stephanie Demetrakopulos believes that Milkman finds himself through the "feminine principle" and women themselves. Men like Macon lose their souls in their search for wealth and power, and can find them only by surrender to the feminine within (*Demetrakopulos NDS* 94). Similarly, Guitar Bains, Milkman's best friend, cuts himself off from the world of women and children by joining the radical black organization Seven Days, a group dedicated to returning white violence with black violence. Significantly, it is Guitar's bullet, meant for Milkman, whom he believes has betrayed the black cause, that slays Pilate. However attractive this interpretation is, though, it should not be construed as feminist separatism. Just as men are damaged by cutting themselves off from the softer parts within themselves, so are women damaged when cut off from the world of men.

For example, Pilate's daughter and granddaughter obviously have been hurt by being raised with no significant males in their lives. Reba knows little about men and is weak and floating, still dependent on her mother in her fifties. Though Morrison suggests Reba may be a little slow-witted, she also tells us that having no father was not good for Reba. In the same way, the spoiled Hagar knows nothing about men, cannot take care of herself, and hopes to find a "Prince Charming" (*BWW* 344). Her society tells her she needs one, and when Milkman enters her life, she invests her entire personality in him. When he leaves her, Hagar lacks the self she needs to survive. Pathetically, she tries to create a self that Milkman will want by buying makeup and clothes, turning her beautiful African hair a horrible orange (Milkman has been dating light-skinned redheads), and generally abasing herself.

As with Pauline and Pecola, with Hagar, Morrison calls attention to the disturbing spectacle of Afro-American women enslaved to white standards of beauty, but she also cautions black culture of the dangers of matriarchy. Yes, black women like Pilate have done their best under formidable odds and they are to be praised for that. On the other hand, girls need fathers to develop other sides of themselves besides the nurturant female sides. Pilate benefited greatly by having her father and, for a while, her brother in her life. Morrison implies that some of Pilate's strength came from them, the female virtues of loving nurturance being nicely balanced with traditional "masculine" qualities of strength and endurance. Somehow, however, that strength has not been passed along to her daughters. Says Morrison:

Pilate is the apogee of all that: of the best of that which is female and the best of that which is male, and that balance is disturbed if it is not nurtured, and if it is not counted on and if it is not reproduced. That is the disability we must be on guard against for the future—the female who reproduces the female who reproduces the female. (BWW 344)

So the beguiling picture of Pilate with her daughter and granddaughter is only one side of the human equation; the other is missing, which leads to profound unhappiness for this matriarchal family. Such a viewpoint, is, of course, very different from that of radical white feminists who urge separation from men. In black culture, says Morrison, men are the ancestors, too, and we separate from them at our peril.

Barbara Rigney suggests that Pilate's negative impact on Hagar's development—it is she who gives her the mirror, a false picture of "self" that convinces her she is worthless—shows a good bit of the "dread of the mother" we find in Nancy Chodorow and the French feminists. As we saw in Chapter 3, Chodorow warns of the tendency some mothers have to keep their daughters too closely by their sides, not allowing them to develop autonomy. Similarly, Julia Kristeva says we must cherish the power of motherhood, and at the same time break away from the "myth of the archaic mother," which in African mythology is symbolized by the Great Mother and her other side by the Hindu goddess, Kali, the Destroying Goddess.[50] In Morrison, characters like Milkman derive strength from the Mother (his actual mother, Ruth, was a negative force, keeping him in an infantile state far too long), but others, such as Plum and Hagar, fail to break away and never achieve individuation. Ironically, Pilate enables Milkman to "fly" but fails her own daughter. Perhaps I should point out here that Morrison does not condemn Pilate—or Ruth, for that matter; neither consciously attempts to hurt her child. If blame falls anywhere, it is on the child who must break away to mature.

Morrison certainly deviates from a sterotypical feminist perspective when she criticizes Hagar's possessiveness as well as Milkman's cruelty. When Hagar and Ruth argue over Milkman, Pilate points out that a man is not a house to be owned. Finally, when Hagar is trying to kill Milkman (not able to possess him, she does not know what else to do), Guitar tells her how wrong she is to base her value on the possession of a man. How can Milkman love her if she is nobody without him? Guitar's speech is ironic, since earlier he has told Milkman that he will defend black women from white men because they are *his*; nevertheless, Guitar is right in this instance. Morrison acknowledges that although men can be cruel to women, women contribute to the situation by being overly possessive and lacking in self-esteem. A white feminist, however, would probably argue that women are possessive because society has told them they are nothing without men, and it is hard for people with little self-esteem to resist the pressures of their culture.

As I have shown, in her first two novels Morrison was critical of black middle-class women who reject their blackness, seeming to show little sympathy with them. However, *Song of Solomon* presents quite a change in its treatment of Ruth and her daughters, Magdelene and Corinthians. Ruth has been victimized first by her family and then by her husband. Losing her mother at a young age and having no friends, she fastened all her love on her grasping, haughty father. Starved for love, she developed incestuous feelings for him and, according to Macon, was caught in bed with her just-dead father, sucking on his fingers.

In punishment Macon withholds sexual contact from his wife for the rest of their marriage, except for a brief interlude when, with the help of a magic potion of Pilate's, Ruth manages to have intercourse with Macon one more time.[51] She had hoped Milkman would restore her to Macon's affections, but since Macon had never really loved her anyway (he married her for the prestige of possessing her), she is unsuccessful. In frustration Ruth nurses Milkman long past the time for weaning, this being the only physical contact she has with anyone. According to Ruth, she never was in bed with her father, and had only kissed his hands on his deathbed. Thus, all these years Macon has been deluding himself about incest that existed in thought only. Terry Otten suggests that the relationship was actually one of "cold indifference" on the part of the father, Ruth developing a sick attachment to him because she led such as empty life (47). This sad woman—she calls herself "small because she was pressed small" (124)—is not really an attractive character, being weak, overly concerned with propriety, regarding her son as a diversion, and having no interest in her daughters because they are female. Nonetheless, Morrison does engage our sympathy by explaining the forces that created Ruth. Belatedly, near the end of his quest, Milkman develops sympathy for his mother's barren life:

If it were possible for somebody to force him to live that way [celibate], to tell him "You may walk and live among women, you may even lust after them, but you will not make love for the next twenty years," how would he feel?...What might she have been like if her husband had loved her? (300)

Morrison creates equally sympathetic characters in Milkman's sisters, showing, as Anne Mickelson asserts, a growth in her feminist consciousness (*RO* 145-146). Magdalene (Lena) and Corinthians (Cory) are raised in a home where all the parental energy is devoted to the pampered son. As girls, they have no function other than to be paraded every Sunday in their best clothes, to sit at home and make roses out of red velvet, and to wait on their brother. Both college educated to be the wives of professional men, Lena and Cory find themselves middle-aged spinsters, no black men in the community wanting highly educated wives. When Lena finds out that Milkman has told their father about Cory's romance with Henry Porter, she comes into her own with a speech to Milkman that rings out as the impassioned cry of every woman supplanted by a man:

Our girlhood was spent like a found nickel on you. When you slept, we were quiet; when you were hungry, we cooked; when you wanted to play, we entertained you; ...You have yet to wash your own underwear, spread a bed, wipe the ring from your tub, or move a fleck of your dirt from one place to another. And to this day, you have never asked one of us if we were tired, or sad, or wanted a cup of coffee. ...Where do you get the *right* to decide our lives? I'll tell you where. From that hog's gut that hangs down between your legs. (215)

Though we do not find out what happens to Lena, from subsequent events we assume that relations between Milkman and his sisters will change. Stephanie Demetrakopoulos states, and I agree, that there are few women who do not respond with an inner "yes!" to this diatribe (*Demetrakopoulos NDS* 95).

Cory's quest tells of the middle-class, educated black woman who rebels against powerful family pressures to be "proper." Tired of being mainly an ornament for the family and ill equipped by her useless education, Cory is forced to take a job as a maid for a fussy elderly white woman poet. At first she hides her romance with Porter, a janitor and member of the Seven Days, but at Porter's pushing, she defies her father and stays out overnight. When we last see Cory, she is entering her home, unafraid of confronting her father. Though later we find that Macon fires Porter, who worked for him, and forbids Cory to leave the house, the reader hopes that at forty-four her newfound spirit will finally enable her to leave. Certainly Porter is no prize, and he seems to have traditional ideas about women; nevertheless,

Morrison clearly tells us that it *is* Cory's life, and that a job, even one beneath her, and a sexual life with Porter are preferable to the living death she experienced with her parents. The pity is that her education did not prepare her for rewarding work that would have permitted her more self-expression.

I have been arguing here that Morrison expresses ambivalence and conflict in her desire to support the black struggle and in her interest and sympathy for women's experience. This tension is most obviously shown in the central metaphor of *Song*—flying. A black man, one of the Seven Days, tries to fly at the beginning of the novel and fails. Milkman discovers that his great-grandfather flew back to Africa, and the ending of the novel finds him soaring, too, toward the arms of his "brother" Guitar. To realize themselves, to achieve individuation, black men must fly. Morrison has said she admires that aspect of black male culture that refuses to be tied down, to knuckle under to a dull, constrained life. While working on *Song* she said: "... black men travel, they split, they get on trains, they walk, they move.... It's a part of black life, a positive, majestic thing." Though she acknowledges that when fathers fly, children are hurt—girls as well as boys—they also remember their fathers, "half in glory and half in accusation." In *Song* the men leave home, and the children remember it, sing about it, and mythologize it.[52]

In the novel Milkman's great-grandfather Solomon's flight from slavery's unbearable conditions back to Africa is seen as beautiful, liberating, a celebration of the human spirit. However, in flying away Solomon left behind a wife and twenty-one children, one of whom was Jake, Macon Dead's father. Milkman is told by Susan Byrd, one of his distant relatives:

And there's this ravine near here they call Ryna's Gulch, and sometimes you can hear this funny sound by it that the wind makes. People say it's the wife, Solomon's wife, crying.... They say she screamed and screamed, lost her mind completely. You don't hear about women like that anymore, but there used to be more—the kind of woman who couldn't live without a particular man. And when the man left, they lost their minds, or died or something. Love, I guess. But I always thought it was trying to take care of children by themselves, you know what I mean? (323)

When black men "fly," they leave behind suffering women and children, and though Morrison tells us the children remember their fathers not only with accusation but also with admiration, the middle-class white feminist feels discomfort with this celebration of male freedom. As she did with Pecola's rape, Morrison asks the reader to remember the pain of black men who hurt women because society offers them so few ways to realize their manhood. Still, it is difficult for someone imbued with white bourgeois values not to condemn the father who deserts his family. Some critics have questioned this tendency in Morrison to celebrate aspects of black male culture that could be seen as damaging.[53] A white critic treads gingerly here; when dealing with Afro-American literature, the worry of saying something racist is very real and causes some white critics to avoid black literature. Morrison has spoken out about white critics who have refused to deal with her work (*BWWW* 121).

Barbara Rigney makes a convincing argument that Morrison's metaphor of flight is more than a simple symbol of freedom for the black male. It involves a flight to a new consciousness, the "wild zone" where language itself becomes unruly, where the human spirit ranges in new and deeper understandings of self and experience. If one remains mentally and emotionally under the sway of the dominant culture's expectations, than full personhood cannot be achieved; "flight" in Morrison, sometimes occurring in dreams, is a way of entering that zone—for the reader as well, it might be added. When reading Morrison, one is always conscious of being touched at levels beyond language and critical discourse, which for a critic sounds like a cop-out; however, any Morrison fan will understand.

Most critics argue that in *Song of Solomon*, Morrison deviates markedly from the traditional quest theme in her concern for black female experience and by having her male protagonist find himself through the feminine. According to Cynthia Davis, however, Milkman's quest is essentially little different from other male heroic quests: he discovers who he is by discovering his forefathers; in his search he relates mainly to other males (Guitar and the men he encounters in the small towns); and females exist as functions: mothers, aunts, sisters, and lovers. Pilate, despite her balance of female and male attributes, her kindness and strength, cannot attain heroic stature because she has no consciousness of her female line or its contributions to her identity. She misinterprets the information given her by her father's ghost, cannot raise her children with her own strengths, and cannot complete her quest without Milkman's help. For women to attain the heroic in literature, they must recognize a past in which women are as central as men.[54] As we have seen in *Sula*, and as we will see in *Tar Baby*, it could be argued that Morrison does not let women "fly" as men do.

TAR BABY: MAMA-SPOILED BLACK MAN AND CULTURE-BEARING WOMAN

In *Tar Baby* (1981) Morrison again tackles issues of black and female identity, but in the context of a cultural clash between two lovers: the beautiful, deracinated Jadine, a Paris model; and Son, a rootless, uneducated man from Eloe in rural Florida. Of all of Morrison's novels, *Tar Baby* received the most mixed critical reception, with a number of reviewers objecting to too obvious a theme (a novel of ideas where the ideas rule the characters) and Morrison's lush, "overly symbolic" style.[55] Also, of all Morrison's novels it most directly confronts the conflict between freedom for women and traditional values.

The novel is set in a perverted paradise, a tropical island off the coast of Haiti called Isle de Chevaliers. Myth abounds with tales of blinded slaves, the chevaliers, riding forever through the forests and mating with the swamp women who lurk in the steamy jungles. Educated at the Sorbonne, Jadine is the niece of black servants Ondine and Sydney, who work for Valerian Street, a retired tycoon, and his bored, much younger wife, Margaret. Jadine lives with the Streets occasionally, almost as their own niece, with her aunt and uncle waiting on her. As a high-fashion model, Jadine has nearly lost her sense of blackness: she admits to being embarrassed by black culture and enjoys Picasso more than African art. Seduced by wealth, she denies the violence of the white culture she loves, a recurring symbol being a baby sealskin coat given to her by a white lover. Recently, though, Jadine feels some guilt for her rejection of her roots; during her last visit to Paris a stately African woman spits on her for so obviously denying her blackness. Jadine admits that she feels "unauthentic" around such a person, and, suspecting that her white lover wants to marry any black girl and not necessarily her, she comes "home" to get in touch with all the family she has.[56]

The hero Son jumps ship, and sneaks into the Street household, ingratiating himself with everyone, including Ondine and Sydney, who are enraged at the entrance of a "swamp nigger" into their domain (Sydney and Ondine have acquired the values of their employers and scorn the native blacks). Son is a number of things in the novel: a natural man (he is able to make the plants in Valerian's greenhouse bloom), untainted by white culture, and comfortable with who he is, the sort of free black man—like Cholly, Ajax, and Guitar—that Morrison finds fascinating:

> In those eight homeless years he had joined that great underclass of undocumented men. . . . They were an international legion of day laborers and musclemen, gamblers, sidewalk merchants, migrants. . . . What distinguished them from other men (aside from their terror of Social Security cards and *cedula de identidad*) was their refusal to equate work with life and an inability to stay anywhere for long. (166)

Son has the ability to make the others look at themselves and discover long-held secrets, to confront dark territories within themselves. In the process, he must look within himself as well.

On one level Son represents the stereotypical black rapist every woman fears. He is not interested in rape, however, at first treating Jadine with contempt and Ondine and Margaret with respect. Jadine reacts with disgust and contempt toward Son; but opposites attract (he is equally attracted to her beauty and civilized aura), and soon they become passionate lovers. Like Nel and Sula, their differences put together could make one balanced

person. Their time together on their home turfs, New York and Eloe, illustrate the clash of cultures that is at the heart of the novel, as well as a
clash between an image of feminism and traditional views of women.

Jadine sees New York as a "black woman's city" full of strong young
women not willing to "take any shit" from any man; Son sees a city where
the "black girls are crying" and "beautiful males . . . had found the whole
business of being black and men at the same time too difficult and so they'd
dumped it" (222, 216). During a visit to Eloe, which Jadine finds restricting
and boring, she is visited by "night women," women from her past and
present holding out breasts and eggs toward her, seeming to accuse her of
losing her womanly function (the African woman in Paris also was holding
eggs, a symbol of female fertility). These cultural conflicts are too difficult
to overcome; Jadine goes back to Paris to adopt the white life she cannot
escape, and the last scene finds Son running "lickety split" into the swamp.
Will he get Jadine's address from the Streets, follow her, and be trapped by
the tar baby made by the white master (Valerian), or will he reject white
civilization and join the blind chevaliers and swamp women? Though critics
have seen it both ways, Morrison has said she left it open ("NM" 424).

Though this brief plot synopsis makes the novel sound clichéd, it is far
more complex. Contrary to what some critics have alleged, Son is more
than the sexually potent black male who awakens a quivering female to her
essence.[57] He represents authentic blackness and a refusal to sell out, as
Jadine has done, to the affluence of white culture, which offers no sense of
identity or closeness of community. Even the white characters Valerian and
Margaret have come to the Caribbean because their neighborhood in Philadelphia is so cold.[58] The variety of critical interpretations shows us Son
and Jadine's complexity. We can see him as the "heroic black male," the
flyer, the rootless wanderer who refuses to reject his roots, and her as the
"tar baby" who almost lures him away from those roots. Others have seen
Jadine as a far more positive character whose "flight" at the end shows she
has escaped her relegation to the powers of nature, represented by the swamp
women who threaten to pull her into their midst. According to this point
of view, Jadine courageously decides to become "subject, rather than object," and Morrison is not being ironic when Jadine thinks that she herself
"*was* the safety she longed for" (290).[59]

However we wish to see him, Son is not a one-dimensional character,
and Morrison does find fault with him. He has a stereotyped view of what
a black woman should be: a recurring fantasy of his is of "yellow houses
with white doors which women opened and shouted Come on in, you honey
you! and the fat black ladies in white dresses minding the pie table in the
basement of the church" (119). Son equates his memories of home with
these sensual, nurturing women, images completely at odds with the liberated Jadine, who long ago decided that she would "never be broken at
the hands of any man" (124). When Jadine talks of "sexual equality," Son

is confused, because all the women he remembers from his past—his former wife, Cheyenne, his mother, and grandmother—could drive trucks, ride horses, build cowsheds (268). These women were able to live active, free lives without losing their womanliness.

Morrison's stance on Jadine's predicament is less ambiguous than some critics have suggested. Clearly, Jadine has adopted a white, middle-class vision of women's freedom that not only makes no sense to Son but also can harm her. Carried to an extreme, it can cause her to lose sight of those wonderful, rich aspects of womanhood such as nurturing and caring for others, not only children but also the elderly. In a scene near the end, Morrison lets us know in no uncertain terms how she feels about Jadine, when Jadine rejects responsibility for Ondine and Sydney. Ondine tells her that a girl must learn to be a daughter before she can become a woman, but Jadine replies that she does not want to be that kind of woman (282-283).

A number of critics have seen the issues in Tar Baby as maternal as well as cross-cultural. As in Sula, Morrison seems to imply that women's freedom is not compatible with motherhood. Critics ask why Jadine is made to choose between nurturing her own family and having a career, and why this "liberated" black woman is portrayed so unattractively, shown masturbating on the sealskin coat and cruelly rejecting her aunt and uncle.[60] Certainly, Morrison usually shows more sympathy for her characters than she does for Jadine. Though Morrison has said that black women can be "ship and safe harbor," in Tar Baby she does not make this possible for her heroine (BWWW 122). The reason for this, however, lies in Morrison's absolute dedication to the survival of the black community and her admiration for the role women have played in the culture; while the men have gone on quests, sometimes forced to do so by the cruelties of white society, the women have been the culture bearers and nurturers of the next generation. For a black woman to deny this aspect of herself is not only to lose any authentic sense of self but also a danger to the survival of the race.

Therese, an old conjure-woman and servant of the Streets (another Morrison ancestor), who gives Son directions into the swamp at the end of the novel, says that Jadine "has forgotten her ancient properties" (305). As Susan Lydon says, she has been educated to think like a man, yet is unable to live like a man without forgetting those "ancient properties."[61] By adopting a white version of women's equality, a version where women worry about whether they are equal to men, Jadine has lost her strong identity as a black woman.[62] Black women know, from their experience in the history of the race, that they *are* equal.

In Tar Baby as well as in the rest of her novels, Morrison advocates the values of cultural feminists who celebrate traditional female virtues and reject the idea that the feminine within themselves is weak and dangerous to their quest for self. Nonetheless, it is difficult for a white woman reader not to sympathize with Jadine and her quandary. As Stephanie Demetrak-opoulos says, Eloe would be seen by her as boring and narrow, with a misogynistic environment. "How do we align the mythic, the racial, the sexual, the fecund, with the achievement ethic?" (*NDS* 133). If we are to achieve as women in *this* society, we must leave Eloe, as young women of all races and ethnic groups have done. Even those of us from middle-class white homes who have opted for careers have left the Eloe of our mothers' lives. We all have our moments of doubt and guilt when we realize the costs of that journey, especially when it comes to raising our children. By posing such universal questions through portraying the lives of black women, Morrison helps all women understand themselves.

Near the end of *Tar Baby* Morrison asks, "Mama-spoiled black man, will you mature with me? Culture-bearing black woman, whose culture are you bearing?" Neither Son nor Jadine has the entire answer to the Afro-Americans' problems. They are attempting to "rescue" each other, not seeing that "one has a past, the other a future" (269), and a balance between both may be valuable for the race. Some of Son's faults are a limited view of women, his pride in his own ignorance, and his lack of any solution to blacks' problems other than rejection of white culture. Is there a way for Son (black men) to move beyond alienation and running? On the other hand, can highly educated, achievement-oriented black women "make it" in the dominant culture without losing their "ancient properties"? Finally, can black culture in the present-day West function by continuing to cement "bonds that work," like the bonds that obviously work in Eloe, and yet permit blacks to exist within the larger culture?[63] These are the basic questions of *Tar Baby*.

One other interesting feature of *Tar Baby* relevant to women's issues is Morrison's sensitive treatment of child abuse. Margaret Street has abused her child, Michael, the abuse being the cause of his long absences from home. Though Morrison does not attempt to excuse child abuse, she shows understanding of its causes, which can be rooted in women's lack of a feeling of control. Margaret, a young working-class Italian girl, married Valerian at seventeen, as an ornament for him. Not allowed to develop a budding friendship with Ondine, resenting the idleness of her life and the complete dependency of the infant—"its prodigious appetite for security"— she surreptitiously begins to abuse the baby, wrongly telling herself she cannot control the impulse (236). Valerian chooses to ignore little Michael's strange behavior, and Ondine, believing she is the "good black woman and Margaret the evil white woman," says nothing. Thus all characters bear some degree of complicity, perhaps Valerian the most for being a "willfully innocent man" (243). Just as she does in *Sula*, Morrison says that evil may lie in saying nothing about the evil others do, just as it does in action. If innocence is willful blindness, then it is evil.

BELOVED: SLAVERY AND BLACK MOTHERHOOD

With the Streets, Morrison created her only fully developed white characters. In her next novel, *Beloved* (1987), which was awarded the Pulitzer Prize, she returns to a black female focus. When working on *Tar Baby*, Morrison suggested that her movement from black girls, to the friendship of black women, to a black man, to the relationship between a black man and woman was "evolutionary" ("NM" 416). Yet in *Beloved* she spirals back to an earlier concern, the particular experiences of black women, in this case in slavery. Set in 1873 Cincinnati, *Beloved* concerns the awful, lingering effects of slavery on black mothers. The protagonist, Sethe, after having endured a horrendous escape from a plantation in Kentucky, attempts to kill her four children rather than allow them to be taken back into slavery. She succeeds in killing one baby daughter before she is stopped; the story concerns the return of this daughter as a ghost, a grown girl of twenty, who demands love and attention from Sethe and finally her self— her own being. In discussing *Beloved,* Morrison said that she wanted to write about slaves developing a feeling of self after slavery; since "women feel themselves best in nurturing," the story of a mother killing her children to keep them from slavery seemed a good one to explore such a theme.[64]

As I have shown in Chapter 3, white feminist writers have explored maternity in a number of ways, some stressing the positive effect nurturing has on women's characters, some examining the visceral pull of mother love and the interference children present to mothers' self-realization. We have seen this theme in all of Morrison's novels as well. In the thinking of the French feminists and Nancy Chodorow, the warm bonding of pregnancy and birth dissolves boundaries between subject and object, and mother and child experience themselves as inextricably one. Every person needs this closeness before emerging into "otherness," what Julia Kristeva calls "the splitting of the subject."[65] Without maternal bonding, people have difficulty establishing human connections in later life. There is danger, however, in this passionate relationship; if the maternal bond is too close, too cloying, the person (often a daughter) will remain dependent and infantile. In her later relationships she will seek this kind of bonding with others, such as men in her life, and will not achieve autonomy.[66] Theorists are just beginning to write about mothers as subjects, and many suggest that the mother bond can be dangerous to the mother as well.[67] In simple terms, women need to see themselves as more than mothers. In a healthy mother-child relationship both must struggle to break this powerful bond.

Though Morrison expresses some of these ideas in her earlier novels, such as in the relationship of Eva and Plum, she makes them a central theme in *Beloved*, where the cruel effects of slavery complicate an already complex psychological situation. In *Beloved* mothers are constantly threatened with losing their children; sometimes they reject their infants if they were fathered through rape. Sethe's "Ma'am," for example, "threw some of her children away" because they were fathered by white rapists, and was not allowed to care for Sethe, having to work in the fields; Baby Suggs, Sethe's mother-in-law, lost half of her children through sales; and Sethe loses her two sons after the attempted killing, as well as the slain daughter. Paul D, the "last of the Sweet Home men," knows that slave women (like slave men) learn "to love everything, just a little bit, so when they broke its back or shoved it in a croaker sack, well, maybe you'd have a little love left over for the next one."[68] Morrison suggests, however, that Paul is wrong. Slave women love their children deeply and suffer greatly when they lose them. They may stuff that love down inside, but it will come back in damaging ways.

As Missy Dehn Kubitschek says, Sethe's situation is complicated by her own lack of mothering. Throughout the novel Sethe recalls the few times she talked with her mother before she was hanged, and longs to see her again. Part of her motivation in killing her children and herself is to rejoin her Ma'am on the "other side," where they will all be free from threats and pain, reunited in those loving bonds of mothering.[69] When Beloved returns, Sethe cannot reject her outrageous demands and let her go, partly out of guilt but partly because she associates her with her own dead mother.

Sethe's greatest sin is believing her children are *hers*; when Stamp Paid later approaches 124 Bluestone Road after the murder, he hears confused voices, from which he can make out only the word "mine." This murder of a child takes maternal possessiveness, the unwillingness of mothers to allow their children autonomy, to the absolute extreme. Even slave owners could not legally kill their slaves. As Paul says, "Sethe didn't know where the world stopped and she began" (164). Unable to see herself as autonomous because of her lack of mothering—she has not been allowed to go through the process of healthy bonding and then breaking away—she tries to keep her children with her any way she can, even to the point of destroying them. In Sethe, Barbara Rigney says, we can see the terrifying power of mothering—the African Great Mother goddess and Kali, the destroyer (69). In Hélène Cixous's terms she is the Phallic Mother who challenges the law of the fathers. For Carol Boyce Davies, Sethe asserts the basic law of mother-right over the bodies of her children in a society which denies her that right.[70] Finally, Sethe defends her actions when Paul tells her that her love is "too thick," saying, "Love is or it ain't. Thin love ain't love at all" (164).

By presenting the calamities of a slave mother's life that might lead her to such a crime, Morrison wants us to sympathize with Sethe and not judge her, but she does *not* believe that Sethe had the right to take her daughter's life.[71] We can see this in the results. The vibrant Baby Suggs turns away from life and dies, Sethe's terrified sons run away, and her daughter Denver grows up self-centered and lonely, fearful of her mother and the world outside her yard. The clearest proof of Sethe's guilt is the events after

Beloved's return. At first she seems just a strange, lonely girl needing love; Sethe gives that love and experiences a complete union of self and Beloved: "I am Beloved and she is mine...I am not separate from her there is no place where I stop"—a preoedipal bonding that seems beautiful (210). But such bonding must end; in fact, it begins to end at birth, when mother and child begin to differentiate and become the Other.

All of Sethe's attention is not enough. Beloved becomes a kind of incubus or demonic force: seducing Paul D; demanding food and love; and sucking the life out of Sethe, who quits her job and serves Beloved, who is still the baby she was at death. Belying her brave assertion—"Beloved, she my daughter, She mine. See: She come back to me of her own free will and I don't have to explain a thing" (200)—Sethe becomes obsessed with explaining her actions. Murder cannot really be justified, though, and Beloved is not interested anyway. Her main complaint is of abandonment; her cry is that of all children left by mothers, and her desire for attention shows the insatiable demand of the infant, who will take from her mother as much as she can get. Unable to see Sethe as an individual (Sethe is completely an object for Beloved), Beloved now becomes a destroyer, a threat to her mother's very being.[72]

At first Denver is delighted with her new friend, recognizing her as her dead sister and dedicating herself to protecting her from Sethe (though she is jealous of Sethe's obsessive attentions to Beloved). However, Sethe grows thin and lethargic, and Denver becomes alarmed, realizing she must protect Sethe from Beloved, to become *her* mother. At this point, the story focuses on Denver's growth in strength as she leaves the yard, the "maternal space" we all must leave, and begs food from neighbors (*VTM* 16). When the neighbors hear of the strange ghost in Sethe's house, they turn from their cruelty; earlier they had ignored the slavers coming to the house because they were jealous of a party Baby Suggs had given to celebrate Sethe's escape. Finally a large group of women (some critics said like a Greek chorus) descend on the house and exorcise the spirit.

Kubitschek sees this final scene of exorcism as a movement into that "wild zone" beyond the words of the patriarchy (174-175). The shout of the women, a cry that goes beyond words, banishes the ghost and, at least to some extent, the horrible memories and effects of slavery. For, as Morrison shows through the stream-of-consciousness memories of Beloved, she is not only the lost daughter, she is all the millions who made the Middle Passage. Morrison says that the women's cry goes back to the beginning where there were no words (259); perhaps (and we are aware that no exorcism is complete) it can banish some of that pain.

Therefore, it would be a mistake to see *Beloved* as only about motherhood, for it is also about slavery and its debilitating effects on all black people, men as well as women. As in all her novels, Morrison shows how social conditions contributed to the gulf between black men and women. Before the escape, Halle, Sethe's husband, must watch from a hayloft while the new master of Sweet Home, Schoolteacher's two sadistic nephews, are allowed to suckle at Sethe's breast. Halle is so unmanned by this assault that he never returns; once again we see a black man leaving his family because of the cruelty of white society. Barbara Rigney suggests that one could see this scene almost as a paradigm for the impotence of the black male, unable to protect his woman (VTM88). In Morrison sometimes women "castrate" men, but it is far more likely that white society does that.

Though Morrison is understanding of Halle's pain—we last see him mad and smearing butter on his face—she emphasizes Sethe's humiliation at this assault on her person, a humiliation that may be best understood by a woman. When Sethe tells Paul D about it, he focuses on Halle's feelings and does not notice Sethe's shame, and also her rage that Halle did not try to stop it. Though Sethe knows rationally that Halle could not help her, her disgust with all men generated by her shame is deflected toward her absent husband and later to men in general. When Paul D says he never mistreated a woman, Sethe replies, "That makes one in the world" (68). Later, when Paul D leaves after finding out about the murder of the baby, Sethe accepts his leaving as inevitable. She always expected it "because she didn't believe any of them—over the long haul—could measure up." She really does not resent men's behavior too much, however, perhaps understanding its cause: "Whatever the reason, it was right. No fault. Nobody's fault" (128). It is part of the "way things are" for black women.

Morrison shows us the degradation of black women through women's eyes. Women slaves are assaulted; Ella is shut in a woodshed for years and made to service a man and his son; they are made to trade sex for services (Sethe couples with the stonecutter who carves Beloved's grave marker because she cannot afford the inscription); and, of course, they suffer worst in the loss of their children. Not only the big cruelties are emphasized but the small ones as well that serve to push down any developing sense of self. When the fourteen-year-old Sethe goes to Mrs. Garner and asks to marry, the young couple is not allowed a ceremony to celebrate their union.

All is not negative in *Beloved*, however. Morrison beautifully stresses the joyful emergence of self in freedom, the tentative feelings of becoming a person. When Baby Suggs crosses the Ohio River into freedom, she seems to see her hands and feel her heart beating for the first time: "Suddenly she saw her hands and thought with a clarity so dazzling, 'These hands belong to me. These *my* hands.' Next she felt a knocking in her chest and discovered something else new: her own heartbeat" (141). Similarly, Sethe feels a pride, a "kind of selfishness" that she got her children out of slavery, and a new, more intense blooming of love for them:

"I was big, Paul D, and deep and wide and when I stretched out my arms all my children could get in between. I was *that* wide. Look like I loved em more when I got here. Or maybe I couldn't love em proper in Kentucky because they wasn't mine to love" (162).

In retrospect, this use of "mine" is ominous, but it also emphasizes the positive qualities of the protective Great Mother whose enduring love gives us all strength and shelter. Morrison also includes joyful scenes of the reunited mother and sisters—the night they go skating for example—that celebrate female connection and unity.

In her earlier novels men tend to be weak, egotistical, or cruel, but with the possible exception of Son, Morrison in Paul D creates her most attractive male character. Paul D is intelligent, kind, long-suffering, and helpful to Sethe's growth in many ways. To a large extent he is responsible for breaking the unhealthy triangle of Sethe, Beloved, and Denver. Paul is "the kind of man who could walk into a house and make the women cry. Because with him, in his presence, they could. There was something blessed in his manner" (17). Clearly he is a man in touch with the feminine within himself, and women recognize this.

Carol Boyce Davies, on the other hand, questions Paul D's entrance into the female triad as a savior and looks askance at his granting of personhood to Sethe. When Sethe says, after Beloved leaves, "She was my best thing," Paul tells her, "You your best thing, Sethe" (273). Davies suggests that Sethe's final question, "Me?" is mocking, because no woman receives self at the hands of another, especially a man. This conclusion to a woman's quest amounts to a reversion to the "heterosexual family romance" in which a dominant male resolves the heroine's problems (53). I, however, agree with Marianne Hirsch that this ending must be seen as positive and healthy for Sethe. Through bonding with another person besides her children, she finds an autonomous self within the community of reconstructed family (198). Sethe is now more than a mother. In addition, one cannot ignore the powerful need for community and connection felt by Afro-American people. It is true that in Morrison, women who live without men experience serious problems; but this situation has been forced on them, so one cannot see it as a chosen "sisterhood," as a white feminist might.

A negative view of Paul D and the novel's resolution ignores the special experiences of black women, who experienced the slavery and cruelties of the past. These experiences forced separations on black couples and forged dissensions between them, contributing to the resentment that each sex felt for the other. Therefore, the coming together of black woman and black man has to be seen as the most hopeful way of exorcising the horrible memories of the past. Further, the process of regeneration in the novel is reciprocal. Sethe is equally Paul's savior. In his sufferings and wanderings, Paul's heart turns into a "rusty tin tobacco can," but Sethe's kindness moves him—she is, he says, "a woman who is a friend of your mind"—and their love blooms softly under freedom (273).

Together, they hesitantly take out their awful memories and examine them: the bit in Paul's mouth, the prison camp, the "taking" of Sethe's milk, and her whipping. Paul has his weaknesses, of course, and the power of Sethe's thick love frightens him, as well as his own guilt over the "cold house" secret: Beloved has seduced him over and over in a kind of incest, and he seems powerless to resist her. The combination of his fear of Sethe's love and his own guilt causes him to leave her, though eventually he returns for the wonderful conclusion, in which, just as Baby Suggs did years before, Paul bathes the wounded Sethe in a baptism. Denver, too, experiences her redemption—Beloved is redeemer as well as devil—and moves forward, an autonomous person, toward her tomorrows with her young man (273).

In *Beloved* Morrison presents a complex picture of the intermeshing of responsibility for sin and suffering. Though most whites are cruel, there are a few decent white characters: Amy, the servant girl who helps Sethe birth Denver, and the Bodwins, the abolitionists who own the house where Baby Suggs lives. In addition, with the exception of Baby Suggs, the black characters all have the capacity to hurt each other. Paul hurts Sethe dreadfully; Stamp Paid, the kindly old man who saves Denver from death, is a meddler who tells Paul about Sethe's crime and later realizes his error; and, as always in Morrison, there is the dark side of the community that fails to warn Sethe of the slavers approaching the farm, and then ostracizes the pariah Sethe after she returns from jail. Just as Nel refuses to accept any guilt in the death of Chicken Little, the community members refuse to recognize their complicity in the death of the baby. The capacity of humans to hurt each other lies in the tendency toward self-aggrandizement and pride. Sometimes this hurt comes from love, for, as Morrison has said, sometimes people do terrible things to each other in the name of love. Even violence can be "a distortion of what, perhaps, we want to do."[73]

As Karen E. Fields says, ultimately this novel can be seen not as a litany of sufferings of slaves but as "a meditation on the nature of love" (159). Not only is there the love of Sethe for her children, of Denver for her mother and sister, and of Baby Suggs for everyone, as well as the love shown by a white character like Amy, there is the tender man/woman love of Paul D and Sethe. This is the only genuinely positive relationship between a man and woman (other than a few between minor characters) in Morrison's novels. Though she still stresses the divisions between black men and black women, sometimes produced by the depredations of white society, she also stresses the redemptive power of love. If black women and black men can realize their strengths and support each other in their sufferings and joys, they can overcome the divisions separating them and move toward hopeful futures. Thus, we can see that, like white women novelists since the 1970s, Morrison has moved from concentrating on male-female divisions to more hopeful and sympathetic views of the possibilities for closeness between the sexes.

JAZZ

At this writing Morrison's *Jazz* (1992) has been available for only a few months, and I have been able to give it only a quick reading. A love triangle set in the Harlem of the 1920s, when Afro-American people were searching for better lives and trying to deal with the still strong memories of slavery, it will likely provide as fertile a field for feminist analysis as Morrison's earlier novels. The character of Dorcas, the sexy young girl who becomes the middle-aged Joe Trace's lover (she is dead in the present of the story), is complex. Though on the one hand she is a femme fatale and home wrecker, Morrison shows us she is actually unsure of her attractiveness, having been rejected by a young man her own age. Dorcas seems to base her sense of worth on her ability to attract men, and turns to Joe to prove this to herself. Her discarding of Joe, a man who really likes women, for the younger Acton, a conceited woman-hater, precipitates Joe's murder of her.

Equally interesting is Violet, Joe's rejected wife, who neglects to have children and then in her fifties finds herself taking a baby from a carriage. She develops a friendship with Dorcas's Aunt Alice that is full of an unspoken closeness both women obviously come to cherish. To some extent, Alice is one of Morrison's "thin brown girls," but she is rendered much more sympathetically than in earlier novels. The most fascinating character is Joe's mother, a crazed wild woman who abandoned Joe as a baby and lives in caves. In an interesting twist on males searching for their fathers, Joe longs to make contact with this enigmatic mother, but he never gets her to speak. She appears to exist in that preverbal "wild zone" that Morrison characters, male and female, sometimes penetrate, usually deriving some revelation beyond the words of the patriarchy. She is a haunting image of the hurt the world inflicts on women (we never discover what she has suffered to cause her to withdraw), but she is also the frightening image of the untamed woman entirely outside the "laws of the fathers."

A CRITICAL ASSESSMENT

Toni Morrison deserves her present status as one of the nation's greatest novelists. Her moral vision continues to expand, and the beauty, passion, and truth of her people and stories are astounding. Truly she has achieved her aim of creating beautiful political writing, writing that takes moral positions on the great issues of our times and soars into that "wild zone" where words express what is inexpressible. I surely have not been able to do her unforgettable women justice in this discussion: not only the sad ones—Pecola, Pauline, Nel, Ruth, and Jadine—but also the amazing Eva, the soft-hearted Hannah, Pilate, sharp-tongued Ondine, and the wonderful Baby Suggs. Baby, another of Morrison's ancestors, is an unchurched preacher up from slavery who tells people not of fire and brimstone but of their lovable bodies: "flesh that weeps, laughs; flesh that dances in grass. Love it, Love it hard" (88). In her is realized the feminist theologian's demand for a spirituality that embraces the body. Over and over in the lives of black people, especially black women, despite the presence of injustice and evil, life is to be celebrated.

Though she has been accused of "selling out" to white feminist values and reveals many attitudes similar to cultural feminists, Morrison cannot be called a feminist writer in the same way as white feminists such as Marge Piercy or even a black "womanist" such as Alice Walker. As I have shown, she is more willing than many white feminists to acknowledge wrongdoing on the part of women. Further, even though she has amply documented black women's experience, expressing a sensibility about life one could certainly call "feminist," she is always attentive to the experiences of her male characters as well. This gives her writing a perspective not found in much white feminist writing. In *Beloved* and her other novels, Morrison has continued to emphasize the uneasy alliance between black women and black men because of their common experience of white oppression. Black women have a concern for their men that many middle-class white women do not have for men of their class. For many white women it is hard to muster up sympathy for white men who seem to be the top dogs in the patriarchal system. We can talk about loss of opportunities to father and the burden of always being strong, but when it comes right down to it, it often looks pretty good to be a white male.

Though dealing frankly with black men's abuse of black women, Morrison has striven to explain the source of that abuse. The juxtaposition of those two themes, as I have shown, sometimes produces tensions and dissonances in Morrison's novels. Nevertheless, human behavior is complex, its causes varied, and tension inevitable. Morrison's understanding of this complexity further contributes to the success of her work. Also, it is likely that her early family life colored her perceptions of male/female relations. As a child she saw a balance and lack of tension between her parents and grandparents. The talents of her mother were not hidden ("NM" 416). Again, therefore, we find that the difference between black and white women's writing can be attributed to authoritative female role models.

Morrison has been accused of placing limitations on her female characters that she does not place on males, of not allowing her women to "fly." Morrison herself, however, has stated that black women writers deal better with aggression and adventure for women, probably because they have experienced more of it. They do not see the conflicts between love and work that white women do: "Black women are able to combine the nest and the adventure" (*BWWW* 122). On balance, despite her obviously ambivalent attitudes toward issues of women's freedom, I would agree with Barbara Rigney that Morrison has taken writing about the experiences of women farther than many white writers. She truly does take us into a "wild zone" where the powers of women are celebrated, their pain is lamented, and the language becomes untamed, expressing aspects of female experience that cannot be expressed.

NOTES

1. Wendy Steiner, review of *Playing in the Dark*, by Toni Morrison, *New York Times Book Review* (5 April 1992), 1, 28, 29.

2. Barbara Rigney, *The Voices of Toni Morrison* (Columbus: Ohio State University Press, 1991). Hereafter abbreviated *VTM*.

3. Rosemary K. Lester, "An Interview with Toni Morrison: Hessian Radio Network, Frankfurt, W. Germany," in *Critical Essays on Toni Morrison*, ed. Nellie McKay (Boston: G. K. Hall, 1988), 45.

4. *VTM*, 3-4; Hélène Cixous, "Laugh of the Medusa," trans. Keith Cohen and Paula Cohen, *Signs* 1 (Summer 1976), 878.

5. Chikwenye Okonjo Ogunyemi, "Womanism: The Dynamics of the Contemporary Black Female Novel in English," *Signs* 11 (Autumn 1985), 64. Ogunyemi explores the distinction between white feminism and black "womanism" as it appears in literature. She says a "feminist" novel protests sexism and the patriarchal system. Some recent novels by black women meet some of these qualifications but have other features that set them apart from white feminist works.

6. Alice Walker, *In Search of Our Mothers' Gardens* (San Diego: Harcourt Brace Jovanovich, 1983), xi.

7. Carolyn Denard, "Toni Morrison," in *Modern American Women Writers*, ed. Elaine Showalter (New York: Scribner's, 1991), 334.

8. In *Black Women Writers (1950-1980), a Critical Evaluation*, ed. Mari Evans (Garden City, NY: Anchor, 1984), 345, hereafter abbreviated *BWW*, Morrison says that the current idea of a novel without a political point of view is "tainted." However, writing can be political and beautiful at the same time.

9. Quoted in Denard, "Toni Morrison," 333.

10. Toni Morrison, "What Black Woman Thinks About Women's Lib?" *New York Times Magazine* (22 August 1971), 14-15, 63ff.

11. For the details of Morrison's life see Denard, "Toni Morrison," 319-322; and Carol Iannone, "Toni Morrison's Career," *Commentary* 34 (December 1987), 59-60.

12. "An Interview with Toni Morrison Conducted by Nellie McKay," *Contemporary Literature* 24 (Winter 1983), 414. Hereafter abbreviated "NM."

13. Barbara Christian, *Black Women Novelists: The Development of a Tradition, 1892-1976* (Westport, CT: Greenwood, 1980), 137. Hereafter abbreviated *BWN*.

14. Mel Watkins, "Talk with Toni Morrison," *New York Times Book Review* (11 September 1977), 50.

15. Stephanie A. Demetrakopoulos, *New Dimensions of Spirituality: A Biracial and Bicultural Reading of the Novels of Toni Morrison*, ed. Karla F. C. Holloway and Stephanie Demetrakopoulos (Westport, CT: Greenwood, 1987), 31, hereafter abbreviated *NDS*; Robert B. Stepto, " 'Intimate Things in Place': A Conversation with Toni Morrison," in *Chant of Saints: A Gathering of Afro-American Literature,*

Art and Scholarship, ed. Michael S. Harper and Robert B. Stepto (Urbana: University of Illinois Press, 1979), 219.

16. Jane Bakerman, "Failures of Love: Female Initiation in the Novels of Toni Morrison," *American Literature* 52 (January 1981), 541.

17. A. M. Umeh, "A Comparative Study of the Idea of Motherhood in Two Third World Novels," *CLA Journal* 31 (September 1987), 31-43.

18. Adrienne Rich, *Of Woman Born: Motherhood as Experience and Institution* (New York: Bantam, 1977), 245.

19. Luise Eichenbaum and Susie Orbach, feminist psychotherapists, expand on this theme in their *Understanding Women: A Feminist Psychoanalytic Approach* (New York: Basic Books, 1983), 43-44.

20. Paula Bennett, "The Mother's Part: Incest and Maternal Deprivation in Woolf and Morrison," in *Narrating Mothers: Theorizing Maternal Subjectivities*, ed. Brenda O. Daly and Maureen Reddy (Knoxville: University of Tennessee Press, 1991), 126-127.

21. Barbara Christian, *Black Feminist Criticism: Perspectives on Black Women Writers* (New York: Pergamon, 1985), 48.

22. Toni Morrison, *The Bluest Eye* (New York: Holt, Rinehart and Winston, 1970), 86.

23. Trudier Harris, *From Mammies to Militants: Domestics in Black American Literature* (Philadelphia: Temple University Press, 1982), 60-63.

24. Joanne Frye, *Living Stories, Telling Lives: Women and the Novel in Contemporary Experience* (Ann Arbor: University of Michigan Press, 1986), 97-108.

25. Elliott Butler-Evans, *Race, Gender, and Desire: Narrative Strategies in the Fiction of Toni Cade Bambara, Toni Morrison, and Alice Walker* (Philadelphia: Temple University Press, 1989), 69. Hereafter abbreviated *RGD*.

26. Madonne M. Miner, "Lady No Longer Sings the Blues: Rape, Madness, and Silence in *The Bluest Eye*," in *Conjuring: Black Women, Fiction, and Literary Tradition*, ed. Marjorie Pryse and Hortense J. Spillers (Bloomington: Indiana University Press, 1985), 176-191. Miner compares Pecola's story with classical rapes of Philomena and Persephone, stressing the "silence" of the victim; Michael Awkward states that Ralph Ellison ignores the daughter's reaction to the rape, and in fact portrays it as a kind of celebration of the power of the black male phallus. "Roadblocks and Relatives: Critical Revision in Toni Morrison's *The Bluest Eye*," in *Critical Essays on Toni Morrison*, ed. Nellie McKay (Boston: G. K. Hall, 1988), 57-67.

27. *Black Women Writers at Work*, ed. Claudia Tate (New York: Continuum, 1983), 125. Hereafter abbreviated *BWWW*.

28. Anne Mickelson, *Reaching Out: Sensitivity and Order in Recent American Fiction by Women* (Metuchen, NJ: Scarecrow, 1979), 176, hereafter abbreviated *RO*. In Chapter 4 I stated that Judith Kegan Gardiner has cited this quality—inability to acknowledge evil in women—as an obvious weakness of feminist fiction by white women.

29. Marianne Hirsch, *The Mother/Daughter Plot: Narrative, Psychoanalysis, Feminism* (Bloomington: Indiana University Press, 1989), 177.

30. *RO*, 126; Terry Otten, *The Crime of Innocence in the Fiction of Toni Morrison* (Columbia: University of Missouri Press, 1989), 26; Naana Banyiwa-Horne,

"The Scary Face of the Self: An Analysis of the Character of Sula in Toni Morrison's *Sula*," *Sage* 2 (Spring 1985), 28. Hereafter abbreviated B-H.

31. Toni Morrison, *Sula* (New York: Knopf, 1974), 52.

32. Meredith Cory, *Different Drummers: New Roles in Old Societies* (Metuchen, NJ: Scarecrow, 1984), 170.

33. Elizabeth Abel, "(E)Merging Identities: The Dynamics of Female Friendship in Contemporary Fiction by Women," *Signs* 6 (Spring 1981), 413-435.

34. See *Desire in Language: A Semiotic Approach to Literature and Art*, ed. Leon S. Roudiez, trans. Thomas Goza, Alice Jardine, and Leon Roudiez (New York: Columbia University Press, 1980), 235-243.

35. Margaret Homans, " 'Her Very Own Howl': The Ambiguities of Representation in Recent Women's Fiction," *Signs* 9 (Winter 1983), 193.

36. *VTM*, 50; Hirsch, *Mother/Daughter Plot*, 182.

37. Cynthia A. Davis, "Self, Society, and Myth in Toni Morrison's Fiction," *Contemporary Literature* 23 (Summer 1982), 340.

38. Stepto, " 'Intimate Things in Place,' " 215.

39. Hortense Spillers, "A Hateful Passion, a Lost Love," in *Feminist Issues in Literary Scholarship*, ed. Shari Benstock (Bloomington: Indiana University Press, 1987), 183.

40. Joseph Wessling, "Narcissism in Toni Morrison's *Sula*," *CLA Journal* 31 (March 1988), 291.

41. In an interview with Bettye J. Parker, Morrison remarked that if women choose to create children, they should not object if men choose to leave, a statement that would appall some white feminists, as it seems to put all responsibility for conception on women. "Complexity: Toni Morrison's Women—An Interview Essay," in *Sturdy Black Bridges: Visions of Black Women in Literature*, ed. Roseann P. Bell, Bettye J. Parker, and Beverly Guy-Sheftall (New York: Doubleday, 1979), 256.

42. In Morrison's *Playing in the Dark: Whiteness and the Literary Imagination* (Cambridge, MA: Harvard University Press, 1991) she argues that white society and white writers use the black as a device to confront the darkness in themselves.

43. Barbara Rigney, *Lilith's Daughters: Women and Religion in Contemporary Fiction* (Madison: Univesity of Wisconsin Press, 1982), 20-21.

44. Dorothy Lee, "The Quest for Self: Triumph and Failure in the Works of Toni Morrison," in *BWW*, 352.

45. Rigney, *Lilith's Daughters*, 22. Rigney sees Sula as Cain *and* Christ.

46. Watkins, "Talk with Toni Morrison," 50.

47. Toni Morrison, *Song of Solomon* (New York: Knopf, 1977), 337.

48. Marilyn Atlas, "A Woman Both Shiny and Brown: Feminine Strength in Toni Morrison's *Song of Solomon*," *The Society for the Study of Midwestern Literature Newsletter* 9 (Fall 1979), 1.

49. *RO*, 136; Bakerman, "Failures of Love," 541-563.

50. Nancy Chodorow, *The Reproduction of Mothering: Psychoanalysis and the Sociology of Gender* (Berkeley: University of California Press, 1978), 100, 183; quoted in Rigney, *VTM*, 15, 68-69.

51. Joseph T. Skerrett, Jr., sees Pilate as a conjure-woman "in touch with the spiritual resources of Afro-American folk traditions." "Recitation to the *Griot*: Storytelling and Learning in Toni Morrison's *Song of Solomon*," in *Conjuring: Black*

Women, Fiction, and Literary Tradition, ed. Marjorie Pryse and Hortense J. Spillers (Bloomington: Indiana University Press, 1985), 195.

52. Watkins, "Talk with Toni Morrison," 50.

53. Mickelson, *RO*, 153, tempers her remarks by saying we should trust the tale, not the artist. Milkman's comments about Pilate not having to leave the ground signify that no one, man or woman, has absolute freedom; in contrast, Iannone says ("Toni Morrison's Career," 61), "There is a strain in [Morrison's] thought which seems not only not to condemn but even to endorse certain pathological elements in black life."

54. Davis, "Self, Society, and Myth," 341.

55. See, for example, Darryl Pinckney, who cites strained language and an unclear evocation of the tar baby myth, "Every Which Way," *New York Review of Books* 28 (30 April 1981), 25; and Barbara Christian, who says the novel is "facile" and uses stereotypes that were not true a century ago, let alone now. "Testing the Strength of the Black Cultural Bond: Review of Toni Morrison's *Tar Baby*," in her *Black Feminist Criticism: Perspectives on Black Women Writers* (New York: Pergamon, 1985), 69.

56. Toni Morrison, *Tar Baby* (New York: Knopf, 1981), 48.

57. Webster Schoot, "Toni Morrison: Tearing the Social Fabric," *Washington Post Book World* (22 March 1981), 1-2, suggests that if *Tar Baby* had been written by a white male, it would be called male chauvinism.

58. Anthony J. Berret, "Toni Morrison's Literary Jazz," *CLA Journal* 32 (March 1989), 281.

59. Susan Corey Everson, "Toni Morrison's *Tar Baby*: A Resource for Feminist Theology," *Journal of Feminist Studies in Religion* 5 (Fall 1989), 77.

60. See, for example, Marilyn Sanders Mobley, *Folk Roots and Mythic Wings in Sarah Orne Jewett and Toni Morrison: The Cultural Function of Narrative* (Baton Rouge: Louisiana State University Press, 1991), 134-167; and Peter B. Erickson, "Images of Nurturance in Toni Morrison's *Tar Baby*," *CLA Journal* 28 (September 1984), 11-32. Though both critics feel the novel is brilliant, they question the limitations Morrison places on Jadine. Erickson feels that Morrison takes cheap shots at her, setting her up as a character we do not like.

61. Susan Lydon, "What's an Intelligent Woman to Do?" *The Village Voice* (1-7 July 1981), 41.

62. According to Karla F. C. Holloway in *NDS*, black women like Therese teach the race how to "survive and remember." Without the pie ladies, black children will have no roots. And if black women withhold these truths, they emasculate as Jadine is attempting to emasculate Son.

63. Christian, "Testing the Strength," 68-69.

64. Walter Clemmons, "A Graveyard of Memories," *Newsweek* 110 (28 September 1987), 75. Clemmons tells how the story was stimulated by a contemporary newspaper clipping telling of a Kentucky runaway slave, Margaret Garner, who tried to kill her children at the home of her mother-in-law in Cincinnati, rather than have them go back to slavery.

65. Julia Kristeva, "Women's Time," trans. Alice Jardine, *Signs* 7 (Autumn 1981), 26.

66. Chodorow, *Reproduction of Mothering*, 100.

67. Jessica Benjamin, *The Bonds of Love: Psychoanalysis, Feminism, and the*

Problem of Domination (New York: Pantheon, 1988), 75, suggests that a too-ready acceptance of the fantasy of the ideal mother can lead to self-abnegation in a woman, an inability to see herself as subject.

68. Toni Morrison, *Beloved* (New York: Knopf, 1987), 45.

69. Missy Dehn Kubitschek, *Claiming the Heritage: African-American Women Novelists and History* (Jackson: University Press of Mississippi, 1991), 170.

70. Carol Boyce Davies, "Mother-Right/Write Revisited: *Beloved* and *Dessa Rose* and the Construction of Motherhood in Black Women's Fiction," in *Narrating Mothers*, ed. Brenda Daly and Maureen Reddy, 48.

71. In a TV interview Morrison said that Sethe had no right to do what she did. *MacNeil-Lehrer Newshour,* PBS, 29 September 1987.

72. Karen Fields, "To Embrace Dead Strangers: Toni Morrison's *Beloved*," in *Mother Puzzles: Daughters and Mothers in Contemporary American Literature*, ed. Mickey Pearlman (Westport, CT: Greenwood, 1989), 160-161.

73. Jane Bakerman, "The Seams Can't Show: An Interview with Toni Morrison," *Black American Literature Forum* 12 (1978), 160.

7

Conclusion

Feminist influence on the contemporary American novel by women goes much farther than the polemical "feminist novel" of the 1970s. In fact, exploration of feminist ideas in the literature has been broad and pervasive since the 1970s. Feminism has changed women's writing by opening up and legitimizing new plots and themes; furthermore, feminist theory has enabled writers to describe many types of female experience with a truth and keen perception seldom seen before. These new insights of feminist theory and the issues and subjects raised by feminism have greatly enriched literature about women's lives.

This new writing has not come from nowhere, of course. Writers have expanded upon the centuries-long tradition in women's literature documented by feminist scholars such as Elaine Showalter, Sandra Gilbert and Susan Gubar, and Hazel Carby, who has shown the legacy that Afro-American women writers owe to the past.[1] Despite this long and rich tradition, however, there were areas left largely unexplored by previous writers; and the insights and theories of the contemporary feminist movement, plus the general interest among the reading public in women and their experiences, have enabled women writers of all ethnic groups and races to enter these new areas. I have not touched in this study, for example, on the marvelous contributions of women writers of Native American ancestry, such as Louise Erdrich, and Chicana writers, such as Sandra Cisneros.

THE 1970s AND 1980s CONTRASTED

In the 1970s some writers put the ideas of radical feminism into fictional form. Interest in the "social construction of femininity" led to the novel of development or *bildungsroman*. In these works, being female was sometimes seen as a negative condition to be overcome by the protagonist in her quest for liberation from socially prescribed roles. Illustrating the idea that "the personal is political," writers such as Marilyn French and Marge Piercy featured sexual politics—male/female power struggles. Sometimes the protagonists were able to overcome what the authors saw as the devastating oppression of being female and to move on to hopeful future lives. In other cases, these novels seemed to hold little hope for women achieving happy, free lives.

Even in the 1970s, however, not all writers echoed the ideas of radical feminism. Some suggested that women's problems were partly of their own making, a result of their own stereotyped thinking or too-eager embracing of patriarchal ideas; some, like Lisa Alther, suggested that radical feminism may be another artificial role preventing a woman from achieving complete self-awareness. Few of these 1970s novels took much interest in women's careers, since "the personal is political," writers suggested that freeing oneself from socially imposed roles within the family and in personal relationships is the first step toward achieving self-identity. Those that did deal with women's careers stressed the connections between jobs and the discoveries protagonists made about their personal lives. Many writers also acknowledged the cost of "liberation" from roles—loneliness, doubt, insecurity. When Isabel in *Final Payments* is freed from serving her father, her freedom is terrifying.

During the 1970s writers took an interest in many specific feminist issues: abortion, rape, the influence of the media on women's images of themselves, discrimination in education, lesbianism, and cultural attitudes toward women. Examination of these issues raised fascinating questions and revealed many paradoxes. For example, Western culture tends to equate women with nature and body, and men with mind and culture. If a woman tries to free herself from the idea that she *is* her body, how does she then come to terms with her sexuality? This is a particular conflict in all of Mary Gordon's novels. If a young woman allows herself to be sexually free, as do the adolescent protagonists of some novels, how does she escape exploitation by men who regard her as an object? One answer is to have sexual relationships with other women, who presumably will regard her as a person. In most mainstream literature, however, protagonists remained heterosexual and experienced pleasure as well as pain in their sexual relations with men. Whether they were dealing with heterosexuality or lesbianism, for the first time in American literature, women writers dealt frankly and expansively with women's sexuality.

Another paradox or problem discussed by women writers was the role of motherhood and women's relationships. In keeping with the feminist theory of the time, which saw motherhood as an institution of patriarchy used to control women, most writers in the 1970s tended to regard motherhood as an impediment to a woman's growth. Relatively few protagonists were mothers, and they tended to find mothering to be immensely restricting to their search for self. However, writers also granted the powerful pleasures of the intimacy of the mother/child relationship. Motherhood was seen as conveying power and vulnerability at the same time.

Novelists in the 1970s also wrote about women's relations with other women, but not as much as they did in the 1980s. In the 1970s the radical feminist writers mainly stressed the concept of sisterhood, the support that women give each other in their struggles to develop and find themselves in male-dominated society. Generally, even radical feminist writers did not feature women's friendships as a central theme; friends often seemed to exist for purposes of comparison, to show role models or anti-models for the protagonists' choices. In the 1970s sexual politics or male-female power struggles remained center stage for most of these writers. One exception to this lack of stress on women's friendships in the 1970s was Toni Morrison's *Sula*, which, although not radical feminist in outlook, featured a friendship between two women as central to their maturation. As some critics have suggested, it could be argued that Morrison is offering her reader an alternative to heterosexual romance for women in their quests. Without this friendship, both women seem to fail in their quests.

Novelists in the 1970s also paid little attention to the relationships between mothers and daughters, another popular topic in the 1980s. When they did feature this theme, mothers were seen mainly as objects with little voice of their own, as "corset tighteners" and representatives of the patriarchy who oppose their daughters' efforts to gain independence. Exceptions to this exist, of course, notably Mrs. Babcock in Lisa Alther's *Kinflicks*, who is allowed to have her own voice in the novel, and who gives her daughter valuable guidance. In Toni Morrison's writing of the 1970s, although there are some positive mother figures, the picture of motherhood is ambiguous at best; mothers are givers of life and love, and destroyers. In Mary Gordon's first novel the protagonist effectively never had a mother.

Although it is no doubt somewhat artificial to make distinctions in types of literature according to decade, as I have done, it is clear that by the 1980s changes were taking place in writers' treatment of issues and in the introduction of new themes. Sexual politics receded as a central theme. Though radical feminist Marge Piercy continued to stress the oppression of women by men, other writers who had treated this theme in the 1970s seemed to veer toward other topics. To some extent we see writers embrace cultural feminist values—a celebration of motherhood; relations between women, including mother/daughter relations; the values of nurturance and female culture in general; and a deemphasis on the negative effects of being a women as well as on the oppression of women by men. Writers like Gail Godwin and Mary Gordon explored the gifts women give each other, their families, and society as a whole.

In my discussion of antifeminist backlash in the 1980s, I described the decade as tough on feminists. Conservatives went on the attack during these years, lambasting feminists for causing social problems such as divorce and teenage drug abuse; in 1982 a coalition of these conservative elements defeated the Equal Rights Amendment. Though I am not suggesting that writers changed their subjects to please conservative critics, I do believe that in part the changed tone of the times caused feminists to regroup and reexamine their ideas. This reexamination led away from an attack on men as representatives of patriarchy and toward a reevaluation of feminine assets; many feminists began to believe that being a woman is not an illness, that motherhood can grant experiences denied to men, that the female values of kindness, concern for the downtrodden, and even passivity may save the species. These ideas are not new to the 1980s, but they did begin to receive more prominence due to the writing of feminist theorists such as Kathryn Rabuzzi.[2] Even such a feminist leader as Robin Morgan, compiler of *Sisterhood Is Powerful*, said in her autobiography that she welcomed the new freedom to come out of the "mother-closet" and admit she loved her child.[3]

These ideas found their way into the popular culture and into the fiction of the 1980s as well. In the 1970s many feminists modeled their struggles toward self-realization on those of men: a woman needed to free herself from the caregiving female role and find work in the public world; feminist writers, of both fiction and nonfiction, celebrated those women who achieved on the public stage of life like men. The problem with this, however, as historian Gerda Lerner says, is that men were still writing the script.[4] By the 1980s we see more understanding of what women may have to give up if they follow the male model of achievement. A character like Jadine in *Tar Baby* sounds a warning to young women who want to escape their femaleness and, in this case, their black roots to achieve in the rat race of affluent, male-dominated society. Though Morrison could be accused of romanticizing the life of the "pie ladies" of Eloe, her warning gets the reader's attention when she feels pulled from traditional values and pleasures toward achievement in her career. Therefore, this sort of conflict in the literature amplifies her own life conflicts for the woman reader. A similar conflict is seen in Gail Godwin's Cate in *A Mother and Two Daughters*: a woman who has achieved status in the outside world yet has an unsettled personal life and sometimes yearns for the quiet rural atmosphere of her past.

Echoing the ideas of "maternalists" such as Adrienne Rich and Sara Ruddick, many of these writers seem to suggest that the qualities needed for mothering (caregiving in general) demand fuller humanity and provide pleasures that most women embrace. These writers answer the criticisms of psychiatrist Ann Dally, who wrote in 1982:

So far the women's liberation movement has failed mothers ... although the movement has much to offer women, until it begins to think and write sensibly about mothers and motherhood it will continue to be a peripheral movement, shunned by most women, supported particularly by those who ignore or dislike motherhood and children and it will continue to be deserted by those . . . who discover that there is more to motherhood than they ever thought or dreamed.[5]

Certainly as of this writing in 1992, it can no longer be said that the feminist movement disparages or ignores mothers. In fact, many of these writers suggest that the qualities which mothering enhances can benefit all of humanity if they are allowed to flourish in the public world.[6] In Godwin's *A Mother and Two Daughters*, the way family members and friends treat each other becomes a model for the way members of a society should treat each other. Many of these writers, such as Mary Gordon in *The Company of Women* and Marilyn French in *Her Mother's Daughter*, celebrate the powerful physical passion of motherhood as well. Though she is frightened by the "diminishment" of marriage, Felicitas in *Company* finds that the celibate, childless life can lead to a "cruelty of judgement" (262). Sue Miller in *The Good Mother* goes so far as to defend the absolute primacy of the mother bond; it is so precious, mysterious, and life enhancing that Anna considers it more important than lover, career, or public truth. Like Adrienne Rich, later women writers acknowledge the restrictions of the *institution* of motherhood but celebrate its potential for enriching life.

On the other side of the question, like writers in the 1970s, novelists in the 1980s have expressed fears of being like their mothers, of reliving their lives. It is this fear that causes daughters to reject their mothers. For Anastasia in *Her Mother's Daughter*, a daughter needs to break her mother's silence, to understand her story and her anger, so that she will not be doomed to repeat it and may even be able to have a closer and more truthful relationship with her own daughter. Similarly, Claire in Godwin's *A Southern Family* must name her mother's experience in order to free herself from the stranglehold her mother's lies have on her own development. Another 1980s novel, Mona Simpson's *Anywhere But Here* (1986), came to my attention only while finishing this study; it powerfully tells of the struggles of the heroine, Ann, to free herself from her loving but neurotic mother, Adele.[7] All these writers reflect the ideas of feminist psychologists like Nancy Chodorow. Though mothering does produce women skilled at personal relationships, it also creates tensions in the woman who steps outside her traditional role. What we need to do is to break the "reproduction of mothering," so that daughters will be free to draw on the strengths of their mothers' experiences and at the same time not have to repeat their lives.

Finally, some novelists have celebrated the strengths of mothers of the past. As Gerda Lerner says, all of our study of women's pasts cannot focus on their diminishment and pain (5). This is one part of women's experience, but it gives a limited, distorted picture of their contributions to human history and their life experiences. In literature, continual focusing on women's sufferings produces the same distortion. So, in a novel like *The Joy*

Luck Club daughters gain strength through their mothers' stories—the joys as well as sufferings—and thus come to acknowledge their debt to their mothers. We see the pain of the concubine, the mother losing her child to war or watching her daughter reject her ways, but we also see the triumphs over background and culture, triumphs that cause a daughter to bow her head in amazement at the vulnerability yet strength of a little warrior mother "with a wok for her armor and a knitting needle for a sword" (204). Such novels ameliorate what Rich calls the "loss of the daughter to the mother, the mother to the daughter . . . the essential female tragedy. . . . [8]

A related new subject of the 1980s is women's friendships, which are linked to the larger issue of "sisterhood," the bonds uniting women in shared experiences that go beyond race and class. First of all, both feminist theorists and novelists have pointed out that our relations to other women are similar to our relations to our own mothers. Second, though many friendships in literature seem to be based on differences, close examination shows that women are drawn together by similarities, not just similarities in life experiences brought about by similar female bodies. Many of the literary friendships I have described here, such as those between Isabel and Liz in Gordon's *Final Payments* and between Claire and Julia in Godwin's *A Southern Family*, are intellectual as well as emotional relationships. Though it could be argued that this stress on close female friendship precludes concern for women beyond one's own sphere, it is equally plausible that realizing the importance of other women to one's own growth is *central* to developing a political consciousness. How are we to believe that what happens to women we do not know matters when we do not realize the importance of our own friends?

Despite this attention to women's friendships, there is not much overt stress on "sisterhood" or women's community in these mainstream novels. Except in radical feminist novels, mostly written in the 1970s, protagonists conduct their quests without the support of an activist feminist community. Though they may identify themselves as feminists, have careers, and form powerful private bonds with other women, most of them do not engage in feminist activism. Though this may be regretted, I think it is an accurate reflection of the lives and consciousnesses of many women in the 1980s; during this period they were interested in the significance of their personal relations. Then, too, novels, even "political" novels, have always been about personal relations rather than depictions of abstract concepts like "women's community." As I have suggested, however, the novel that concentrates on women's friendships and relations with female relatives *can* have the political function of calling the reader's attention to larger issues of women's community, as does a novel like *The Color Purple*.

Not all feminist critics are agreed that this change in themes and emphasis from sexual politics to cultural feminist values emphasizing motherhood and women's friendships is beneficial for the Women's Movement. At a recent conference, when I read a paper titled "Mothers and Daughters in Contemporary Fiction," a colleague wondered if all the stress on the "tender ties" of motherhood would throw women back toward traditional roles and a limited view of themselves. Paulina Palmer, in *Contemporary Women's Fiction*, believes that this stress on the pleasures of motherhood can romanticize an activity that is "burdensome and humdrum."[9] Similarly, Gayle Greene has little positive to say about much of the fiction of the 1980s, stating that the work of writers like Mary Gordon and Sue Miller shows "the privatization and depoliticization of their concerns, the sentimentalization of the family, the resignation to things as they are." As she sees it, even the "feisty" feminist writers like Marge Piercy have abandoned the struggle to challenge the world and have turned inward to "character and relationship."[10] In this view, writers may have turned toward such subjects out of frustration: since women cannot achieve much in the public world, they will concern themselves with the one area where they do have power. Obviously, I do not agree, feeling that all aspects of women's experience need to be examined with truth and sympathy. As Ann Dally and many of these novelists have said, not all women experience motherhood as mostly a burden, and their experiences deserve exploration.

Another aspect of this new fiction that I have not stressed, perhaps because it seems obvious, is the greater variety of types of women used as subjects. Like older fiction, we still have plenty of stories of young, middle-class women and their relationships with men, but there are many older women, single women who are single by choice, lesbians, working-class women, and women of varying ethnic and racial backgrounds. It is hard to imagine a novel like *The Color Purple* achieving the prominence it did prior to 1970. Though women writers like Zora Neale Hurston paved the way for Alice Walker and Toni Morrison, the Women's Movement with its stress on the inclusion of all women, regardless of color or class, legitimized such subjects and made it possible for novels about many types of women to achieve a wide readership. As a result, this writing has increased middle-class women's understanding of the similarities and differences between themselves and women of other classes and races. Examining these similarities and differences can guide women in determining the changes our society needs.

During the period between 1970 and 1990, a number of writers created fictional utopias, such as those of Marge Piercy, where cultural feminist values have triumphed, female values are celebrated, and the sexes live together in harmony. These writings satisfy to some extent the reader's desire to see feminist goals realized. Though some critics have called for more speculative feminist fiction and fiction in which strong role models are featured, most mainstream writers have stuck to describing women's present situations. Similarly, few writers have illustrated feminist proposals for alternative methods of child rearing and so on. To my mind, this is not a situation to be deplored but, rather, an accurate reflector of human experience, what novels have always tried to do. As a reader, I find the utopias thought provoking but am more drawn to fiction that describes contemporary women's present struggles and triumphs.

NEW VERSIONS OF WOMEN'S EXPERIENCE

How effective has this new fiction been in portraying women's lives? I have argued that a major reason for its popularity is that it *has* accurately documented the lives and consciousnesses of many types of contemporary women. And, although I can offer only anecdotal evidence, I feel confident in asserting that by "telling women's lives," as Joanne Frye says, it has *changed* lives. This experience is immensely varied, of course, and it would be hazardous to posit a universal female experience that literature has amplified. There are, however, themes reaching across lines of race and class: struggles and love with men, especially husbands and lovers; the power and danger of motherhood; conflicts and love between mothers, daughters, and sisters; the important role played by female friendship in women's lives; for some women of all classes and races, the potential of sexual love with women; the difficulty of attaining self-esteem when surrounded by male-dominant values.

As I have shown, women in contemporary fiction have been on quests since the 1970s, but the contexts of those quests are very different and the specific problems they face are complicated by class and race. Some of the issues and problems faced by Celie, Sula, Pilate, and Jing-mei are quite different than those of Isadora, Stephanie, Ginny, and Anastasia. If it has done anything, the renaissance of literature by and about women shows that sweeping generalizations about what is "Woman" and her experience are very problematic. One point here deserves special stress: although it would indeed be dangerous to allege a universal female experience, enough commonalities exist that women of different types can see themselves in the fiction. That is why this writing, whether of middle-class white women, poor black women, or Chinese immigrants has been so immensely popular.

When I began this study, I stated my intention to make some artistic judgments about the novels and writers I would discuss. After reading and rereading many novels, I find that writers are most successful when they avoid a direct transcription of feminist political theory into fiction. Political theories, after all, describe general conditions; they cannot adequately account for the infinite variety of human experiences. To me, the works that are *obviously* radical feminist in orientation are less successful as literature and even as vehicles to promote feminist ideas. Though I am often swept away by the power of Piercy's and French's pleas for the abused women of the past and present, I also find their portraits of women's experience to be incomplete. But in making that judgment I fall back on my own experience— life was not like that for me; some of it was, but there was much joy in being female and in being human that I find missing from the radical feminist novel.

These issues are amplified in one of Lisa Alther's later novels *Other Women* (1984). Alther presents her plot mostly as series of conversations between her protagonist, Caroline, a radical lesbian feminist, and her analyst, Hannah, a less radical heterosexual feminist. Caroline is outraged, saddened, and obsessed with the cruelties of life and the injustices suffered by the downtrodden, mostly women and children, at the hands of men. Hannah tells her to look at the beauty, pleasure, and miracles of life: for every young girl who is raped by an idiot there are "also pileated woodpeckers."[11] The beauties of life are all around if only one takes one's eyes off the horrors for a moment. Paulina Palmer finds Hannah's advice here "mawkishly sentimental" (62), but I find myself agreeing with it. The outrages perpetrated against women are always present in my consciousness, but to concentrate so relentlessly on them as does radical feminist fiction produces an inaccurate picture of women's experience. Though Palmer judges works that veer from the radical feminist viewpoint to be "ideologically confused," for me they are more successful as literature because they create more truthful versions of the complexity of human experience. I realize, however, that in making such judgments, I reflect my own limited view.

A VARIETY OF STYLES

It is a commonplace in literary criticism that women do not write postmodernist fiction. In the course of my work I have indeed found that most American feminist-influenced writers have employed a realistic style, particularly those who reflect radical feminist theory. I feel, as does Palmer, that this is one reason why some of these writers have been rejected or ignored by the critics who prefer experimental modes. Palmer divides feminist fiction into radical, usually "realist," fiction and psychoanalytic fiction, which employs experimental techniques such as discontinuous narration. Because psychoanalytic fiction is concerned with the "fractured self," the conflicting forces at work on the individual psyche, psychoanalytic writers show women trapped in the "phallocratic structures" of society but do not portray them engaging in collective acts of resistance (162). Palmer and other critics believe the realist text does more to change women's status.[12]

A number of scholars have devoted a good deal of effort to showing that much of the "realistic" women's fiction is actually more experimental than the "metafictions" of male postmodern writers, fictions in which the work comments on the nature of its own literary conventions (often the protagonist is a writer), where there is little unitary sense of "character," and where traditional plot patterns of development are ignored. Scholars such as Rachel Blau DuPlessis, Molly Hite, Patricia Yaeger, and Gayle Greene argue that in their narrative strategies of "writing beyond the ending" by radically altering traditional plots, in their invention of different types of women characters, and in their questioning of traditional assumptions about sexual roles, some women writers are truly postmodern and experimental. Greene points out that there has always been a strong strain of didacticism in women writers, and this has led them to create texts that are accessible to a wide audience, texts that are described as realistic but are actually experimental.[13]

Greene, however, excludes American feminist writers such as Marge Piercy and Lisa Alther from her study, saying they are not metafictional. She also excludes black writers, who, she says, do not write feminist metafiction, and concentrates on Doris Lessing, Margaret Drabble, Margaret Atwood, and Margaret Laurence. My own belief is that many of the American writers I have discussed in this study, although employing realistic modes, do "write beyond the ending" and challenge traditional assumptions about their societies and sexual roles. One thing this scholarship does show is the degree to which the realistic novel has fallen in esteem among the literary establishment, where scholars must go to great lengths to prove that the texts they are working with are "postmodern" and "experimental." Certainly one may argue that the writers Greene works with are better writers than the Americans I have discussed, but that they are more effective as feminist writers seems a more debatable assertion.

Though the majority of the mainstream American authors I have studied employ a realistic approach to fiction, there are many variations. Writers as different as Piercy and Godwin are Victorian in the sweep and scope of their plots and characters. A few, such as Erica Jong and Francine du Plessix Gray, have occasionally employed an experimental style, liberally using discontinuous narrative and other nonrealistic devices. Barbara Rigney argues that despite the "magic realism" label, in Toni Morrison's use of multiple narrators and discontinuous narrative (*Song of Solomon* is the only novel with a traditional plot), her impressionistic use of language, and her rejection of a unified "self," she is a postmodernist, deconstructionist writer.[14] In her early novels Mary Gordon seemed to be consciously drawing on the legacy of the great nineteenth-century women writers; at the same time she also revealed a psychoanalytic approach to personality with liberal use of Freudian theory, but still had some characters who broke out of patriarchal structures. However, despite these variations, in these popular mainstream American novels realism predominates, whether in radical feminist works or in works only influenced by feminism.

This leads me to make an assertion that certainly will not go unchallenged: at least in literature, mainstream American feminism tends to be less radical than European or other types of Anglo feminism. Though we have plenty of women writers of a more radical bent, such as Paule Marshall, Cherrie Moraga, and Kathy Acker, we do not have feminist writers who have achieved the prominence of Margaret Atwood, Doris Lessing, or Fay Weldon. Another point seems clear as well: feminism as reflected in American mainstream literature by women often tends to be less radical than the feminist theory that influences it. Feminist theory often criticizes present social arrangements and suggests alternatives to them. Fiction writers with radical feminist leanings must therefore concentrate on women's problems and sufferings or create fictional utopias where alternative lifestyles have come into being. As we have seen, radical writers like Piercy and French have done that. Others, however, less concerned with promoting feminist issues and more concerned with representing a variety of themes, have incorporated feminist themes in a more diffuse way.

SOME POSSIBLE NEW DIRECTIONS

I intended to conclude by speculating on how feminism may influence women's writing into the 1990s. Because of the present state of the Women's Movement, I find that to be a more difficult task than I had supposed. There is cause for both pessimism and optimism. First, it seems clear that the radical feminist novel of the 1970s was a passing phase, if you will, a response to the theoretical ideas promoted by the early Women's Movement. Though such novels continued to be written into the 1980s, they did not achieve a great deal of prominence either in critical studies or on the best-seller lists. Sexual power struggles are less important in the fiction, and men are now being portrayed more sympathetically; there is a tacit understanding that masculinity, too, is a social construction of society. Also, authors today, especially those who write about middle-class women, are more likely to subscribe to the idea of each woman's responsibility for her own destiny; too much portrayal of women as victims encourages passivity and perpetuation of the status quo.

As I have suggested, this situation is deplored by some critics who feel the turn from women's sufferings toward personal relationships in the 1980s shows insensitivity to those who *are* victims. If middle-class women stop believing that all women have been victimized by patriarchy, they will turn their backs on their less fortunate sisters who are still victims. This can be a dangerous attitude that I see in some younger women, who feel that the world is their oyster and are not aware of the suffering of many of the world's women. Perhaps, as Gloria Steinem has said, they will need to have their consciousness raised by encountering their own problems.[15] I do not feel, however, that writers' declining attention to the injustices suffered by women shows insensitivity to women's problems; rather, it is simply a turning to unexplored subjects. Writers often do not like to cover ground already covered, and feminism opens up many areas to explore besides women's sufferings.

I believe that the issues raised by the cultural feminist novels of the 1980s will continue to be discussed for some time. Female friendship, motherhood,

mothers and daughters and sisters all have been far from exhausted as
subjects, and there seems to be relatively little in either the literature or
theoretical writing on sisters; this is an area that writers might consider
exploring. As I pointed out, many writers concentrated mainly on the negative influences of mothers on daughters; more novels like Amy Tan's *The
Joy Luck Club* might be welcomed by women readers. As a mother of sons
and daughter of my father, I would like to see writing about relationships
between women and their fathers and sons. There have been male writers
who have written about their relations with their mothers, but it seems few
contemporary women writers have written about their sons or fathers. Is
there a place for novels about women and men that show them living
together in intimacy and respect in these difficult times of fluctuating roles?

Another area that deserves exploration is women's relationships to careers
other than homemaking. With more than 50 percent of women working,
even those with young children, this certainly could be an apt subject. If
more women writers do deal with women's careers, it is likely they will
continue to stress the connections between work and personal life, as does
Mary Gordon. Feminism resists the separation of human experience into
private and public speres, and argues that more women at higher levels in
the workplace will humanize public life.

Whatever subjects writers choose, the Women's Movement and the related
literary revolution have opened up many possibilities for subjects and themes
previously off limits for writers. Their responses have been as varied as the
radical approach of Marge Piercy, and the cultural feminist approach of
Mary Gordon, and as ambivalent as Toni Morrison's. Morrison's work
reminds us that the feminist vision of women of all races and classes united
in working for a better world is still only a beautiful ideal.

FEMINISM AND LITERATURE: A CASE FOR OPTIMISM

I mentioned there was cause for optimism and pessimism for the Women's
Movement. In view of the recent inroads on women's reproductive freedom
by the Supreme Court, continuing sexist portrayals of woman in the media,
and the continuing "feminization of poverty" due to the position of women
of color and white working-class women, it is possible to be very pessimistic
about the future of the Women's Movement. Seen in this light, the decline
of the political feminist novel can be viewed as a surrender to the status
quo; Greene sees this quietism in the recent work of British and Canadian
novelists as well. One could also argue that films such as *Fatal Attraction*,
portraying crazed career women and stable housewives, or *Baby Boom*,
which certainly does sentimentalize motherhood, do far more to influence
public opinion than do novels. The burgeoning of feminist theory could be
viewed as alarming: instead of *doing* feminism, thousands of busy academics

are writing about it, inventing ever-proliferating theories that do little to change the status of the average woman. To provide them with material, women writers produce more and more fiction exploring ever-widening aspects of female experience, again doing little to help the "woman in the street" who watches *Fatal Attraction* and *Baby Boom*.

As I argued at the beginning of this study, however, the Women's Movement is in large part an intellectual revolution, a revolution in individual thinking. It is important for women to name their experience, to evaluate their sufferings and joys, their weaknesses and strengths, and to see how these are reflected in other women's lives. All feminist writing, but fiction especially, because of its capacity to represent experience, has the ability to help women do this. True, there is always a danger in any political movement that the intelligentsia, in this case the academics, will forget that "average woman," but luckily popular fiction writers are speaking to large numbers of these women in ways feminist criticism cannot. Such fiction keeps the new ideas about women in circulation and helps women to expand and grow in their struggles with self and society. The continual growth and expansion of this fiction and its readership is a sign of the vitality of the feminist movement.

Further, the fact that many thousands of people marched in Washington to protest the Supreme Court's abortion rulings, and even in my small town a sizable group rallied to protest Michigan's "parental consent" law, suggests that the genie will not be stuffed back in the bottle. Though the mass media continue to churn out plenty of traditional images of women, there is also Murphy Brown. The changes that the Women's Movement has brought about will continue and deepen, and there will continue to be cross-fertilization between the movement and literature.

There is cause for concern, of course. One troubling aspect of today's Women's Movement is the divisions that exist between "liberals," radicals, lesbians, and so on. We see this division even in academe in literary criticism, where some works are rejected as "reactionary." It is ironic that apparently some critics would like to channel this outpouring of varied artistic interpretations of female experience; we have complained that women writers have been restricted in subjects and themes, but now that they have been freed, we do not always like what they are saying. In Chapter 2 I argued that the novel representing female experience as restricted and painful is to be equally valued with one that celebrates the "liberated" woman; novelists should not be expected to supply protagonists who are role models for the reader. And, if one function of literature is to teach, surely a work showing the sufferings of women can teach a reader as much as one where the protagonist conquers all obstacles.

On the other hand, writers must be free to celebrate and explore all aspects of woman's experience, including the traditional, in order to expand our understanding; not all female experience is negative, and to portray it as such is untruthful and can damage the Women's Movement by rendering its ideas incredible. This is why feminist critics, whether "radical," or po-litically more moderate, should strive to be open in their evaluations of the female experience they see portrayed in literature. To dismiss as reactionary or counterproductive writing that deals with family and personal relation-ships seems as biased as to dismiss a novel that has strong, politically activist resonances. It is unlikely that feminists are going to settle all their differences, but they can resolve to tolerate and respect varying points of view both in the narrow world of literary criticism and in the larger political movement. From listening to each other we grow; a vital and varied literature by women can be a continued support to the political aims of the movement.

In her essay on *The Bluest Eye*, Paula Bennett argued that since the work of Carol Gilligan and Nancy Chodorow there has been a tendency in the Women's Movement to overvalue the feminine qualities of interconnect-edness and caring for the Other; blurring of ego boundaries is seen as beneficial to women and humanity; and the male qualities of separation and autonomy are seen as damaging. These cultural feminist thinkers are forgetting that this is only one side of the human equation; Chodorow has also argued that women *need* to differentiate, to see themselves as separate from others. If we forget this need, we end up with the fantasy of the ideal mother, the woman who always puts herself last. Full growth involves a woman's learning to assert her subjectivity, as Jessica Benjamin says, to expect that others see her as an autonomous being. Otherwise, too often women will remain silent victims.[16]

If we apply this analysis to literature, it suggests that if we want literature to have the power to change lives, we need both types of writing, writing that deals with both sides of the human equation. Fiction celebrating tra-ditional female qualities of interconnection and caring shows us the beauty and strength of those values; yet we also need writing that celebrates women as separate, autonomous, active, struggling to change their lives and the world. Though I have argued that literature of the 1980s expresses important feminist insights, I do miss the "feisty" heroines of the 1970s. My personal hope is to have fiction incorporating both parts of the human equation, as well as a continuation of the contributions of nonwhite, lesbian, and ethnic writers whose voices are so welcome.

CONCLUSION

In 1975, in "The Laugh of the Medusa," Hélène Cixous called on women to break their silence and make a shattering entry into history. This will not involve adopting male discourse but developing a feminine practice of writing that will "write the body." Although this practice cannot be defined, it will avoid the "struggle for mastery" that is the hallmark of phallocratic values; it will celebrate woman's sexuality, her difference, and her joy. As of 1992 it seems that Cixous's call for women to write their own experience in their own language is being answered. Rather than appropriating the symbolic constructs of men, the *écriture feminine* they are writing is partly a language of the "preoedipal mother" and of the body. It emphasizes not just sufferings and exclusions; it also affirms women's difference, joys, and gifts, as well as embracing the Other.[17] For the most part, the rage against men that we see in earlier women's writing has been left behind; present women's writing for the most part implies an incorporation of female values into the culture, rather than separation. The result is a new richness in contemporary literature that we can only hope will thrive and expand.

NOTES

1. Hazel Carby, *Reconstructing Womanhood: The Emergence of the Afro-American Woman Novelist* (New York: Oxford University Press, 1987).

2. Kathryn Rabuzzi, in *The Sacred and the Feminine: Toward a Theology of Housework* (New York: Seabury, 1982), 151, argues that the stasis needed to perform domestic activities can be a positive quality, compared with the active domination reserved for the male; one could see the manipulative aspects of masculine values as being detrimental to humanity and the environment.

3. Robin Morgan, *Going Too Far: The Personal Chronicle of a Feminist* (New York: Vintage, 1978), 8.

4. Gerda Lerner, *The Creation of Patriarchy* (New York: Oxford University Press, 1986), 13.

5. Ann Dally, *Inventing Motherhood: The Consequences of an Ideal* (London: Burnett, 1982), 185.

6. Sara Ruddick ("Maternal Thinking," *Feminist Studies* 6 [Summer 1980], 348-350) believes that nurturant activities demand a passive attitude of preservation. Since the mother has little control over the object of her care, she learns qualities of waiting and supporting. These attitudes are more beneficial to humanity and the environment than are active male activities of questing and manipulation. Similarly Evelyn Fox Keller says that such male qualities seen in science and technology have made a mess of the planet. "Feminism and Science," *Signs* 7 (Spring 1982), 599-601.

7. Mona Simpson, *Anywhere But Here* (New York: Knopf, 1986). In this novel the mother, Adele, is so smothering and manipulative that the heroine Ann must escape her to emotionally survive; nevertheless, Ann's love for Adele is passionate.

8. Adrienne Rich, *Of Woman Born: Motherhood as Experience and Institution* (New York: Bantam, 1977), 240.

9. Paulina Palmer, *Contemporary Women's Fiction: Narrative Practice and Feminist Theory* (Jackson: University Press of Mississippi, 1989), 165.

10. Gayle Greene, *Changing the Story: Feminist Fiction and the Tradition* (Bloomington: Indiana University Press, 1991), 199-200; Elinor Langer, "Whatever Happened to Feminist Fiction?" *New York Times Book Review* (4 March 1984), 35.

11. Lisa Alther, *Other Women* (New York: Knopf, 1984), 243.

12. See also Olga Kenyon, *Women Novelists Today: A Survey of English Writing*

in the Seventies and Eighties (New York: St. Martin's Press, 1988); and Joanne Frye, *Living Stories, Telling Lives: Women and the Novel in Contemporary Experience* (Ann Arbor: University of Michigan Press, 1986), 199.

13. Greene, *Changing the Story*, 3-5.

14. Barbara Rigney, *The Voices of Toni Morrison* (Columbus: Ohio State University Press, 1991), 105.

15. In 1983 Steinem suggested that today's younger generation of women will have to go through their own consciousness-raising. Many young women have not yet encountered the "real world" and the problems women still face. "Why Young Women Are More Conservative," Gloria Steinem, *Outrageous Acts and Everyday Rebellions* (New York: Henry Holt, 1983), 211-218.

16. Paula Bennett, "The Mother's Part: Incest and Maternal Deprivation in Woolf and Morrison," in *Narrating Mothers: Theorizing Maternal Subjectivities*, ed. Brenda Daly and Maureen Reddy (Knoxville: University of Tennessee Press, 1991), 134-136; Jessica Benjamin, *The Bonds of Love: Psychoanalysis, Feminism, and the Problem of Domination* (New York: Pantheon, 1988), 78.

17. Hélène Cixous, "Laugh of the Medusa," trans. Keith Cohen and Paula Cohen, *Signs* 1 (Summer 1976), 875-893.

Selected Bibliography

PRIMARY SOURCES CITED

Alther, Lisa. *Kinflicks*. New York: New American Library, 1975.

———. *Other Women*. New York: Knopf, 1984.

Ballantyne, Sheila. *Norma Jean, the Termite Queen*. New York: Bantam, 1975.

Chase, Joan. *During the Reign of the Queen of Persia*. New York: Harper & Row, 1983.

French, Marilyn. *The Women's Room*. New York: Jove, 1978.

———. *The Bleeding Heart*. New York: Summit, 1980.

———. *Her Mother's Daughter*. New York: Summit, 1987.

Godwin, Gail. *The Odd Woman*. New York: Knopf, 1974.

———. *Violet Clay*. New York: Knopf, 1978.

———. *A Mother and Two Daughters*. New York: Viking, 1982.

———. *A Southern Family*. New York: Morrow, 1987.

Gordon, Mary. *Final Payments*. New York: Ballantine, 1978.

———. *The Company of Women*. New York: Ballantine, 1980.

———. *Men and Angels*. New York: Ballantine, 1985.

———. *The Other Side*. New York: Viking, 1989.

Gray, Francine, du Plessix. *Lovers and Tyrants*. New York: Simon & Schuster, 1976.

Jong, Erica. *Fear of Flying*. New York: Holt, Rinehart, and Winston, 1973.

———. *Fanny: Being the True History of the Adventures of Fanny Hackabout-Jones*. New York: New American Library, 1980.

Kaufman, Sue. *Diary of a Mad Housewife*. New York: Random House, 1967.

Leffland, Ella. *Rumors of Peace*. New York: Harper & Row, 1979.

Lessing, Doris. *The Golden Notebook*. New York: Simon and Schuster, 1962.

Miller, Sue. *The Good Mother*. New York: Harper & Row, 1986.

Morrison, Toni. *The Bluest Eye*. New York: Holt, Rinehart and Winston, 1970.

———. *Sula*. New York: Knopf, 1974.

———. *Song of Solomon*. New York: Knopf, 1977.

———. *Tar Baby*. New York: Knopf, 1981.

———. *Beloved*. New York: Knopf, 1987.

————. *Jazz.* New York: Knopf, 1992.

Piercy, Marge. *Going Down Fast.* New York: Fawcett Crest, 1969.

————. *Dance the Eagle to Sleep.* Garden City, NY: Doubleday, 1970.

————. *Small Changes.* New York: Fawcett Crest, 1972.

————. *Woman on the Edge of Time.* New York: Fawcett Crest, 1976.

————. *The High Cost of Living.* New York: Fawcett Crest, 1978.

————. *Vida.* New York: Fawcett Crest, 1979.

————. *Braided Lives.* New York: Fawcett Crest, 1982.

————. *Fly Away Home.* New York: Fawcett Crest, 1984.

————. *Gone to Soldiers.* New York: Fawcett Crest, 1987.

————. *Summer People.* New York: Knopf, 1989.

————. *He, She and It.* New York: Knopf, 1991.

Plath, Sylvia. *The Bell Jar.* New York: Harper & Row, 1971.

Roiphe, Anne Richardson. *Up the Sandbox!* New York: Simon and Schuster, 1970.

Rossner, Judith. *Looking for Mr. Goodbar.* New York: Simon and Schuster, 1975.

Shulman, Alix Kates. *Memoirs of an Ex-Prom Queen.* New York: Bantam, 1972.

Tan, Amy. *The Joy Luck Club.* New York: G. P. Putnam's, 1989.

Walker, Alice. *The Color Purple.* New York: Washington Square Press, 1982.

WORKS ON FEMINISM, LITERARY CRITICISM, AND CONTEMPORARY WOMEN'S WRITING

Abbandonato, Linda. "A View from 'Elsewhere' ": Subversive Sexuality and the Rewriting of the Heroine's Story in *The Color Purple. PMLA* 106 (October 1991), 1106-1115.

Abel, Elizabeth. "(E)Merging Identities: The Dynamics of Female Friendship in Contemporary Fiction by Women." *Signs* 6 (Spring 1981), 413-435.

————. *The Voyage In: Fiction of Female Development.* Ed. Elizabeth Abel, Marianne Hirsch, and Elizabeth Langland. Hanover, NH: University Press of New England, 1983.

Allen, Mary. *A Necessary Blankness: Women in Major American Fiction of the Sixties.* Urbana: University of Illinois Press, 1976.

Atlas, Marilyn. "A Woman Both Shiny and Brown: Feminine Strength in Toni Morrison's *Song of Solomon.*" *Society for the Study of Midwestern Literature Newsletter* 9 (Fall 1979), 1-13.

Atwood, Margaret. "That Certain Thing Called the Girlfriend." *New York Times Book Review* (11 May 1986), 1, 38-39.

Banner, Lois W, *Women in Modern America: A Brief History.* 2nd ed. New York: Harcourt Brace Jovanovich, 1984.

Banyiwa-Horne, Naana. "The Scary Face of the Self: An Analysis of the Character of Sula in Toni Morrison's *Sula.*" *Sage* 2 (Spring 1985), 28-31.

Bartkowski, Frances. *Feminist Utopias.* Lincoln: University of Nebraska Press, 1989.

Baruch, Elaine Hoffman. *Women, Love, and Power: Literary and Psychoanalytic Perspectives.* New York: New York University Press, 1991.

Beauvoir, Simone de. *The Second Sex.* Trans. and ed. H. M. Parshley. New York: Vintage, 1952; 1989.

Bell, Roseann P., Bettye J. Parker, and Beverly Guy-Sheftall, eds. *Sturdy Black Bridges: Visions of Black Women in Literature*. New York: Doubleday, 1979.

Benjamin, Jessica. *The Bonds of Love: Psychoanalysis, Feminism, and the Problem of Domination*. New York: Pantheon, 1988.

Bennett, Paula. "The Mother's Part: Incest and Maternal Deprivation in Woolf and Morrison." In *Narrating Mothers: Theorizing Maternal Subjectivities*, 125-138. Eds. Brenda O. Daly and Maureen T. Reddy. Knoxville: University of Tennessee Press, 1991.

Berlant, Lauren. "Race, Gender, and Nation in *The Color Purple*." *Critical Inquiry* 14 (Summer 1988), 831-859.

Bernikow, Louise. *Among Women*. New York: Harper & Row, 1980.

Bloom, Harold, ed. *Modern Critical Views: Toni Morrison*. New York: Chelsea House, 1990.

Braendlin, Bonnie Hoover. "Alther, Atwood, Ballantyne, and Gray: Secular Salvation in the Contemporary Feminist *Bildungsroman*." *Frontiers* 4 (1979), 18-22.

Brownmiller, Susan. *Against Our Will: Men, Women, and Rape*. New York: Simon and Schuster, 1975.

Butler-Evans, Elliott. *Race, Gender, and Desire: Narrative Strategies in the Fiction of Toni Cade Bambara, Toni Morrison, and Alice Walker*. Philadelphia: Temple University Press, 1989.

Carby, Hazel. *Reconstructing Womanhood: The Emergence of the Afro-American Woman Novelist*. New York: Oxford University Press, 1987.

Castro, Ginette. *American Feminism: A Contemporary History*. Trans. Elizabeth Loverde-Bagell. New York: New York University Press, 1990.

Chesler, Phyllis. *Women and Madness*. New York: Doubleday, 1972.

Chodorow, Nancy. "Mothering, Object-Relations and the Female Oedipal Configuration." *Feminist Studies* 4 (1978), 137-138.

———. *The Reproduction of Mothering: Psychoanalysis and the Sociology of Gender*. Berkeley: University of California Press, 1978.

———. "Feminism and Difference: Gender, Relation and Difference in Psychoanalytic Perspective." *Socialist Review* 46 (1979), 51-69.

Chodorow, Nancy, and Susan W. Contratto. "The Fantasy of the Perfect Mother." In *Rethinking the Family*, 54-75. Ed. Barrie Thorne and Marilyn Yalom. New York: Longman, 1982.

Christian, Barbara. *Black Women Novelists: The Development of a Tradition, 1892-1976*. Westport, CT: Greenwood, 1980.

———. *Black Feminist Criticism: Perspectives on Black Women Writers*. New York: Pergamon, 1985.

Cixous, Hélène. "The Laugh of the Medusa." Trans. Keith Cohen and Paula Cohen. *Signs* 1 (Summer 1976), 875-893.

Cory, Meredith. *Different Drummers: New Roles in Old Societies*. Metuchen, NJ: Scarecrow, 1984.

Coward, Rosalind. "Are Women's Novels Feminist Novels?" In *The New Feminist Criticism: Essays on Women, Literature, Theory*, 225-239. Ed. Elaine Showalter. New York: Pantheon, 1985.

Cramer, Carmen. "Anti-Automaton: Marge Piercy's Fight in *Woman on the Edge of Time*." *Critique* 27 (Summer 1986), 229-233.

Cranny-Francis, Anne. *Feminist Fiction: Feminist Uses of Generic Fiction*. New York: St. Martin's Press, 1990.

Dally, Ann. *Inventing Motherhood: The Consequences of an Ideal*. London: Burnett, 1982.

Daly, Brenda O., and Maureen T. Reddy, eds. *Narrating Mothers: Theorizing Maternal Subjectivities*. Knoxville: University of Tennessee Press, 1991.

Daly, Mary. *The Church and the Second Sex*. Boston: Harper, 1968.

———. *Beyond God the Father: Toward a Philosophy of Women's Liberation*. Boston: Beacon, 1973.

———. *Gyn/Ecology: The Metaethics of Radical Feminism*. Boston: Beacon, 1978.

Davis, Cynthia. "Self, Society, and Myth in Toni Morrison's Fiction." *Contemporary Literature* 23 (Summer 1982), 323-342.

Denard, Carolyn C. "The Convergence of Feminism and Ethnicity in the Fiction of Toni Morrison." In *Critical Essays on Toni Morrison*, 171-178. Ed. Nellie McKay. Boston: G. K. Hall, 1988.

———. "Toni Morrison." In *Modern American Women Writers*, 317-335. Ed. Elaine Showalter. New York: Scribner's, 1991.

Diamond, Arlyn. "Flying from Work." *Frontiers* 2 (1977), 18-23.

Dinnerstein, Dorothy. *The Mermaid and the Minotaur: Sexual Arrangements and Human Malaise*. New York: Harper & Row, 1976.

Donovan, Josephine. *Feminist Theory: The Intellectual Traditions of American Feminism*. New York: Frederick Ungar, 1985.

DuPlessis, Rachel Blau. *Writing Beyond the Ending: Narrative Strategies of Twentieth-Century Women Writers*. Bloomington: Indiana University Press, 1985.

Eichenbaum, Luise, and Susie Orbach. *Understanding Women: A Feminist Psychoanalytic Approach*. New York: Basic Books, 1983.

Eisenstein, Hester. *Contemporary Feminist Thought*. Boston: G. K. Hall, 1983.

Ellmann, Mary. *Thinking About Women*. New York: Harcourt Brace Jovanovich, 1968.

Erickson, Peter B. "Images of Nurturance in Toni Morrison's *Tar Baby*." *CLA Journal* 28 (September 1984), 11-32.

Evans, Mari, ed. *Black Women Writers (1950-1980), a Critical Evaluation*. Garden City, NY: Anchor, 1984.

Everson, Susan Corey. "Toni Morrison's *Tar Baby*: A Resource for Feminist Theology." *Journal of Feminist Studies in Religion* 5 (Fall 1989), 65-78.

Faludi, Susan. *Backlash: The Undeclared War on American Women*. New York: Crown, 1991.

Ferguson, Mary Anne. "The Female Novel of Development and the Myth of Psyche." In *The Voyage In: Fictions of Female Development*, 228-243. Ed. Elizabeth Abel Marianne Hirsch and Elizabeth Langland. Hanover, NY: University Press at New England, 1983.

Firestone, Shulamith. *The Dialectic of Sex: The Case for Feminist Revolution*. New York: Morrow, 1970.

Friday, Nancy. *My Mother/My Self: The Daughter's Search for Identity*. New York: Delacorte Press, 1977.

Friedan, Betty. *The Feminine Mystique*. New York: Norton, 1963.

Friedman, Susan Stanford. "Creativity and the Childbirth Metaphor: Gender Difference in Literary Discourse." *Feminist Studies* 13 (1987), 49-82

Frye, Joanne. *Living Stories, Telling Lives: Women and the Novel in Contemporary Experience*. Ann Arbor: University of Michigan Press, 1986.

Gallop, Jane. *The Daughter's Seduction*. Ithaca, NY: Cornell University Press, 1982.

Gardiner, Judith Kegan. "The (US)es of (I)dentity: A Response to Abel on '(E)Merging Identities.' " *Signs* 6 (Spring 1981), 436-442.

———. "Evil, Apocalypse, and Feminist Fiction." *Frontiers* 7 (1983), 74-80.

Garrard, Nikki. *Into the Mainstream: How Feminism Has Changed Women's Writing*. London: Pandora, 1989.

Gilbert, Sandra M., and Susan Gubar. *The Madwoman in the Attic: The Woman Writer and the Nineteenth-Century Imagination*. New Haven: Yale University Press, 1979.

Gilead, Sarah. "Mary Gordon's *Final Payments* and the Nineteenth-Century English Novel." *Critique* 27 (Summer 1986), 213-226.

Gilligan, Carol. *In a Different Voice: Psychological Theory and Women's Development*. Cambridge, MA: Harvard University Press, 1982.

Gordon, Mary. "Coming to Terms with Mary." *Commonweal* (15 January 1982), 11-14.

———. "Getting Here from There: A Writer's Reflections on a Religious Past." In *Spiritual Quests: The Art and Craft of Religious Writing*, 27-53. Ed. William Zinsser. Boston: Houghton Mifflin, 1988.

Gornick, Vivian. "The Conflict Between Love and Work." In *Essays on Feminism*, 128-139. Ed. Vivian Gornick. New York: Harper & Row, 1978.

Greene, Gayle. *Changing the Story: Feminist Fiction and the Tradition*. Bloomington: Indiana University Press, 1991.

Greer, Germaine. *The Female Eunuch*. New York: McGraw-Hill, 1971.

Griffin, Susan. *Pornography and Silence: Culture's Revenge Against Nature*. New York: Harper & Row, 1981.

Hansen, Elaine Tuttle. "The Double Narrative Strategy of *Small Changes*." In *Contemporary American Women Writers: Narrative Strategies*, 209-228. Ed. Catherine Rainwater and William J. Scheick. Lexington: University Press of Kentucky, 1985.

Harris, Trudier. *From Mammies to Militants: Domestics in Black American Literature*. Philadelphia: Temple University Press, 1982.

Harstock, Nancy. *Money, Sex and Power: Toward a Feminist Historical Materialism*. New York: Longman, 1983.

Heilbrun, Carolyn. *Reinventing Womanhood*. New York: W. W. Norton, 1979.

Hirsch, Marianne. *The Mother/Daughter Plot: Narrative, Psychoanalysis, Feminism*. Bloomington: Indiana University Press, 1989.

Hite, Molly. "Writing—and Reading—The Body: Female Sexuality and Recent Feminist Fiction." *Feminist Studies* 14 (Spring 1988), 121-142.

———. *The Other Side of the Story: Structures and Strategies of Contemporary Feminist Narrative*. Ithaca, NY: Cornell University Press, 1989.

Holloway, Karla F. C., and Stephanie A. Demetrakopoulos. *New Dimensions of Spirituality: A Biracial and Bicultural Reading of the Novels of Toni Morrison*. Westport, CT: Greenwood, 1987.

Homans, Margaret. " 'Her Very Own Howl': The Ambiguities of Representation in Recent Women's Fiction." *Signs* 9 (Winter 1983), 186-205.

Hymowitz, Carol, and Michaele Weissman. *A History of Women in America*. New York: Bantam, 1978.

Janeway, Elizabeth. *Man's World, Woman's Place: A Study in Social Mythology*. New York: William Morrow, 1971.

Johnson, Nora. "Housewives and Prom Queens, 25 Year Later." *New York Times Book Review* (20 March 1988), 1, 32-33.

Keller, Evelyn Fox. "Feminism and Science." *Signs* 7 (Spring 1982), 589-602.

Kenyon, Olga. *Women Novelists Today: A Survey of English Writing in the Seventies and Eighties*. New York: St. Martin's Press, 1988.

———. *Writing Women: Contemporary Women Novelists*. Concord, MA: Pluto Press, 1991.

Kessler, Carol Farley. "*Woman on the Edge of Time*: A Novel 'To Be of Use.'" *Extrapolation* 28 (1987), 310-318.

Keyishian, M. Deiter. "Radical Damage: An Interview with Mary Gordon." *The Literary Review* 32 (Fall 1988), 69-82.

Kimball, Gayle, ed. *Women's Culture: The Women's Renaissance of the Seventies*. Metuchen, NJ: Scarecrow, 1981.

Koedt, Anne. "The Myth of Vaginal Orgasm." In *Radical Feminism*. Ed. Anne Koedt, Ellen Levine, and Anita Rapone. New York: Quadrangle Books, 1973.

Kristeva, Julia. *Desire in Language: A Semiotic Approach to Literature and Art*. Ed. Leon S. Roudiez. Trans. Thomas Goza, Alice Jardine, and Leon Roudiez. New York: Columbia University Press, 1980.

———. "Oscillation Between Power and Denial." In *New French Feminisms: An Anthology*. Ed. Elaine Marks and Isabell de Courtivron. New York: Schocken, 1981.

Kubitschek, Missy Dehn. *Claiming the Heritage: African-American Women Novelists and History*. Jackson: University Press of Mississippi, 1991.

Langer, Elinor. "Whatever Happened to Feminist Fiction?" *New York Times Book Review* (4 March 1984), 1, 35-36.

Lerner, Gerda. *The Creation of Patriarchy*. New York: Oxford University Press, 1986.

Levy, Bronwen. "Women and the Literary Pages: Some Recent Examples." *Hecate* 11 (1985), 6-7, 11.

Lidoff, Joan. "Tangled Vines: Mothers and Daughters in Women's Writing." *Women's Studies Quarterly* 11 (Winter 1983), 16-19.

Ling, Amy. *Between Worlds: Women Writers of Chinese Ancestry*. New York: Pergamon Press, 1990.

Mainardi, Pat. "The Politics of Housework." In *Sisterhood Is Powerful: An Anthology of Writings from the Women's Liberation Movement*, 447-454. Ed. Robin Morgan. New York: Random House, 1970.

Mbalia, Doreatha Drummond. *Toni Morrison's Developing Class Consciousness*. Cranbury, NJ: Associated University Presses, 1992.

McKay, Nellie, "An Interview with Toni Morrison Conducted by Nellie McKay." *Contemporary Literature* 24 (Winter 1983), 413-429.

———, ed. *Critical Essays on Toni Morrison*. Boston: G. K. Hall, 1988.

McLaughlin, Andrée Nicola. "A Renaissance of the Spirit: Black Women Remaking the Universe." In *Wild Women in the Whirlwind: Afra-American Culture and the Contemporary Literary Renaissance*, xxxi-xlix. Ed. Joanne M. Braxton and Andrée Nicola McLaughlin. New Brunswick, NJ: Rutgers University Press, 1990.

McNaron, Toni A. H., ed. *The Sister Bond: A Feminist View of a Timeless Connection*. New York: Pergamon Press, 1985.

Michie, Helena. "Mother, Sister, Other: The 'Other Woman' in Feminist Theory." *Literature and Psychology* 32 (1986), 1-10.

Mickelson, Anne. *Reaching Out: Sensitivity and Order in Recent American Fiction by Women*. Metuchen, NJ: Scarecrow, 1979.

Miles, Angela. *Feminist Radicalism in the 1980's*. Montreal: Culture Texts, 1985.

Miller, Jane. *Women Writing About Men*. New York: Pantheon, 1986.

Millett, Kate. *Sexual Politics*. Garden City, NY: Doubleday, 1970.

Mitchell, Juliet. *Women's Estate*. New York: Pantheon, 1971.

Mobley, Marilyn Sanders. "A Different Remembering: Memory, History and Meaning in Toni Morrison's *Beloved*." In *Modern Critical Views: Toni Morrison*, 189-199. Ed. Harold Bloom. New York: Chelsea House, 1990.

———. *Folk Roots and Mythic Wings in Sarah Orne Jewett and Toni Morrison: The Cultural Function of Narrative*, 134-167. Baton Rouge: Louisiana State University Press, 1991.

Modleski, Tanya. *Loving with a Vengeance: Mass Produced Fantasies for Women*. Hamden, CT: Archon Books, 1982.

Morgan, Ellen. "Humanbecoming: Form and Focus in the Neo-Feminist Novel." In *Images of Women in Fiction: Feminist Perspectives*. Ed. Susan Koppelman Cornillon. Bowling Green, OH: Bowling Green State University Popular Press, 1972.

Murray, Meg McGavran, ed. *Face to Face: Fathers, Mothers, Masters, Monsters— Essays for a Nonsexist Future*. Westport, CT: Greenwood, 1983.

Neary, John. "Mary Gordon's *Final Payments*: A Romance of the One True Language." *Essays in Literature* 17 (Spring 1990), 94-110.

Ogunyemi, Chikwenye Okonjo. "Womanism: The Dynamics of the Contemporary Black Female Novel in English." *Signs* 11 (Autumn 1985), 63-80.

Otten, Terry. *The Crime of Innocence in the Fiction of Toni Morrison*. Columbia: University of Missouri Press, 1989.

Palmer, Paulina. *Contemporary Women's Fiction: Narrative Practice and Feminist Theory*. Jackson: University Press of Mississippi, 1989.

Pearlman, Mickey, ed. *Mother Puzzles: Daughters and Mothers in Contemporary American Literature*. Westport, CT: Greenwood, 1989.

Pearlman, Mickey, and Katherine Usher Henderson, eds. *Inter/View: Talks with America's Writing Women*. Lexington: University Press of Kentucky, 1988.

Perry, Ruth. "Mary Gordon's Mothers." In *Narrating Mothers: Theorizing Maternal Subjectivities*, 209-221. Ed. Brenda O. Daly and Maureen T. Reddy. Knoxville: University of Tennessee Press, 1991.

Piercy, Marge. "In the Fifties: Through the Cracks." *Partisan Review* 41 (1974), 202-216.

———. *Parti-Colored Blocks for a Quilt*. Ann Arbor: University of Michigan Press, 1982.

Powers, Meredith. *The Heroine in Western Literature: The Archetype and Her Reemergence in Modern Prose.* New York: McFarland, 1991.

Pryse, Marjorie, and Hortense J. Spillers, eds. *Conjuring: Black Women, Fiction, and Literary Tradition.* Bloomington: Indiana University Press, 1985.

Rabuzzi, Kathryn Allen. *The Sacred and the Feminine: Toward a Theology of Housework.* New York: Seabury, 1982.

———. *Motherself: A Mythic Analysis of Motherhood.* Bloomington: Indiana University Press, 1988.

Rapping, Elayne. "A Novelist's Career." *The Women's Review of Books* 7 (February 1990), 13.

Regan, Nancy. "A Home of One's Own: Women's Bodies in Recent Women's Fiction." *Journal of Popular Culture* 11 (Spring 1978), 772-788.

Rich, Adrienne. *Of Woman Born: Motherhood as Experience and Institution.* New York: Bantam, 1977.

Rigney, Barbara. *Lillith's Daughters: Women and Religion in Contemporary Fiction.* Madison: University of Wisconsin Press, 1982.

———. *The Voices of Toni Morrison.* Columbus: Ohio State University Press, 1991.

Roller, Judi. *The Politics of the Feminist Novel.* Westport, CT: Greenwood, 1986.

Rosenfelt, Deborah Silverton. "Getting into the Game: American Women Writers and the Radical Tradition." *Women's Studies International Forum* 9 (1986), 363-372.

Ruddick, Sara. "Maternal Thinking." *Feminist Studies* 6 (Summer 1980), 342-367.

———. *Maternal Thinking: Toward a Politics of Peace.* Boston: Beacon, 1989.

Schweickart, Patrocinio. "Reading Ourselves: Toward a Feminist Theory of Reading." In *Contemporary Literary Criticism: Literary and Cultural Studies*, 118-141. Ed. Robert Con Davis and Ronald Schleifer. New York: Longman, 1989.

Shinn, Thelma. *Radiant Daughters: Fictional American Women.* Westport, CT: Greenwood, 1986.

Showalter, Elaine. "Women Writers and the Double Standard." In *Woman in Sexist Society.* Ed. Vivian Gornick and Barbara K. Moran. New York: Basic Books, 1971.

———. *A Literature of Their Own: British Women Novelists from Bronte to Lessing.* Princeton, NJ: Princeton University Press, 1977.

———. *The New Feminist Criticism: Essays on Women, Literature, Theory.* New York: Pantheon, 1985.

———. *Sister's Choice: Tradition and Change in American Women's Writing.* Oxford: Clarendon Press, 1991.

———, ed. *Modern American Women Writers.* New York: Charles Scribner's, 1991.

Shulman, Alix Kates. "Books: The 'Taint' of Feminist Fiction." *Ms.* (November/December 1991), 72-75.

Skerrett, Joseph T., Jr. "Recitation to the *Griot*: Storytelling and Learning in Toni Morrison's *Song of Solomon*." In *Conjuring: Black Women, Fiction, and Literary Tradition*, 192-202. Eds. Marjorie Pryse and Hortense J. Spillers. Bloomington: Indiana University Press, 1985.

Sochen, June. *Enduring Values: Women in Popular Culture.* New York: Praeger, 1987.

Spacks, Patricia Meyer. *The Female Imagination.* New York: Knopf, 1976.

———, ed. *Contemporary Women Novelists: A Collection of Critical Essays.* Englewood Cliffs, NJ: Prentice Hall, 1977.

Spencer, Jane. *The Rise of the Woman Novelist: From Aphra Behn to Jane Austen.* Oxford: Basil Blackwood, 1986.

Spender, Dale. *The Writing or the Sex?* Elmsford, NY: Pergamon Press, 1989.

Spillers, Hortense. "A Hateful Passion, a Lost Love." In *Feminist Issues in Literary Scholarship*, 181-207. Ed. Shari Benstock. Bloomington: Indiana University Press, 1987.

Stepto, Robert B. " 'Intimate Things in Place': A Conversation with Toni Morrison." In *Chant of Saints: A Gathering of Afro-American Literature, Art and Scholarship*, 213-229. Ed. Michael S. Harper and Robert B. Stepto. Urbana: University of Illinois Press, 1979.

Suleiman, Susan Rubin. "On Maternal Splitting: A Propos of Mary Gordon's *Men and Angels*." *Signs* 14 (1988), 25-41.

——. "Writing and Motherhood." In *The (M)Other Tongue: Essays in Feminist Psychoanalytic Interpretation*, 352-357. Ed. Shirley Nelson Garner, Claire Kahane, and Madelon Springnether. Ithaca, NY: Cornell University Press, 1985.

Syfers, Judith. "Why I Want a Wife." *Ms.* (31 December 1971).

Tate, Claudia. *Black Women Writers at Work.* New York: Continuum, 1983.

Trebilcot, Joyce, ed. *Mothering: Essays in Feminist Theory.* Totowa, NJ: Rowman and Allanheld, 1989.

Umeh, A. M. "A Comparative Study of the Idea of Motherhood in Two Third World Novels." *CLA Journal* 31 (September 1987), 31-43.

Wagner, Linda W. "Toni Morrison: Mastery of Narrative." In *Contemporary American Women Writers: Narrative Strategies.* Ed. Catherine Rainwater and William J. Scheick. Lexington: University Press of Kentucky, 1985.

Weaver, Mary Jo. *The Contemporary Challenge to Traditional Religious Authority.* San Francisco: Harper & Row, 1988.

Wessling, Joseph. "Narcissism in Toni Morrison's *Sula*." *CLA Journal* 31 (March 1988), 281-298.

White, Barbara. *Growing up Female: Adolescent Girlhood in American Fiction.* Westport, CT: Greenwood, 1985.

Woolf, Virginia. *A Room of One's Own.* New York: Harcourt, Brace & World, 1929; 1957.

Wymward, Eleanor B. "Mary Gordon: Her Religious Sensibility." *Cross Currents* 37 (Summer/Fall 1987), 147-158.

Yaeger, Patricia. *Honey-Mad Women: Emancipatory Strategies in Women's Writing.* New York: Columbia University Press, 1988.

Zimmerman, Bonnie. "What Has Never Been: An Overview of Lesbian Feminist Criticism." In *Making a Difference.* Ed. Gayle Greene and Coppelia Kahn. New York: Routledge, 1985.

Index

About the Author

KATHERINE B. PAYANT is Professor of English and Director of the Gender Studies Program at Northern Michigan University, Marquette. She has published essays on related subjects in anthologies and scholarly journals.